Wealth and Power

Wealth and Power

Survival in a Time of
Global Accumulation

Duran Bell

ALTAMIRA
PRESS

A Division of Rowman & Littlefield Publishers, Inc.
Walnut Creek • Lanham • New York • Toronto • Oxford

AltaMira Press
A division of Rowman & Littlefield Publishers, Inc.
1630 North Main Street, #367
Walnut Creek, California 94596
www.altamirapress.com

Rowman & Littlefield Publishers, Inc.
A wholly owned subsidiary of The Rowman & Littlefield Publishing Group
4501 Forbes Boulevard, Suite 200
Lanham, Maryland 20706

PO Box 317
Oxford
OX2 9RU, UK

Copyright © 2004 by AltaMira Press

British Library Cataloguing in Publication Information Available

Library of Congress Cataloging-in-Publication Data

Bell, Duran, 1936–
  Wealth and power : survival in a time of global accumulation /
Duran Bell.
     p. cm.
Includes bibliographical references and index.
  ISBN 0-7591-0489-1 (hardcover : alk. paper)—ISBN 0-7591-0490-5
(pbk. : alk. paper)
  1. Wealth—Cross-cultural studies. 2. Exchange—Cross-cultural
studies. 3. Saving and investment—Cross-cultural studies. 4.
Wealth—Social aspects. 5. Social structure—Economic aspects. 6.
Capitalism—Social aspects. 7. Globalization. 8. Economic
anthropology. I. Title.

  HB251.B45 2003
  339.2—dc21

                                                        2003011076

Printed in the United States of America

♾™ The paper used in this publication meets the minimum requirements of American
National Standard for Information Sciences—Permanence of Paper for Printed Library
Materials, ANSI/NISO Z39.48-1992.

CONTENTS

PREFACE

This series of lectures was presented in written form to a class of graduate students at the Institute for Sociology and Anthropology, Peking University, during the fall semester of 2001. These lectures were supplemented by other readings and discussed each week. One or more students would assume leadership responsibilities with prepared written comments on the assigned material.

The opportunity to present this material to students at Peking University has provided me the exceptional focus and excitement that was required to complete a unified treatment of materials that I have been developing over the last fifteen years. Some of this work has been published in academic journals, such as the *Journal of Quantitative Anthropology*, the *Journal of Socio-Economics*, and *Current Anthropology*. However, this book contains a number of significant social scientific discoveries that have not yet been published elsewhere. It is, in fact, the unpublished materials contained herein that are most consequential for our understanding of social relations and social process, and I am pleased to be able to publish them first in this form.

I have had the good fortune of having as my teaching assistant, Liang Yongjia, who has functioned as a wise informant on Chinese culture and politics and as a frequent companion. He is also responsible for translating these lectures and facilitating their publication in China. I would like to thank the director of the Institute for Sociology and Anthropology, Professor MA Rong, whose consideration and hospitality enabled me to teach this course. And I have special thanks and appreciation for the students in the class. Some of them are recognized by footnotes in these lectures as a result of their comments in class, but all were an inspiration for me. And in that regard I should like to say one thing: In this book I address a number of fundamental scientific errors that emerge from what I impolitely call the "tribal mythologies of the West." Among these "myths" are an analytically debilitating "norm of reciprocity," a useless bourgeois conception of "wealth," an ideologically contrived definition of capitalism, ethically self-serving myths about friendship relations, and so forth. All of these myths have been eagerly adopted by the world in general, including China in particular. People generally make the mistake of accepting the "dirty bath water" out of a desire for the baby. Since I feel that these myths, if accepted by Chinese intellectuals, will weaken China as it emerges onto the world stage, I have been eager to share my thoughts with the students of Peking University. And with the publication of this book, perhaps my thoughts may be even more broadly shared.

ACKNOWLEDGMENTS

Although this version of *Wealth and Power: Survival in a Time of Global Accumulation* was prepared for graduate students in China, the students whose diligence, insights, patience, and creative comments were most important to its development were undergraduate students at the University of California, Irvine. For a number of years, various manifestations of this book have been presented as "required reading" for a course called The Economics of Traditional Societies. And, indeed, Irvine students in the same course will be among the readers of this book—freeing me, finally, to move forward into my next project. It is impossible for me to express the gratitude that I feel toward them and toward students of years past.

I am also deeply indebted to several reviewers of the manuscript, solicited for that purpose by the fine editors of AltaMira. A very timely review by Josiah McConnell Heyman was particularly useful, as was that of an anonymous reviewer. But special thanks must be extended to Kalman Applbaum. Not only did he review this manuscript for AltaMira, but he also was the only nonstudent reader of a much earlier version of this work. Such selflessness is rare. I greatly treasure his advice, his useful criticism, and his positive regard. To be sure, I failed to be fully responsive to the comments of these reviewers, and the remaining faults are my own.

And, finally, I offer a note of appreciation and admiration to Gyula Derkovits (1894–1934). His works at the beginnings of each chapter have challenged me to make the chapters deserving of his presence. And I am grateful to the directors of the Hungarian National Gallery for providing me permission to feature Derkovits, herein.

CHAPTER ONE
A TIME OF GLOBAL ACCUMULATION

Marchers by Gyula Derkovits. Dózsa-Series I. (1928) Woodcut, 400 × 495 mm, Hungarian National Gallery, Budapest.

A conspicuous feature of the moment is an effort to transform the systems of state-managed capitalism into a global system of accumulation under the domination of leading centers of capital. Given the awesome economic resources in support of that effort, success is ensured. The economic dislocation, impoverishment, and death that must attend that success are beyond speculation. There can be no doubt at this point that this evolving system will manifest severe inequalities in access to capital and, consequently, increase differences among individuals in access to consumption goods and, hence, in the power to survive. Differences in survival probabilities that I can now observe at the national level will explode into the future both within and among nations. In the same way that the "primitive accumulation" of industrial capital featured the impoverishment of a newly developed proletariat, the primitive accumulation of global capital must impoverish nations and societies, as well as classes within nation-states.

These inequalities will be greater, I believe, to the extent that a single center of capital is globally controlling. My objective is to contribute, albeit modestly, to an effort to avoid that outcome by developing a broader conception of social processes so that any non-Western society may chart its unique, culturally specific participation in this phase of capitalist expansion.

Clearly, the effort toward monolithic control is well under way. Uniform sets of economic and "moral" rules have been announced, the intellectual and military arsenals have been mobilized, and the body counts among the enemies are mounting. The many international organizations that advance the hegemony of Western interests (the United Nations and its various agencies, the International Monetary Fund, the World Trade Organization, and innumerable "nongovernmental organizations") demand the adoption of "postindustrial" ideologies and social processes of the West, regardless of the cultural foundations and paths of development to be followed by various nation-states. While it is clear that a uniform global "playing field" is facilitative of Western economic interests, it is plausible that the precipitous adoption of such rules of action by "developing" societies will not most effectively advance their interests. The potential value of the theoretical work presented herein is to create a social scientific basis for the legitimization of alternative "rules of the game."

An Analytical Framework

The wide range of social relations that can be presented by the ethnographic record will inform our vantage point on the contemporary present. Hence, our interest in capital accumulation will be informed primarily by analyses of other forms of "wealth-accumulation." Over most of the period of their existence, Homo sapiens have lived as hunter-gatherers. As such, they were able to increase their physical security and increase the flow of consumables by increasing their demographic presence. Unlike the hunter-gatherers of today, all of whom must survive in economically marginal areas, our ancestors were free to experience the benefits of fertility. However, the management of fertility, as a basis for differences in power among groups, becomes more evident at a rather advanced level of development—with lineage organization. And we are well aware of those who thrive to accumulate animal stock and attempt to benefit from the fertility of stock.

Land and industrial machinery contain no intrinsic forms of fertility, but under certain social arraignments, they, too, can be objects of accumulation. Thus, fertility of humans and of other animals, land, and "means of production," operating as forces of accumulation, may become "wealth-assets." In order to advance this characterization, I shall require a conceptualization of wealth-assets that is transportable across social systems, and such a conception has not existed, heretofore. I am aware of no other serious attempt to address this problem, given the virtually universal tendency to impose concepts of wealth that derive from capitalism.

Once we have delineated the four necessary and sufficient conditions that must apply to any form of wealth within any social formation, we shall be in a position to define the power of a wealth-asset and to determine power of one asset relative to another. We also discover that the possession of *more powerful forms* of wealth may be the basis of the power of one social system over another and of one category of person over another (e.g., of males over females). These are discoveries that are unavailable in the absence of a general characterization of wealth-assets.

Given the importance of wealth, as defined, we can appreciate the efforts of a system's management in developing codes of morality and rules of social relations that more effectively facilitate its accumulation. Indeed, we shall demonstrate that the prevailing and dominant systems of social relations and the regulated set of moral valuations at household and community levels are structured in relation to the exigencies of wealth-accumulation—this being true for any social formation that is organized around wealth. We shall show that the probability that any individual is able to survive (i.e., have access to the means of survival from domestic resources) is a function of his or her location in the social system of "wealth-accumulation."

We shall find that all social formations are structured by the principles of exchange (between individuals or groups) and by the principles of sharing (among individuals within groups). Exchanging and sharing, broadly conceived, will be shown to constitute the foundations for *all* forms of resource allocation, including forceful appropriation and theft. The exchange-reciprocity paradigm that has dominated Western social science has been responsible for logically insupportable analyses of sharing, or pooling, processes, and this paradigm has clouded and confused the analysis of exchange. We present here, for the first time, a new conception of *balanced exchange*. Other students of exchange have been unable to provide a solution to this problem for the general case. We not only find the necessary and sufficient conditions for an exchange relation to be balanced, but we show that any alternative conception must be incorrect. Given a clearer representation of exchange and reciprocity, we may more effectively consider otherwise intractable issues in Chinese social organization.

Systems of sharing will be shown to be derived from *socially imposed* systems of rights and responsibility, and we shall prove that such processes should not be characterized by reciprocity. Much of the confusion that has bedeviled this issue is the result of a failure to distinguish the responsibilities that accrue to social position from the obligations that are derived privately. Confucian thought presents an elegant and sophisticated system of rights and responsibility, and it is an ethical system that is hostile to (balanced) exchange as an aspect of personal relations. However, in Western ethics the exchange-reciprocity paradigm is fundamental, beginning with Aristotle's elevation of a friendship relation as a balanced exchange between "good" men. Unfortunately, students of Chinese society who are trained in the West are often unable, or unwilling, to recognize the uniqueness of the Chinese philosophical tradition. Graduate students in the Institute of Sociology and Anthropology at Peking University are familiar with the thoughts of Fei Xiaotung and with the argument that there are fundamental differences between Chinese and non-Chinese forms of social interaction. My work begins with those insights.

It would appear that the discussion of social relations that dominates the latter portions of this book is unrelated to our discussion of wealth. However, wealth is considered herein as a feature of social structure, having social entailments as intrinsic elements of being. Wealth will be characterized as a managed resource whose value is captured by groups and shared within groups by culturally articulated rules. If we are to understand wealth as a feature of social structure, we must understand *sharing* as a fundamental social process. However, to understand sharing we must also understand exchange (reciprocity), which we shall present as a well-defined alternative to sharing.

A popular but muddled conception of reciprocity and, consequently, a failure to recognize *sharing* as a central feature of culture, have led to analytical misrepresentations of Chinese social relations. This failure has been, in a sense, engineered by bourgeois ideologies of capital accumulation. Particularly today, at a time of global accumulation (of capital), a denial of the *possibility* of sharing in the wealth and consumption domains has become an academic religion, a religion to be exported around the world in a new (hegemonic) civilizing mission. This new religion is called *methodological individualism,* and it advances its principles by denying the existence of corporate groups and by requiring that individuals be the only unit of action. Yet, if individuals are the units of action, an understanding of sharing (within groups) cannot be advanced, preventing us from understanding the relationship of wealth to social structure.

Individualism

Prior to the 1800s Western philosophical values featured a strong communalism and a focus on responsibility to the group, be it the family, the estate, or the guild. The premodern West and contemporary China have featured philosophic traditions that fully recognized individual responsibility toward others as central virtues (Munro 1985). St. Thomas Aquinas argued that a person's love of God was to be manifested in "charity" toward other persons. He suggested that it was through charity that individuals were able to reciprocate, repay, God for His benefaction. And as you well know, the Confucian ideal was a man of virtue who was responsible to superiors and dutiful toward subordinates.

The individualism of the contemporary West emerged as a particular strategy for capital accumulation. The philosophical roots can be found in Adam Smith's (1776) analogy about the "invisible hand" of capitalism that ensures a positive societal outcome from socially indifferent and entirely irresponsible behaviors. Feudal norms of responsibility for the welfare of serfs that the aristocracy had espoused were inconsistent with the new system of wages. Since increases in capital lead to increases in consumer goods, it could be argued that social welfare is advanced (in the long run) by the suppression of the living standards of the great mass if their impoverishment facilitates the accumulation of capital.

The indifference that capitalists were enjoined to have toward workers was not, initially, to be generalized to all forms of relations. A man was still expected to be responsible for his family, and the household was recognized to be an essential element of the social system. However, in the postindustrial contemporary context the household is being rendered asunder by market forces, thereby allowing the irresponsibility of the invisible hand to become applicable to the household. This movement has reached a philosophical extreme in the form of methodological individualism, an approach to social analysis that is increasingly affecting the social sciences.

> The starting point for the individualist paradigm is the simple fact that all social interactions are after all interactions among individuals. The individual in the economy or in the society is like the atom in chemistry; whatever happens can ultimately be described exhaustively in terms of the individuals involved. Of course, the individuals do not act separately. They respond to each other, but each acts within a range limited by the behavior of others as well as by constraints personal to the individual, such as his or her ability or wealth. (Arrow 1994: 3)

Kenneth Arrow's characterization of the individual readily dismisses socially derived responsibility. According to him, the only constraints are "personal to the individual." Virtue has no place here. And, although he does not say so, explicitly, this individual is not connected to others via the sharing of household resources or wealth. Arrow's attempt to convey the reasonableness of the individualist perspective leads him to hide the most critical implication of this paradigm: that scarce resources are necessarily the possession of individuals—that rights to such resources cannot be jointly held, they cannot be *shared*. This hidden assumption must be hidden because it is obviously false.

I might never have noticed this critical assumption had economists not roundly attacked me for presenting a model in which African pastoralists jointly held rights to a herd of cattle. The concordance of my assumption with ethnographic fact was irrelevant. Quoting again from Arrow (1994: 1): "Our behavior in judging economic research, in peer review of papers and research, and in promotions, includes the criterion that in principle the behavior we explain and the policies we propose are explicable in terms of individuals, not of other social categories."

Hence, a model that addresses the strategies of corporate groups of herders is not to be allowed; one must assume that rights to cattle are individual. Arrow's individual cannot share rights with members of a group without violating the presumed independence of that individual. Therefore, the community property of husbands and wives that exists in most states of the United States must not be recognized in formal models.

Tools for the Other (at a Time of Global Accumulation)

These theoretical inclinations are not accidental; they are the products of an overarching capitalist ideology to which everyone within the West becomes subjected. A worldview has evolved that is appealing to the owners of capital; it is increasingly required for corporate- and state-controlled research grants, and it becomes a condition for hiring and promotion. It is an ideology that is useful for the global accumulation of Western capital. The fact that it is scientifically invalid does not threaten its role as a powerful and effective hegemonic ideology. It gains it effectiveness to the degree that the social structures of the Other can be challenged and disrupted by reference to its implications. For example, "individual human rights" can be interpreted to imply that younger family members should have full rights to their market earnings and should not be expected to share those earnings with other family members with whom they live. Under the guise of liberating children from parental domination, we have here a proposition that would deliver those children into the clutches of atomistic market forces.

Systems of accumulation can reach their potential only when there is a socially disabled Other whose role is to contribute to the accumulation of wealth. We shall see that this is a basic principle, not only for the various periods of capital accumulation but for any regime of wealth. The imposition of Western values of "freedom," "democracy," "human rights," "women's rights," and the "right to life" constitute a veritable team of Trojan horses with which the Other is to be rendered helpless in the face of globalizing capital. The problem is not so much that these are intrinsically bad ideas, but that they are advanced strategically and selectively as bases for undermining the legitimacy of recalcitrant authority. When it is useful to do so, the very inverse of these principles may be supported. It is in this way that the period of colonialism gives way to a different and broader terrain of exploitation, in a new civilizing mission.

There is an often essential moral myopia that posits the correctness of a prevailing morality for all past and future time. In this suprahistorical conception of morality, the postindustrial ideologies of the contemporary West can appear to be best, not only for the contemporary West, but for all peoples and for all of historic time. This kind of cultural ethnocentrism is to be expected of the elite and the masses, but it is now becoming the religion of an academic establishment that should certainly know better. This transformation is a clear response to the dictates of capitalist globalization, which demands a level playing field within which to operate throughout the world. Having abandoned strategies of accumulation that could exploit societal differentiation under colonialism, there is now a new strategy of declaring the illegitimacy of alternative systems of rights and responsibility.

For this reason the perspective taken in this book will disturb many readers. They will often demand that I express a postindustrial valuation on the cultural practices of societies in other times and places. If the fertility of women is exchanged for animal stock, I am expected to decry the practice; if women and children are first to die from limited food availability or if some are slaves to be bought and sold by others, I should express moral outrage. The principal reason for my refusal should be clear from the foregoing remarks—I refuse to join the systematic and strategic delegitimization of the Other in the new civilizing mission of the West.

The purpose of this book is to provide a basis for understanding the structural dynamics of systems of wealth-accumulation. In that context we inquire into the processes of the corporate groups that give social integrity to the management of wealth-accumulation. Those group processes are always configured as "rights and responsibilities." It is not my intention to suggest any set of policies or any system of morality to Chinese or to any other national culture. All such matters of social construction derive from complex interactions that are unpredictable. My goal is only to increase the salience of certain essential parameters of social organization, thereby furthering the ability of the Other to survive in the face of global power.

CHAPTER TWO
WEALTH, POWER, AND CORPORATE GROUPS

Insurgent Peasant by Gyula Derkovits. Dózsa-Series IV. (1928) Woodcut, 487 × 440 mm, Hungarian National Gallery, Budapest.

C hapter 2 introduces the most fundamental concept of our discussion: wealth. We all use the term in common speech; however, I am unaware of an analytically useful characterization of wealth— a conception of wealth that could be used for the study of all forms of society. In a capitalistic economy, "wealth" is almost anything of monetary value that one accumulates in sufficient quantity. Unfortunately, social scientists have naively imposed this bourgeois conception of wealth on other forms of society, including those societies that lack a general translation of value into money. Therefore, they have failed to find the special significance that we shall discover for "wealth-assets."

By having a conception of wealth that applies to any society, we will be able to discover its role in social structure. Wealth will be shown to be fundamental to the formation of lineages and tribal organizations. It is foundational to the relative power of one gender over another and of relative rank of other categories of person, and wealth is the focus of management efforts of the leadership of dominant groups within society. By observing the implications of wealth on a cross-cultural and multisocietal basis, we can gain new insights into the implications of capital formation during this period of global accumulation.

The material in this chapter will be presented in a sequence that corresponds to a logic that is only now available to me. Certainly, the path of discovery was a different one. Years ago, I began with an interest in the allocation of consumption goods and "work-effort" within households. The current status of that issue will be central to chapter 6. I focused next on bridewealth and dowry, thereby coming into contact with the strategies of African, Asian, and Oceanic lineages. It was here that the basic findings of this chapter arose. Earlier versions of some elements of this chapter can be found in Bell (1997, and especially 1998) and Bell and Song (1994). The findings were slow in coming, and a full explication of the foundations of this chapter has not been published heretofore.

Wealth

Although "property" should be recognized to have limited ethnographic applicability,[1] *wealth*, if suitably characterized, is a term with nearly universal applicability. It can be shown to be foundational to the power of the dominant gender, social caste, or class in every society. Wealth will be shown to form a basis, directly or indirectly, of the power of one tribe over another, of one matrilineage or patrilineage over another, and of the power of men over women (or vice versa). Indeed, matrilineages and patrilineages do not exist except as entities organized around wealth-assets. And the nation-state that is familiar to our age has been created as a foundation for the management of wealth in the form of capital. Wealth generates greater capacity to produce consumption goods, adding to a group's power to survive, and in every case, one feature of this "power" is the ability to induce or force those lacking in wealth to devote their efforts and lives to the augmentation of wealth-assets held by others. Wealth informs social structure.

Given the centrality of wealth in the social experience of people (and of some nonhuman mammals), it is essential that our understanding of it not become blurred by careless attribution. I shall present a set of necessary and sufficient conditions by which to characterize any resource as an item of wealth. By reference to this set of characteristics, we will be able to identify wealth-assets in any society and elevate our understanding of wealth beyond the level of common cultural usage. Consequently, many references to wealth in the literature are implicitly challenged herein. By going beyond common usage, we can discover characteristics of social process never before observed.

There are four fundamental characteristics of wealth-assets:

1. Growth Criterion: A wealth-asset must have a capacity to grow in number, value, or size over time, as evidenced by the growth rate of human and animal populations (fertility) or by rates of return on capital assets.

2. Consumption Criterion: A wealth-asset must generate a flow of consumption benefits to *a set of individuals who have rights to them*. This set of individuals is a consumption group, the most obvious example being a domestic group. But in relation to certain resources, consumption groups may be manifested at community and at national levels.

3. Marginal Value Criterion: A wealth-asset must be scarce in the sense that marginal increases in its size or value must have positive social valuation.

13

These three (of the set of four) characteristics apply to wealth-assets without reference to the social structures within which they may be embedded; yet each can be realized in practice only by means of appropriate management. A herd can be managed as wealth—and subjected to a process of long-term growth (satisfying the Growth Criterion)—or it may be slaughtered for a feast and become no more than a consumption good. On the other hand, wealth that provides no consumption benefits has no social value. The management of a herd as wealth must be fully consistent with use of the herd as a source of meat, milk, and hides for those who have rights to enjoy such consumption benefits (satisfying the Consumption Criterion). And unless the number of animals is so large that available grazing capacities are exhausted, the birth of offspring will be a valued addition to the herd (satisfying the Marginal Value Criterion).

Certainly, capital also satisfies the Growth, Consumption, and Marginal Value criteria. Under socially and ecologically fortuitous conditions, capital has proven to be a preeminent form of wealth, having the capacity to grow at a relatively high exponential rate, even when other potential forms of wealth have met serious constraint (usually a violation of the Marginal Value Criterion). Human fertility is not wealth with the arrival of the demographic transition, animal fertility ceases to be wealth in the case of a severe shortage of forage areas for herds, and capital ceases to be wealth when processes of capitalist accumulation induce its redundancy, reducing long-run profits to zero.

It is not so readily evident, however, that the properties of wealth apply to land. Land does not grow in size or number; it lacks any "natural" form of self-augmentation. This is also true of capitalist "means of production"—machines. However, under facilitating social circumstances, circumstances that permit the expropriation and subjugation of others, *the quantity in the hands of particular groups or individuals can grow* (to the disadvantage of others). A possible role and reason for state-level power may be to facilitate the maintenance of infrastructures that promote land as wealth. However, land is at best a weak form of wealth. It is more likely to become an essential resource that permits the fuller "wealth-expression" of another resource, such as animal or human fertility.

One of many exceptions may be the role of land during the period of China's imperial expansion. Here, we find elaborate administrative machinery for an expansion of the arable as the population increased, and there were further expansions in the form of colonial domination. Yet this land expansion process was oriented toward aggrandizing the state, not constituent groups. Land functioned more effectively as wealth at the imperial level than at the local. Indeed, one of the classical problems of Chinese statecraft was to discover how to strengthen the state relative to those powerful overlords who might seek to usurp state prerogatives.

The role of land in social structure is highly variable, and it is difficult to assign to it an unambiguous characterization. Land is wealth inchoate. It may be subject to accumulation by some and not others in a given society; it may be subject to accumulation by the tribe or state (and perhaps not by subgroups); and it may appear to be subject to accumulation by no social entity. For example, English feudalism was oriented toward stability and order, rather than accumulation, at both the local and state levels. The Catholic Church, on the other hand, was concerned to prevent further erosion of territory to the forces of Islam and eventually promoted geographic expansion beyond Europe. It was only in this larger domain that land clearly functioned as a wealth-asset.

The criterion to be adopted here is that land should be treated as a wealth-asset if its growth or maintenance or both require active efforts. Hence, in the weakest case, land fails to increase in quantity or value, but a significant effort is required to avoid its diminution at the hands of others. Hence, land is a wealth-asset for those who lose land as well as for those whose land may increase steadily over time. The process matters, even for those who are unsuccessful. It is clear, however, that the dynamics of land acquisition are usually connected with population pressures and, thus, with the expression of fertility. Consequently, the interaction of fertility and land, as jointly articulated wealth-assets, are what must be managed in some fashion. And often this process involves violence.

Implicit in the preceding three characteristics of wealth has been the manner in which the asset is managed and the existence of a set of individuals who have rights thereto. In order for an asset to realize its potential as wealth, there is an additional essential characteristic:

4. Indefinite Life Criterion: The (growing) asset must be exploitable over an indefinite time horizon by the entity that possesses rights to its accumulation over that horizon.

15

Although one could imagine wealth as the possession of a single individual, such that it atrophies with the death of that individual, it is unlikely that any noncapitalist society has ever been so poorly organized. If the asset has a potential for indefinite increases in quantity or valuation much beyond the life of individuals, there will always be methods of capturing those benefits within a socially designated collectivity. Hence, when we speak of a wealth-asset, we have in mind the entire "time-path" of valuation, not simply its value at an arbitrary point in time. This implication is clear in reference to a herd of cattle. A given herd continues into the future, changing in numbers and composition. It is the same herd, even when every specific element has changed, and it is the underlying dynamics of fertility that are the unifying forces linking future elements to the past.

Noncapitalist social formations have been able to exploit the long-term growth properties of wealth-assets by allowing a resource of indefinite life to be associated with culturally pre-prescribed sets of "rights-holders" that also have indefinite life, that is, through the medium of clearly specified inheritance rules: A system of inheritance exists only when there is a system of devolution such that particular individuals, identified by characteristics of parentage, gender, and, perhaps, birth order, are socially predetermined as the appropriate recipients of socially predetermined shares of the relevant assets.

The set of rights-holders that results *conceptually* from this chain of devolution constitutes a (multigenerational) wealth-holding corporate group, for which unilineal descent groups are the best-known representation. Lineages are often defined in terms of kinship and "kin terms." However, they exist as socially meaningful collectivities only to the extent that their members hold joint inheritance claims for *shares* of resources.

Modern business corporations accommodate the Indefinite Life Criterion without having to construct multigenerational corporate groups. This is accomplished by the development of a standard of account ("money") that can be exchanged against wealth-assets as well as against consumption goods and by creating "shares" of capital assets. The "money-value" of a share reflects at each point in time the collective (market) expectations regarding the future growth in the value of the underlying assets. In other words, the price of a share is a measure of the indefinite life of the assets, discounted to the present. Astoundingly, the future can be purchased in the present. This possibility is a form of magic, and we should not allow the magical nature of this thing to be obscured by the fact that it is well established in the contemporary period. In any case, the value of shares, the discounted value of the future, depends on the effectiveness of capital in the production of consumer goods, which are also valued in terms of money. In this way, an owner of shares becomes functionally equivalent to the preceding "intergenerational entity," holding rights to the "indefinite life" of the asset.

Corporate Groups

A *corporate group* is the set of individuals who jointly hold rights to a given set of wealth-assets or consumption goods and services. The minimal conception of the corporate group presented here lacks any cultural articulation. In fact when we use the term "lineage" there is no implication of a culturally recognized association of any kind, and in the normal case, most of its members are yet unborn. In our discussion, then, a wealth-holding corporate group, or lineage, is an abstraction that is associated with a form of rightful access. It is not an identifiable set of individuals. All that is required is that there be a socially predictable mechanism by which certain individuals gain rights to a wealth-asset. Unfortunately, corporate group is a term in common use in anthropology and in most cases it entails cultural features that are not presumed here.

Furthermore, we will refer to domestic groups as corporate groups. In this case, the groups are concrete, but perhaps only at a point in time. That is, individuals may belong to one such group today and another tomorrow depending on where they happen to be at that moment. Thus, at the home of one's parents and at the home of one's parents-in-law, one may have rights to a share of available foods. And it would not be meaningful to have rights to shares of food in both places simultaneously, because otherwise one's share would remain unconsumed in one of those places or someone who possesses no right to it would claim it (illegitimately).

It is very important, then, that rights to consumer goods and rights to wealth-assets be recognized separately. And similarly, wealth-holding groups must be recognized as distinct from domestic groups. I say this even though a compounding of these two groups is the common practice of anthropology. For example, anthropologists commonly claim that in patrilineal, patrilocal societies women are incorporated into the lineages of their husbands, whereas it is clear that they become members of domestic groups that are connected to the lineages of their husbands.

The Consumption Criterion suggests that wealth-assets must generate a flow of consumption benefits to those who have rights to them (in domestic groups). While the individuals who belong to wealth-holding groups are usually among those with rights to these consumption benefits, as a matter of ethnographic fact, it is not an analytical necessity. Rather, it is essential that the flows of consumption goods that arise from wealth provide a consumption benefit at least indirectly to members of the wealth-holding group. For example, we could imagine a society in which members of a wealth-holding elite consider milk ritually polluting and suitable only for slaves, who are themselves a wealth-asset. In this case the consumption flow from cattle is complementary with another wealth-asset, and this second asset is productive of consumption goods of value to wealth holders. At some point in this chain of benefits, wealth holders must gain benefits of consumption. This must be so if the wealth-asset is to have "value."

Although the wealth-holding corporate group must always benefit directly or indirectly from the flow of consumption benefits produced by wealth, it is never the case that those benefits are limited to this group.

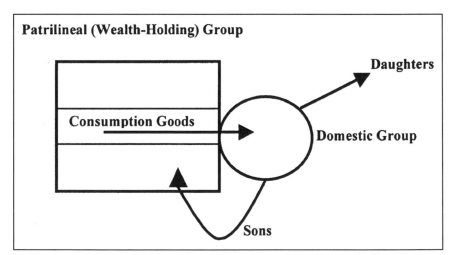

Figure 2.1. Relationship Between Wealth-Holding and Domestic Groups in a Patrilineal Setting

There will always be others who have a claim on this flow. Hence, while a lineage of male heirs may have exclusive rights of inheritance to cattle, their wives and female children can expect to receive meat, milk, and hides as members of associated households. As members of households, these individuals have a socially supported "demand-right" to the basis of subsistence, in much the same way that heirs have socially supported demand-rights to shares of wealth.

While wealth-assets may generate consumption goods for the subsistence of domestic groups, it is always true that domestic groups yield outputs that accrue to wealth-holding groups. The most obvious example would be the case of domestic groups benefiting from animal stock while wealth-holding groups obtain the benefits of fertility from domestic groups—a supply of lineage members and a supply of daughters who can be exchanged for animal stock (see figure 2.1). These criteria make it possible to identify wealth as it may arise in any society, human or nonhuman. And we shall see that any asset that meets these qualifications has distinct consequences for social organization. I can also claim that if in the future a previously unimagined form of wealth were to be developed as the foundation of a postcapitalist social formation, this wealth-asset will have the characteristics indicated in the preceding. However, were I to "define" wealth, I would necessarily limit its properties to those that seem to have been presented by known forms of wealth. That is, a definition would describe "wealth as we have known it," whereas my criteria provide us with the capability of "knowing wealth when we see it." I do not believe that it is possible to accomplish these two things simultaneously.[2]

Inheritance

It is common for English speakers to use the term "inheritance" to refer to systems of bequests, as well as to systems of inheritance. This conflation arises from the fact that the term "inheritance" continued to be used in England even after the Church of the Middle Ages had forced on it a system of bequests. No doubt, the church encouraged this confusion in order to minimize the significance of the new requirements. A system of bequests, expressed through the medium of "wills," or testaments, allows an individual to claim fully the right of alienation with respect to wealth-assets. Hence, an Englishman could bequeath his entire landed estate, complete with serfs and slaves, to the church, and he was more likely to do so if in life his deeds promised an eternity in hell. A priest would show no reluctance in alerting him to these options.

Of special relevance to our discussion is the fact that a system of bequests, to the extent that it disinherited offspring, is a fatal attack on the integrity of wealth-holding corporate groups. With the abandonment of "rightful heirs," it implies individual ("private") ownership. Since individual ownership is inconsistent with effective wealth management under precapitalist conditions, devolution to offspring continued to be socially encouraged. But this fact does not change the fact that the right of sons had been abandoned and, hence, the system of inheritance no longer existed.

A system of inheritance is one in which the claims on a person's estate are socially prescribed by unambiguous rules of devolution. In such systems, one's heirs, however they may be designated, have rightful claims on assets that arise from their positions within wealth-holding corporate groups. Indeed, their positions within such groups are defined by reference to those rights. And in the absence of a formal process of disinheritance by which an heir is socially divested of eligibility, the choices of an anterior generation are strongly circumscribed. The existence of an inheritance process reduces any current possessor of a resource to the role of a corporate trustee of an estate that has indefinite duration. The individuals who now control it do not have the right to alienate the wealth-asset, except as part of a strategy of effective wealth augmentation—"in the interest of the family." That means that wealth should be alienated only in exchange for another form of wealth whose flow of benefits to future generations is expected to increase.

While systems of inheritance are among the least problematic corporate structures for the management of wealth, there are other forms. For example, devolution in colonial Guatemala was by bequest of the "patrimonial estate" to a single son or daughter. The patrimony would devolve to a daughter if it could be instrumental in arranging her marriage to a native Spaniard, thereby generating prestige and social connections in Spain of enormous value. Such a marriage could also advance a marriage to a Guatemalan of good position. This movement of the patrimony did not affect the management of the estate. However, it clearly meant that a man who did not belong to the patrilineal line would contribute sons and daughters to the group. These new members would be a drain on the income of the estate, but if daughters married appropriately, the group would experience a counterbalancing inflow of wealth.[3]

Defining the Power of Wealth-Assets

A central and defining characteristic of wealth is its capacity to grow in value, magnitude, or number over time. We will designate the *natural rate of growth*, r, of a form of wealth to be the rate at which it can grow under effective management when there are no reductions whatsoever for consumption and use. Hence, the r of cattle is the rate at which a herd will grow under *commonly prevailing* environmental and ecological conditions, good management, and in the absence of any use of healthy reproductive females for consumption, gifts, or bridewealth. This means that if the size of the herd (or any other asset) is initially W_0, then after the passage of time (t) the amount of wealth is potentially

$W(t) = W_0 e^{r\,t}$, where e is the base of the natural logarithm.

This characterization applies to a herd of cattle, to a human population, and to any other unit of wealth, provided that limits on growth do not intervene during the process. For example, if there are no epidemic diseases, droughts, or limitations on grazing land, a herd should be able to grow indefinitely at its natural rate. The actual rate of growth that is feasible may prove to be substantially below its natural rate. Nevertheless, since we cannot predict the actual rate of growth, we shall use its natural rate as a defining characteristic of the resource.

The natural rate of growth of population defines the power of fertility as a wealth-asset. This power is expressed through women, but it accrues to the corporate group that holds rights to it. In the cases of matrilineal organization, women are among those rights-holders. In the cases of patrilineal organization, they are not. In any case, the power associated with a wealth-asset accrues to a corporate group. In fact, the power of wealth is the power that it provides to a group, because the growth of the resource has no social significance in the absence of the related set of rights-holders. The necessary assistance that women require from men does not mean that male insemination has the properties of wealth. This is because under normal conditions the availability of insemination capability is redundant, in violation of the Marginal Value Criterion. That is, under conditions that would allow the access of a single male to the sexuality of a multiplicity of females, a reduction in the number of men need not affect the effective fertility of women. Women are the limiting resource on population growth, not men. It is for this reason that in the context of the simplest production systems, only female fertility is wealth, often leaving men bereft of any counterposing form of wealth.

Levi-Strauss (1969 [1949]) has suggested that the exchange of women by groups of men is among the most primal of social processes. However, this is surely incorrect. It is the circulation of males into groups that contain related females, not the exchange of females among groups of related males, that dominates the scene among mammals, and it was common among American "Indians" and remains the practice in a small number of African, Asian, and South American societies. It is inconceivable that it was not predominant among Homo sapiens until archeologically recent times.

Now that we have distinguished wealth in the form of fertility from domestic consumption goods, such as sex, we can readily see the confusion in the literature regarding marriage. While it is true that marriage is oriented toward the securing of rights to domestic services on the part of the principals, the *social organization of marriage is always defined by reference to the interests of outsiders*. Men are driven to secure special, rightful access to the sexuality of women, but for outsiders it is fertility and the flow of benefits from fertility that are central. And in the absence of another form of wealth (or "community defense," to be discussed in the proceeding) that can be counterposed in exchange for fertility, claims to it will remain within a woman's natal group.

In most cases this group includes her siblings, her parents, her maternal grandmother, the siblings thereof, and so forth—a matrilineal group. This kind of multigenerational collectivity may claim, *by default*, the fertility of women. And this group will make use of its claim as a means of extracting "work-power" from men in an institution called marriage. Matrilineal groups *exploit* men by inducing them to contribute to the growth of a matrilineage to which those men do not belong. It is a straightforward example of "surplus value" that is left unrecognized by Friedrich Engels (1972 [1884]).

There are three ways for a group of males to gain control of fertility and secure fertility as a foundation for patrilineal organization. First, men may gain control over a more powerful asset—an asset with a higher rate of growth. Second, they may become the essential protectors of their community and, hence, of those who are blessed with fertility, so the number of fighting men, not the number of nubile women, determines the rate of population growth. Or, finally, men may raid other groups and seize possession of their female members. In principle, the capture rate of females can overwhelm the internal growth rate, once again making the number of raiding men the more powerful locus of population growth.

Men without Endowment

While both men and women embody work-effort, only women are blessed with fertility. This proves to be a problem for men when the "wealth-value" of female fertility is controlled in the interest of a group, such as a matrilineage, because this group's interest intrudes conspicuously onto the mating efforts of men, forcing them into the service of the group.

The exploitation principle: Those who control wealth always have the power to extract work-effort from others, thereby augmenting their own rate of "wealth-accumulation." Since the exploitation of those without wealth is an essential condition for the maximization of its rate of accumulation and, hence, of effective management of wealth-assets, this power will not be left unused.

A most pitiable example comes from Africa, where a man of the Cewa tribe submits to a life of agricultural work on the land of his wife's people. According to Audrey Richards (1950: 233–34):

> Mitchell says that unsuitable husbands are dismissed with compensation and sent away. He adds that the husbands of the women of a village are often away visiting and are definitely not reckoned as members of the community. Stannus states that a widower is usually given a present with the suggestion that he go elsewhere since he no longer has any standing in his wife's village.
>
> Marwick indicates that Cewa marriage ties sit loose and speaks of a man and his sister and "her current husband." The Cewa talk of the father as a stranger. "He is a beggar; he has simply followed his wife." At divorce he leaves his wife's village with his hoe, his axe, and his sleeping-mat and has no right to any of the children of the marriage, even if he may have begotten as many as seven children.

A similar story can be told about men in Rembau, one of the nine states of Negri Sembilam, Malasia. Here we find not only matriliny but also matriarchy, where all clan land is inherited by women only. The position of men in marriage is predictably low:

> But if the responsibility for a husband's welfare rests with his wife, his relative position is one of inferiority. He is at the beck and call of his relations by marriage; his mother-in-law boasts that she can find some use for any sort of son—the clever may be cajoled, and the fool bullied; the blind man can be put to pound the rice; the cripple to mind the padi drying in the sun; the deaf to fire the cannon and the braggart to take the hard knocks. . . .
>
> The mother's dominance in the home is patent to her children and has prevented the growth of a sincere filial affection for the father. (Parr and Mackray 1910: 87)

The Rembau case is unusual in that the wealth-holding corporate group consists only of women; and these women are endowed with wealth in land as well as with the wealth-value of their own fertility. The Cewa, on the other hand, are more typically matrilineal in that brothers are admissible into membership. Hence, men have status at the home of their mothers, even though they are without power at the homes of their wives.

Such is the consequence for men having no wealth. A different structure is found among the Inuit. In this case the awesome environment that yields an often meager and always uncertain supply of food undermines the value of female fertility. Depending on location and season, men may be hunters or fishermen or both, while women transport and maintain the household, process and prepare food, and make clothing. The tasks of women are demanding, but achievable only so long as men are successful in hunting. And while every man wants sons and, perhaps, daughters, not many children can be maintained. Infanticide, especially of females, is common. This fact implies the social redundancy of women's fertility and implies that its marginal social valuation is zero.

> Infants are only potentially productive. If conditions permit, the Eskimos will always endeavor to raise their babies to adulthood. Too often, however, harsh circumstance does not permit it. It is then up to each family to decide for itself: Are its present resources (both human and

material) sufficient to maintain the baby through its nonproductive years? There will be no social blame or legal sanction if a negative decision is reached and acted upon. (Hoebel 1967: 74)

Census data collected by Weyer (1962; cited by Hoebel [1967]) indicate that in eight of ten groups studied, there was a (male to female) sex ratio of 1.40 or higher among surviving infants, compared to the customary 1.05 figure. Nevertheless, as a result of accidents in hunting and homicide, adult women greatly outnumbered adult men.

Among Inuit marriage was easily and informally established and abandoned. Once established, however, men exercised great control over their wives. A measure of the strength of this control is the fact that men would lend their wives to friends quite readily—the wife's sexuality being fully the possession of the husband, and he could kill her without consequence. There was little sexual jealousy, and both spouses were expected to take lovers during the occasions when the husband was away hunting. Nevertheless, there appears to have been frequent combat over women, leading on many occasions to homicide. Challenging a man for possession of a woman, via flagrant adultery or by "theft," was a mark of power and prestige for the interloper and a source of outrage and shame for the husband. Contests for women were the ultimate status game made possible by the ease of divorce that limits the rights of husbands and by the limited wealth-value of women that prevents the development of wealth-holding groups that would control their fertility and secure more effective, rightful access to them.

Since Inuit culture strongly sanctioned selfish acquisition, a man would need special reasons to refuse the sexuality of his wife to a friendly visitor. On the other hand, men had limited rights in women; they had only that which their charisma could deliver. Among the Inuit, the contest between men was simply one on one. In the best of cases, the conflict took the form of a "song contest" in which each attempted to depict in song the inferiority and depravity of the other. In other cases, physical combat and, perhaps, homicide could erupt, to be followed by the vengeance of kin. These facts are beautifully illustrated in a recent film, "Fast Runner." It appears, then, that Inuit men could make claims on the services of their wives only to the extent that they and their kin were physically able. The weakness of fertility as a form of wealth is obvious. But were men not powerful? Well, not really. Social position was maintained only by personal effort and charisma. At any moment his wife could pack her things and disappear into the hut of another. On the other hand, women were disadvantaged, not only by their lack of independent economic viability but also by the social redundancy of their fertility. It was this weakness that promoted their vulnerability, not the absolute strength of men.

Defense of Community

If the survival of a wealth-holding group were threatened by outside aggression, then the demographic growth of the group generally becomes dependent on the defensive actions of men, so increasing the rate of population growth would depend on the number of (armed) men. Under these conditions, it is men who advance the group's fertility, and military activity becomes a basis of power and a foundation for patrilineal organization. However, it is wrong to believe that violence itself is the basis of power. The relevant wealth-asset remains fertility, whose expression now depends on male intervention.

Military activity can be extended further when men capture and incorporate women from other groups in "local warfare" (Harris 1993). Both the defense and capture of women have created conditions for the *fecundation* of men among the Comanche. However, raiding and plunder were problematic methods of population growth because of the high probability of injury and death that they entailed. Comanche society in the nineteenth century was constantly recouping its losses by incorporating captives into the tribe. Such captives were taken as children and mildly exploited as houseworkers, if they were girls, or put to work as herders, if boys. The girls were ultimately married by their captors and so acquired full citizenship. The boys were allowed to join war parties, and they, too, were incorporated after a time into the kinship system through adoption as "brothers" or "sons" by their captors or some other Comanche friend (Hoebel 1967: 136–37).

The conditions existed among the Comanche for the development of patriliny, not based on moveable wealth-assets, but based on community defense and raiding. However, a cultural transformation so great as patriliny may have required more time and more social stability than was available to them. In their transition from the matrilineal organization that existed prior to the disruption of European intrusion, they had assumed a simple "band" form of organization. And relative to the matrilineal form that they had maintained earlier, the band represented a state of disorganization, a state that may well have been appropriate to their chaotic life of raiding and marauding.

The Baruya is an example of a society where male defense is the basis for preserving both land and fertility as wealth, and where male defense has become a firm basis of patriliny. Maurice Godelier (1986: 3–4) describes

> the flight of the Baragaye refugees to Marawaka . . . around the end of the eighteenth century. . . . They decided to grab the territory of the local groups that had given them shelter . . . and took the name of one of the clans of the victorious refugees, the Baruya clan, and absorbed certain lineages of the vanquished local groups.

Patrilineal clans hold land, aggressively acquired, and maintaining and expanding this land is a precondition for the survival and growth of the group. Hence, the military activity of men makes feasible the preservation of fertility and land. Since female fertility and land are held hostage by the warfare of men, it is the number of men that determines the fertility rate. Analytically, it is men who are fertile. This analytical fact is stridently recapitulated, among the Baruya, by the ingestion of sperm for strengthening women, producing children, and converting boys into men. It symbolizes the fecundation of men made possible by warfare in defense of women (and others). On this basis, men can claim rights to fertility within patrilineal groups. In societies, such as the Baruya, men exchange women among patrilineal groups, and it may have been a focus on this form of society that led to Levi-Strauss' theory that marriage begins with an exchange of women. Lacking wealth other than fertility and prone to violence, they would appear to be emblematic of the primitive.

There seems to be an almost universal presumption that control over women and their fertility is gained by men through a direct attack on women. In short, men are said to "dominate" women and "oppress" them by force. In chapter 6 we show that physical force against women is characteristic of weak men. Careful attention to the facts of the matter makes

27

clear that men gain domination over women by having power over other men. For the Baruya the power over other men is through warfare. In societies containing wealth other than fertility, it is control over those other forms of wealth that becomes a basis for ranking among men. There are no exceptions to this rule.

The importance of community defense as a basis of male dominance is further illustrated by salient exceptions, cases in which women are central to community defense and warfare. Two celebrated examples are the military activity and leadership of Vietnamese women in their nearly two thousand years of struggles against Chinese, French, and American colonialism and the "Amazons" of precolonial Dahomey who are credited by many to have been important in fighting the French.

Herskovits (1967) devotes two volumes to his economic anthropology of Dahomey. However, this society is so very complicated and sophisticated that many more volumes would hardly have sufficed. At the level of the king, it was a slave empire with annual raids against neighboring societies for the gathering of slaves to the benefit of his retainers and for the massive workforce that he required in his own fields. Slaves were required, at least two were sacrificed each day to complement the king's prayers for periodic massive elaborate sacrifices to propitiate the ancestors, and the sale of slaves to Europeans was the source of revenue that powered economic process. The slave trade provided the king with guns with which to raid others, other goods, and with cowries for use as money. This was a society devoted to the trading of internally produced goods as well as the goods of neighboring societies, made possible with cowries. Slaves were not a major source of fertility for marriage to free persons, and the fertility of the women of Dahomey remained an important wealth-asset. However, the sale of slaves provided the cowries that could then become essential as marriage payments. One might say that the fertility of women was exchanged against the bodies of exported slaves.

Herskovits (1967) describes Dahomey as patrilineal. However, the significance of women in warfare was mirrored by their significance in social structure. It appears that many women of the upper classes chose to establish their own compounds, using money that they earned in trade or from inheritance, to secure wives and develop a lineage. They became female husbands with children sired by relatives, and their eldest sons inherited their daughters, and their eldest daughters inherited their sons.

These younger sons and daughters (who might share no parent in common) would intermarry to produce the next generation, and all of these children would belong to the sib of their deceased grandmother. Then, after this first generation, the eldest daughter would assume the name of the founder, and the whole process would be repeated. While there are certainly some unanswered questions here, my main point is that Dahomey was also matrilineal for a large percentage of upper class and otherwise wealthy women.

By the mid-nineteenth century, the Amazons were a fully established institution. The army possessed two parts: the right and the left. On the right were two components, the male and the Amazon, as pairs with equivalent rank. The Amazon was the "mother" of the male, and "the male soldier, when accused, appeals to his 'mother' to speak for him" (F. E. Forbes; cited by Herskovits 1967: 84). The female soldiers were also called wives of the king and hence the "mothers" of all others. They were the trusted bodyguards of the king, and they were celibate. According to R. F. Burton (1864: vol. 2, 49; cited by Herskovits 1967: 86):

> The regimen in which these women are compelled to live doubtless increases their ferocity in fight. It is the essence of training every animal, from a game cock to a pugilist, and a married she-soldier would be useful only as a mother of men. Commander Forbes thus explains the action of forced celibacy: "The extreme exercise of one passion will generally obliterate the very sense of the others; the Amazons, whilst indulging in the excitement of the most fearful cruelties, forget the other desires of our fallen nature." . . . Of course they are savage as wounded gorillas, more cruel than their brethren in arms. For men at most differ as heaven and earth; But women, worst and best, as heaven and hell.

According to Edgerton (2000: 15):

> Before they were killed almost to the last woman by much better armed French troops in the early 1890s, for some 200 years Dahomey's "Amazons" had achieved a well-earned reputation for loyalty to their monarch, and during the nineteenth century, they repeatedly displayed ferocity, bravery, and skill in battle. During the 1840s, they led Dahomey's army to several victories, including one in which its male soldiers fled under fire, forcing the Amazons to fight and win the battle alone.

Illustration of an Amazon musketeer, holding a severed male head, dripping blood. Source: Forbes, Frederick Edwyn (1851, vol. 1, opp. p. 23).

Females were not only the counterpart of males in the army but also were at the highest levels of royal administration.

> At the Court of Dahomey every man must have at least one mother, and she may be twenty years his junior. (Burton 1864: vol. 1, 213). . . .
>
> No office under government is paid, and the offices, although hereditary, are subject to much espionage. In the house of each minister lives a King's daughter [the minister's "mother"] and two officers: these superintend the minister's trade, on which he pays tribute according to their report. (Burton 1864: vol. 1, 34–35)

It is clear that men and women were strongly differentiated in position and function. Amazons tended to occupy the inside, being located within the palace walls in times of peace, and as the king's "daughters" in government, they had the confidence of the king as advisors and fiscal protectors. We should not be surprised, then, that in private life, other women may have independent wealth, they may have wives of their own (wealth in the form of fertility), and they may act as the founders of lineages.

Another society featuring a tradition of women warriors is Vietnam. According to Nancy Wiegersma (1988: 27–28), the status of women in early Vietnamese society was more equal to men than in subsequent periods of Vietnamese history up to (and possibly including) the present era. Women fought in the Vietnamese military in this early period. In fact, the Vietnamese women-military and political leaders are the ones who mounted attacks on the Chinese in the first several centuries of Chinese rule.

In addition to the famous rebellion by Trung Trac and Trung Nhi that was temporarily successful against the Chinese in A.D. 40, there was another insurrection against the Chinese led by a woman military leader, Trieu Thi Trinh, two hundred years later. After this, the anti-Chinese leaders were men, and this change reflected the influence of Confucianism on Vietnamese Society. In addition to these indications of high female status, there is considerable contemporary cross-cultural evidence, presented by Ester Boserup (1965), that the more "primitive" farming systems are female and that men gain ascendancy in agricultural societies only after the introduction of the metal plough. The Vietnamese may have had a primitive version of a plough before Chinese intervention, but the Chinese claim to have introduced an improved metal plough into Vietnamese agriculture.

> Women were the early agriculturists in Vietnam and are reputed to have discovered rice cultivation. A woman named Sao Chi is supposed to have introduced rice cultivation into Vietnam: "One day, she discovered a grass with white grains. She picked off the grains and scattered them on the mud. More plants grew from them and then more grains." There were temples erected to the women discoverers of other crops also, for example Lady Soya, Lady Mulberry, and Lady Bean.

31

Vietnamese soldier: Young women were said to be excellent warriors. Source: *The Vietnam Archive at Texas Tech University.*

In this early Vietnamese society, children did not know their fathers and, even later, after several centuries of Chinese influence, did not bear the name of their fathers. There was no parental interference with their progeny's marriage decisions in this early period, since this epoch was before the establishment of private property, and there were no economic factors for the parents to consider. The husband, when married, went to live with the wife in her family home. (Taylor 1999: 27–28)

Even the Chinese influenced Lê Code of the Lê Dynasty (1428–1788) manifested distinct recognition of rights for women, relative to Confucian standards. Indeed, during this period there was an effort to retrieve much of traditional Vietnamese tradition after a thousand years of Chinese efforts to instill hierarchy and patriarchy. However, after ousting the Chinese in 939, Vietnamese kings carried out a six-century long process of southward movement whose frontier encountered and subdued the Champa kingdom (Gotter 1968). This military expansion was not a manifestation of "community defense" and did not feature women warriors. We would guess that it only strengthened male supremacy.

The Communist Party initiated a new period of national defense with women as full participants during the 1930s. It was felt that the liberation of women from "feudal ideology" required their political education and military involvement (Taylor 1999). However, similar involvement of women in Communist struggles is rare, so one must associate their more recent involvement with an honored cultural tradition of heroic women and with the importance that women continued to maintain in Vietnamese agriculture.

Ester Boserup (1965) noted a correlation between the use of metal plows in agriculture and male ascendancy. However, plows are only tools for the production of food and cannot be a basis of power. On the other hand, the plow leads to increased productivity of *land* and increases the potential level of productive surplus that an organized elite may extract from direct producers. If men are the principal users of the plow, then there will tend to be increased efforts by elites to exploit men. Boserup calls this "agricultural intensification." Effective exploitation of men requires a division of labor and an ideology of female service that facilitates the efforts of this direct producer. It is not unlike the role of women in their support of men during the period of industrial capital. In the agrarian system, however, land (not capital) becomes the dominating wealth-asset, joining with fertility in a regime of accumulation.

However, the story in Vietnam was different. The Chinese did not seek direct control over male producers; rather, they accepted the villages as units of exploitation, allowing many traditional forms to remain intact therein. In that traditional system, a system of communal land tenure prevailed, along with periodic redistribution as a function of family size. And women were arguably as important as men as direct producers within that system. Quite possibly, a more intensive level of surplus extraction by the Chinese might have forced greater specialization within families, thereby isolating males as direct producers.

Vietnam did not develop patrilineal inheritance. Many authors mistakenly refer to Vietnam as patrilineal, but it would be more correct to say that it has been patriarchal. For example, husbands were allowed to beat their wives (so long as there were no serious injuries), while wives were forbidden to complain to husbands. Moreover, men were usually chosen to succeed their fathers in the possession of "worship" land whose product was intended to aid in the veneration of ancestors. *But patriliny must be identified by reference to the structure of wealth-holding groups.* "Patrilineal" is a term with reference to the manner in which wealth is transmitted across generations. In spite of the clearly subordinate legal status of women in traditional Vietnam, sons and daughters inherited equally. Furthermore, the property of wives remained separate from that of their husbands, both during and after marriage. It would seem that the case of Vietnam is one where Chinese patriarchy (and its ideology) has been imposed on traditional matrilineal organization, resulting in a compounded form. In any case, we should not confuse succession with inheritance. Vietnam featured patrilateral succession, but not patrilineal inheritance.

It should be made clear that I offer here no "explanation" for the appearance of female warriors in these two exceptional societies. But there is a general denial in Western social science of these seemingly intrusive facts. Edgerton (2000: 1) cites John Keegan, *A History of Warfare* (1993: 73) as an example of this denial: "Women, however, do not fight. They seldom fight among themselves and never, in any military sense, fight men. If warfare is as old as history and as universal as mankind, we must now enter the supremely important limitation that it is entirely a masculine activity."

Amazing. It is possible that this expert on warfare is reluctant to recognize the achievements of non-European women, whose efforts involved military defeat of European men. Certainly, the efforts of Vietnamese women were well advertised by posters and photographs during their war with the United States. How can such publicly available facts remain unknown to those who know the most? We find a similar denial among some feminists, for whom a strictly male inclination to violence is believed to be the primary basis of male domination. In the contest between fact and ideology, the latter always wins.

What, then, are the implications of this discussion for the position of women in society? Does it imply that the position of women in contemporary societies would be advanced by the placement of women into military combat? The answer is no. Notice that our argument is that "community defense" becomes a basis of male domination because it has the result that the *number of men*, not the number of nubile women, determines the rate of population growth. Fertility, directly expressed, or militarily defended, is the basis of power in these societies. However, fertility is not a contemporary basis of power. Capital is now the ruling wealth-asset, and technological capability is the deciding feature in military success. "The number of men" is no longer the critical issue, and with the passage of time, it becomes even less important. The position of women under capitalism depends on their social location relative to capital and technology.

The Power of Animal Stock

We now consider the common case where a movable wealth-asset in the possession of men becomes the basis of patriliny. A patrilineal wealth-holding group is the set of males who have rightful claim, via processes of inheritance, to some set of wealth-assets. Daughters and wives are assets of such groups, not members, since they have no rights of inheritance. Moreover, women's fertility becomes a patrilineally held wealth-asset when (as I shall demonstrate) men hold another wealth-asset that possesses greater power than fertility.

Consider a herd of cattle that grows at a "normal" rate of 3.4 percent per annum under normal conditions of health and food availability (Dahl and Hjort 1976). Over time this herd, growing at an exponential rate, will become rather large. If the population of the pastoral society also grows rapidly, there would be no problem in managing this growing herd. However, it can be shown that growth of the human group (operating in a pre-modern demographic growth environment) will not match herd growth unless the average woman produces over ten surviving offspring (Bell and Song 1994).

Cattle can be used as bridewealth—securing the transfer of fertility from one group to another—only when cattle reproduce at a rate that exceeds the growth of the human population. This condition leads me to say the fertility of the herd is *more powerful* than the fertility of women. This greater power provides men with the capacity to secure the wealth-asset embodied in women. The "power" associated with holding wealth in the form of cattle is a function of its rate of growth. This analytical fact becomes clear when one imagines the contrary. If the fertility of women exceeds the fertility of cattle, then over time the population becomes poorer and poorer on a per capita basis, especially when cattle are employed as bridewealth, thereby increasing population growth and reducing herd growth. Engels (1972 [1884]: 65–68) recognizes this power of animal stock and associates it with a transition from matrilineal to patrilineal organization.

> Here [in the Old World] the domestication of animals and the breeding of herds had developed a hitherto unsuspected source of wealth and created entirely new social relationships. . . . But to whom did this new wealth belong? Originally, undoubtedly to the gens. But private property in herds must have developed at a very early stage. . . .
>
> Just as the once so easily obtainable wives had now acquired an exchange value and were bought, so it happened with labour power, especially after the herds had finally been converted into family possessions. The family did not increase as rapidly as the cattle. More people were required to tend them; the captives taken in war were useful for just this purpose, and, furthermore, they could be bred like the cattle itself. . . .
>
> According to mother right, that is, as long as descent was reckoned solely through the female line, and according to the original custom of inheritance in the gens, it was the gentile relatives that at first inherited from a deceased member of the gens. The property had to remain within the gens. At first, in view of the insignificance of the chattels in question, it may, in practice, have passed to the nearest gentile relatives—that is, to the blood relatives on the mother's side. The children of the deceased, however, belonged not to his gens, but to that of their mother. In the beginning, they inherited from their mother, along with the rest of their mother's blood relatives, and later, perhaps, had first claim on her property; but they could not inherit from their father, because they did not belong to his gens, and his property had to remain in the latter. On the death of the herd owner, therefore, his herds passed, first of all, to his brothers and sisters and to his sisters' children or to the descendants of his mothers' sisters. His own children, however, were disinherited.
>
> Thus, as wealth increased, it, on the one hand, gave the man a more important status in the family than the woman, and, on the other hand, created a stimulus to utilize this strengthened position in order to over-

throw the traditional order of inheritance in favour of his children. But this was impossible as long as descent according to mother-right prevailed. This had, therefore, to be overthrown, and it was overthrown; and it was not so difficult to do this as it appears to us now. For this revolution—one of the most decisive ever experienced by mankind—need not have disturbed one single living member of a gens. All of the members could remain what they were previously. The simple decision sufficed that in future the descendants of the male members should remain in the gens, but that those of the females were to be excluded from the gens and transferred to that of their father. The reckoning of descent through the female line and the right of inheritance through the mother were hereby overthrown and male lineage and right of inheritance from the father instituted. As to how and when this revolution was effected among the civilized peoples we know nothing. It falls entirely within prehistoric times. . . .

The overthrow of mother-right was the *world-historic defeat of the female sex.* The man seized the reins in the house also; the woman was degraded, enthralled, the slave of the man's lust, a mere instrument for breeding children. This lowered position of women, especially manifest among the Greeks of the Heroic and still more of the Classical Age, has become gradually embellished and dissembled and, in part, clothed in a milder form, but by no means abolished.

We should not readily accept Engels' presumption that the transition from "mother-right" was effected with ease. We know that matrilineal organization prevailed over much of human existence and that it was supported by an abundance of ritual and ideology. Furthermore, Engels does not recognize fertility of women as wealth, although the fertility of slaves and cattle is so recognized. Hence, he fails to see that women remained the carriers of wealth, even as that wealth became subject to exchange against animal stock. As a result, he suggests that "as wealth increased, it, on the one hand, gave the man a more important status in the family than the woman." Since he does not recognize women's fertility as wealth, he cannot address the relative power of the women's fertility relative to that of animal stock. It is a difficult issue, since this comparison does not rest on the greater importance of animals over women. Indeed, the importance of animal stock arises in large part from the fact that it facilitates a systematic claim on women.

Engels claims that animals were "private property," implying individual ownership, and he claims that the "family" held the rights to this "property." This is a most serious error, because it fails to recognize that patrilineal organization is based on wealth as the possession of a group (of indefinite duration) in much the same way as the "gens." Unlike a share of contemporary corporate stock for which private ownership is conventional, a herd of cattle cannot be the possession of a single, mortal man. He can only manage it in the interest of the larger collectivity.

The demographic advantage of holding cattle depends on the existence of other groups that are poor on cattle and willing to sacrifice daughters (and their own demographic growth) for the sake of accumulating cattle, thereby facilitating the relatively greater demographic growth of a "rich" tribe or lineage. It is for this reason that we say that possession of cattle provides greater power than the possession of the fertility of women. Simply put, a well-managed patrilineage will grow faster than a similarly placed matrilineage. And with that demographic advantage, it will overwhelm matrilineal groups. In other words, the power of a group comes from having more people and not from having more animals. But by judicious use of animals as bridewealth, a group may use animals as the means of accumulating more women and, hence, more people. In this context women are the foundational form of wealth, and the desire for cattle emerges as an indirect desire for women.

We can see, then, that a bridewealth regime is a complex and sophisticated mechanism for the management of two interacting forms of wealth: animal herds and human fertility. Unfortunately, the sight of African elders arguing vociferously over alternative dispositions of cattle has led some to presume that bridewealth regimes are simple and primitive. If, however, those elders manage the bridewealth regime with an implicit awareness of the relevant variables, as delineated in Bell and Song (1994), it is a very sophisticated process indeed (and the elders have much to argue about).

The problem faced by men with herds is an eventual shortage of grazing land. This shortage develops in part, of course, from the growth of herds; but perhaps equally it develops from intrusions into grazing land by agriculturists. In either case, the Marginal Value Criterion intervenes to drive down the growth and wealth-value of animal stock. A second and related problem is that the social technology of herding societies is not

conducive to the development of centralized military power. While nomadic hordes have occasionally been able to assume control over the military establishments of agriculturists, they are unlikely to have a militarily
powerful state based on animal stock. This often proves to be a fatal weakness for the social technology of herding societies.

Land as Wealth

As a wealth-asset, land is weak; at least, it is weak relative to animal stock.
Such a statement must appear peculiar in the face of the great civilizations
and the powerful aristocracies and dynasties that appear to have been the
product of land: Ancient Egypt, Imperial China, feudal Europe, and the
Inca Empire. Until the development of modern industry and capitalism,
control over land and its product has been preeminent as a form of wealth.
So, in what sense can land be weak as a wealth-asset?

The problem with land is that if it is equally distributed, it can be no
more than a basis of subsistence for its users. And as a source of subsistence, it has little capacity for self-augmentation. That is, one would seldom be able to use the product of land as a basis for making claim on
additional land. Land can become wealth only under particular forms of
social organization and only under well-designed forms of social technology. In particular, land can become a source of wealth only when it is
combined with the work-power of a dispossessed category of workers
(satisfying the Exploitation Principle) and when the latter can be controlled with the use of military power. Hence, a very elaborate caste of
supporting characters is required of those who would make land into
wealth. Only when many men must toil for the sake of others, generating a food surplus that can be claimed, rightfully, by well-placed others,
only then is land the foundation of powerful empires and enriched aristocracies.

For example, Chinese social structure developed in an open agrarian
plain, accessible to marauding nomads from the north. The efforts of men
to defend their settled communities from nomads led to a transformation
of a matrilineal system based on land and fertility into a patrilineal system in which those wealth-assets were under the protection of military
power. Once so organized, these Han clans were able to subjugate their
agrarian neighbors and force them into slavery. This enslavement was

feasible only with a military state that could monitor and punish the reluctant and the rebellious. And given that capacity, land could be transformed into a powerful asset around which to build patrilineal organizations and state power.

The development of feudalism in Europe is an example of a supranational locus of land expansion. The critical antecedent of European feudalism was feudalism in the world of Islam. Feudalism is a system in which privileged categories of individuals are offered an income-generating asset in return for the provision of military service and equipment. (This income is the fee to which the "feu" in feudalism refers.) The Church of Rome had witnessed with horror the lightning spread of Islam in the eighth century. It spread by the Book and the sword, and the sword was supported by the granting of lands and serfs to military personnel. In the face of the collapse of the Roman Empire, the social structures presented by Islamic societies constituted the state of the art for suprastate-level territorial expansion. While the feudalism of Europe was differently structured to reflect the particular hierarchical structure of the church, it was nevertheless a structure learned from observation of Islam.

From the sixth to the ninth centuries, Europe was in the Dark Ages, while the lands of Islam enjoyed a vibrant and sophisticated civilization. So in the same way that nations today mimic the capitalism of the West in their efforts to find a mechanism for accumulating capital, the church mimicked the Middle East in order to find a mechanism for accumulating territory. However, the feudalism of Europe was not particularly successful. Of course, it failed in its main purpose—the development of a fighting force (the Crusades) that would capture the lands of the East for the church. But besides that problem, Rome's construction was unstable and began to unravel after only a few centuries. There was, in my view, nothing "natural" about the appearance of feudalism in Europe as a stage in sociohistorical evolution, as the Marxist would claim. Rather, it was a failed strategy of the church. It failed, I believe, because it permitted only the church any opportunities for wealth-accumulation. This is not the forum for addressing the issue, and I strongly urge additional research, but I would suggest that both China and Islam maintained more effective agrarian formations than Rome's version of feudalism.

Capital and Wages

Animal stock is an asset that tends to dominate the power of human fertility. Hence, it generates patrilineal organizations that overwhelm matrilineal forms, which are invariably organized, in part, around fertility. Moreover, groups that are rich in animal stock can make claim against work-power of groups lacking in such wealth—a power of men over other men. However, there has never been a form of wealth more powerful than industrial capital.

We should not take the power of capital for granted. Machinery, like land, will fail the Growth Criterion in the absence of facilitative social technologies. The effective management of "free enterprise" has required very active legislative and administrative structures, an intensity of management not required of other systems of accumulation (other than bureaucratic communism). However, the most important aspect of this facilitative technology has been a system of wage rates by which to implement the Exploitation Principle. The system of wages is truly revolutionary. We forget that, with the exception of a small minority of particularly unfortunate types, agricultural and manufacturing workers of an earlier time owned the product of their work or at least a portion thereof. The serf may appear to us as a miserable wretch, but he did own at least half of his output (or time) to be used for the provision of his domestic unit. So, the well-being of the common folk was further depressed with the birth of the industrial system and wage labor. Only with the aid of a powerful and violent state were the new captains of industry able to force a majority of their fellows into a wage-earning collectivity that lacked any rights in the product of their work.

The genius of this new system lies in the possibility that workers can be made to become dependent on wages as the basis of consumption and then to compete with each other to drive down the level of wages. Since the product of their work does not belong to them but to the owners of capital, this new system makes possible a previously unimaginable level of surplus. And as Karl Marx (1906) has pointed out, their surplus could then be used for the formation of additional capital. In other words, we have here a new system of wealth-augmentation—capital producing more capital through the intermediary efforts of dispossessed workers.[4] Workers, like subaltern categories

41

in most systems of wealth-accumulation, suffer the tragedy of strengthening the agency of their own domination.

Marx believes that capital accumulation is both the defining driving force of the system and the source of its destruction. Capitalists are driven to accumulate, he argues, but in consequence capital becomes too large relative to capitalistic requirements, and the rate of profit falls to zero (violating the Marginal Value Criterion). "Capital as wealth" ceases to exist, I would say, when its redundancy eliminates profitability in much the same way that fertility loses wealth-value with the demographic transition. To return to Marx: lacking profit as an engine of capital accumulation, capitalists bring production to a halt, and, at this point, hungry workers seize the means of production and produce a flow of consumer goods without concern for profit.

Given the brilliance of Marx's theory, it is dangerous to dismiss it, even with the collapse of Soviet "communism" and the opening of China to the world market. All other systems of wealth have eventually become overwhelmed by more powerful systems or suffered from internal weakness when the Marginal Value Criterion could no longer be satisfied. So, it would be naive to dismiss a concern for the future of capitalism.

In relation to the future of capitalism, what can we say about global accumulation? We have now characterized a number of social formations in terms of their foundations in wealth-accumulation. And we have begun to make it clear how wealth provides a basis of power for those with rightful claims to it. We shall elaborate on these characteristics in the next two chapters.

We know that the death of capitalism has been long anticipated and that at critical points it has always found new life. Lenin proclaimed imperialism to be the "highest stage" of capitalism, with the implication that the Marginal Value Criterion would not continue to be satisfied beyond the end of that stage. Capitalism would come to an end, not because of successful revolts against imperialism and colonialism, but because of a failure of colonialism to maintain a system of effective accumulation.

We now know that imperialism was not the highest stage of capitalism. There is at least one additional stage that is commonly called "globalization" and that we will refer to as "global accumulation" in order to focus attention on capital as a wealth-asset. While colonialism reduced the costs of production (thereby raising profits) by moving lower-cost raw materials and natural resources to the centers of capital, global accumulation reduces cost by allowing capital to move to locations that feature low-cost labor. The geopolitical implications of this change are enormous. Colonialism required subordinate states (colonies) that were incorporated into the economy of the master state. Not only did this give primacy to the nation-state idea, but also it forced each master state to guard jealously its colonial prerogatives, leading those states into warfare as they struggled to continue the accumulation process. Global accumulation, on the other hand, encourages cooperation among the master states and requires an effort to construct an international labor market that can be utilized by the capital. And it is the homogenization of this market that underlies the cultural hegemony of the contemporary period.

If global accumulation proceeds to its full extent, the results will be unlike those that seem to be most widely expected. First, we must understand that the nation-state, as we know it, is the product of industrial capital. And with the exception of several "export-oriented" states, the purchasing power of its citizens has been the foundation of consumer demand and of industrial expansion. Indeed, it is often pointed out that in the United States consumer demand is the essential stimulant of investment and the growth of capital. However, in the context of global accumulation, where capital moves toward lower-cost labor, there must be a downward pressure on the purchasing power of labor in each state. The fact that falling real wages is demand reducing for the citizens of a given state might not be very important if there is a viable international market for output. However, this reduction in demand for output in the older centers of capital must be more than replaced by increases in demand from the rest of the world.

As I see it, global accumulation cannot survive under current nation-state management, since each state spoils the market for others. In the same way that Keynesian economics emerged as a theory for the management of national economies, there must now appear the agencies and theories for the management of a wealth-asset that is no longer rooted within the nation-state. Policies must be developed that will maintain continued capital accumulation.

A super state is not the answer. It seems more likely that the current tendency of agency proliferation will continue. That is, we shall have a United Nations for some purposes, a Group of Seven, the World Trade

Organization, the World Bank, and so forth, for other purposes, in which the Group of Seven, or some such core group, gains power within each agency—linking them together as an effective coordination. Most importantly, the New World Order will not be an American Empire, and an apparent attempt to create such an empire within the George W. Bush administration will be viewed with derision by future observers. While certain elements within the United States stand to profit greatly by this imperial strategy in the short run, the general citizenry of the United States will pay the price in blood, indebtedness, and economic viability.

The capacity to bully and attack defenseless peoples—the emergence as the single world power—appears to be inducing North Americans onto a path of oblivion. It is inducing a reliance on an awesome but superficial availability, while promoting an avoidance of the fundamental and relatively intractable. One must never forget the central lesson of this chapter: power resides in wealth-accumulation.

CHAPTER THREE
CAPITALISM AND THE RIGHT TO SURVIVE

Slaughtered Peasants *(unfinished) by Gyula Derkovits. Dózsa-Series XIa. (1928)* Woodcut, *439 × 512 mm, Hungarian National Gallery, Budapest.*

The social theorist whose ideas are discussed in this chapter is Karl
Polanyi, a person whose contributions to economic anthropology
are widely acclaimed.[1] He is credited with insights into the characteristics of the "precapitalist" system, especially the suggestion that economic process in those systems tends to be institutionalized by social
relations—redistribution and reciprocity. His discussion of capitalism is
questioned in this chapter. It is suggested that he has fallen prey to the obfuscation of bourgeois ideologies that hide the roles of workers under capitalism in deference to a glorification of the roles of merchants and
capitalists. The problem with this approach is that it denies the most fundamental aspect of capitalism—its role in the accumulation of capital and
the particular manifestation of the Exploitation Principle (see chapter 2)
that arises with the introduction of a system of wages. I would say that we
should not approach this period of global accumulation with such a distorted and limited understanding of the system at hand.

Several years ago, it was my practice to assign to students in my undergraduate class in "traditional systems" a book by Polanyi called *Dahomey
and the Slave Trade*. Of course, I was aware that Melville J. Herskovits had
produced the real ethnography. However, the book by Herskovits was in
two thick volumes, promising to tell more about this ancient kingdom than
anyone could reasonably want to know. It was only later that I realized how
straightforward and readable it was (volume 1 would have sufficed for my
purposes), and only later did I begin to develop theoretical differences with
Polanyi.

What Polanyi had discovered in reading Herskovits was that Dahomey was a sophisticated and complex African kingdom, featuring a
well-planned economy, an effective army "including an awesome regiment
of Amazons," and important elements of an exchange economy, especially
in the domain of cooked food and other consumption goods. Given the
prominence of market processes in Dahomey, it might appear that this
"Negro" kingdom on the coast of Africa contained the beginnings of a
market economy, and Polanyi's study of Dahomey is oriented toward dis-
pelling this impression.

I would be pleased to argue with Polanyi on this point. I would de-
light in demonstrating that Dahomey was the original capitalist state and
that like so many things of great importance, capitalism breathed its first
vibrant breath on African soil. Unfortunately, I cannot make such an ar-

gument. Indeed, I consider it a rather silly issue, but it is an issue never-theless—created by Polanyi's peculiar characterization of capitalism as a "market economy."

Polanyi's Capitalism

In their preface to *Trade and Market in Early Empires*, Polanyi and Arensberg (1957) said that

> We asked, abstractly and analytically, what social action does the free market entail? . . . they [the economists] agreed with us upon the following tentative formulation: In the free market of supply and demand, a man can reverse roles, being supplier or demander as he can or wills. A man can go to this market or that as he sees his advantage; he is free of fixed and static obligation to one center or one partner, he may move at will and at random, or as prices beckon. He can offer to all and any comers, dole or divide among them, "corner the market" so that they all pay his price and so dance to his tune. At another turn of prices, or in a next transaction or market, formally, he is one of a similar "crowd" and dances in unison to the tune called by another who may in his turn have "cornered the market" from them all. . . . Where outside the recent Western world, in the ethnographic record, would we find anything resembling or parallel to this? (viii–ix)

Capitalism is depicted here as a system of traders and merchants, or some would grandly say entrepreneurs seeking profitable opportunity. This depiction is so focused on merchants that we are left unaware of the nature of the system of production. The production process is entirely hidden from view and relegated to the specific optimization routines of those who own the machines. Polanyi is keenly aware of workers and the need for a labor market under capitalism. A fundamental anomaly of capitalism, he claims, is that capitalism requires a market for labor and that this market cannot be a naturally occurring and freely functioning entity. In *The Great Transformation*, Polanyi (1944) argues with great eloquence that capitalism, defined as a purely self-regulating market system, can never exist. It must be constructed and protected by the powers of the state, because the natural processes of the market are inconsistent with the preservation of labor. The conversion of labor into a commodity is destructive in the absence of strategic state intervention that might provide protection. For the sake of capitalism, capitalism must be restrained.

The state is essential, also, to the integrity of land and money, neither of which can emerge from pure market processes, because they cannot be valued at their costs of production. For these reasons, according to Polanyi, a fully self-regulating market system is impossible, and, hence, ideal capitalism is impossible—impossible in part because labor is an unavoidable blemish on the face of a putative ideal. Nevertheless, we are told that the actually existing forms of capitalism resemble and are parallel to his picture of free and enterprising entrepreneurs, and consequently, the blemishes created by labor, land, and money fail to destroy the essence of capitalism as a system of self-regulating markets.

Were we to follow Polanyi and define capitalism by reference to market processes, we would be unable to distinguish it from market socialism. Polanyi was familiar with the then very prominent discussion of market socialism being pursued by Oscar Lange and Fred Taylor (1938), Abba Lerner (1944), Henry D. Dickinson (1939), and others, continuing with important work by Benjamin Ward (1967). Market socialism would not be a pure system of fully self-regulating markets; however, it need not be less pure than actually existing market systems. And although this debate about market socialism was at its height while Polanyi (1944) was writing *The Great Transformation*, he failed to mention it.

According to Peter Rosner (1990), Polanyi contributed considerable attention to the challenge from Ludwig von Mises (1920) on the impossibility of rational resource allocation under socialism. It was the von Mises' paper that had given rise to the initial debate, and Polanyi had been an early participant in the fray, offering an organizational framework within which socialism might function efficiently. Yet, we do not find in *The Great Transformation* any suggestion that a socialist formation might be able to realize the advantages of unregulated markets. Had he addressed those debates, he might have been forced to consider *relations of production* as necessary factors in the characterization of social systems.

Polanyi and the Condition of Labor

In *The Great Transformation*, Polanyi (1944) focuses on the construction of the English working class and, therewith, the creation of a market for labor power. In his analysis, the labor market came fully onto center stage with the abandonment of the Poor Law in 1834.

The Poor Law had been established in 1795, a time of great social distress, when a group of men met in Speenhamland, just outside of Newbury, England, and

> decided that subsidies in aid of wages should be granted in accordance with a scale dependent on the price of bread, so that a minimum income can be assured to the poor *irrespective of their earnings* [Polanyi's emphasis]. . . . Very soon it became the law of the land over most of the countryside, and later even in a number of manufacturing districts; actually it introduced no less a social and economic innovation than the "right to live" and until abolished in 1834, it effectively prevented the establishment of a competitive labor market. Two years earlier, in 1832, the middle class had forced its way to power, partly in order to remove this obstacle to the new capitalistic economy. Indeed, nothing could be more obvious than that the wage system imperatively demanded the withdrawal of the "right to live" as proclaimed in Speenhamland. (Polanyi 1944: 78)

The "right to live" was not an innovation that came on the scene with Speenhamland; it was the custom of the countryside and of the feudal period that members of the parish or estate would be availed the resources by which to secure a living. The parish serfdom that was installed by the Act of Settlement of 1662 had the function of binding the common folk to the village (Polanyi 1944: 78), but fortunately the village contained a variety of common resources from which life could be ensured, except under the worse conditions. However, with the expulsion of village folk by the enclosures that divorced the people from their means of survival, the traditional elite sought another way to ensure the "right to life." Hence, Speenhamland.

Polanyi (1944) argues that the ultimate destitution of the workers of England was not the result of class exploitation. The employer offered employment and the workers accepted it voluntarily. The workers' destitution arose, he says, from the destruction of the traditional culture and groups to which they had belonged, not from meagerness of wages:

> There is no starvation in societies living on the "subsistence margin." The principle of freedom from want was equally acknowledged in the Indian

village community and, we might add, under almost every and any type of social organization up to about the beginning of sixteenth century Europe, when the modern ideas on the poor put forth by the humanist Vives were argued before the Sorbonne. It is the absence of the threat of individual starvation that makes primitive society, in a sense, more human than market economy, and at the same time less economic. (p. 164)

But what, I ask, is the problem with capitalism that makes traditional rights to life so problematic? Why is it that capitalism is associated with the destruction of traditional communities both at home and abroad? Given that capitalism is associated with a massive increase in society's productive potential, is it necessary that (as Karl Marx suggests in *Wage, Labor and Capital*) the "forest of uplifted arms demanding work becomes ever thicker, while the arms themselves become ever thinner?" The answer is that capitalists are expected to pay the lowest wage consistent with securing the services of a worker, without reference to the requirements of survival for the worker and his family. It would make sense, then, to allow workers to have alternative modes of survival, such as private plots of land from which to secure certain staples.

We find such structures in Latin America, where native producers seek out work on the latifundia only for ancillary expenditures and tax payments. The provision of family plots makes it possible to reduce wage rates to a much lower level. Yet, in the construction of the English working class, it was presumed that workers simply would not work unless threatened with starvation and driven by hunger. This partly explains his attack on Speenhamland. His argument is that the squires of England only made things worse by attempting at Speenhamland to remove the essential foundation of the labor supply.

To later generations nothing could have been more patent than the mutual incompatibility of institutions like the wage system and the "right to live," or, in other words, than the impossibility of a functioning capitalistic order as long as wages were subsidized from public funds. Polanyi presumes that the industrial system *must* impose a heavy a price on the common people, and he presumes that the labor market must be forced into existence by the state against the resistance of traditional conceptions of the right to life. Only with the removal of this traditional right could modern capitalism come into existence.

While there were certainly serious problems with Speenhamland as a form of public policy, it would be useful to reconsider capitalism *as a social formation* before addressing issues of labor regulation. Labor is a feature of capitalism. For Polanyi it is an unfortunate adhesion to the system because it is ineluctably connected to the human material that is its source. So while it may not matter that the price of widgets goes to zero, it does matter if wages follow that course, leading to the destruction of the human community. Hence, the state must stand ready to protect labor from the ravages of free markets. One should not allow labor to be part of the self-regulating mechanism by which capitalism is defined.

The beginning of a more powerful understanding of capitalism could begin with the last paragraph of *The Grundrisse*, 1857–1858, where Marx declares that

> [i]t requires no great penetration to grasp that where e.g. free labour or wage labour arising out of the dissolution of bondage as the point of departure, there machines can only arise in antithesis to living labour, as property alien to it, and as power hostile to it; i.e. that they must confront it as capital. (Marx, in Tucker 1972: 293)

With Marx the contradiction between labor and capital is not based on free versus non-free markets, but on the fact that workers who are remunerated by wages are thereby denied any claim on the product of their efforts. It is based on this fact that in the course of capital accumulation, capital can grow relative to labor and, as the property of an alien class, become an instrument for the subjugation of labor. To the extent that workers are successful in extracting a social product from the forces of nature, to that extent they also build the power that controls and dominates them.

This argument may seem at first to be an overly dramatized and radicalized image of the worker's position. However, accepting that characterization does not entail any particular consequence or suggest any particular ethical valuation. Rather, the central thesis of this chapter is that the relationship, observed by Marx, between workers and capital is also reflected under other institutional formations that are structured hierarchically in terms of a wealth-asset. It is simply a most fundamental analytic fact that in *any system of wealth*, a class of direct producers is impressed into service by the owners of wealth in such a way as to facilitate an augmentation of the wealth held by those owners. In some systems, the strategic use of "direct producers" is only ancillary to the process of wealth-accumulation, and in other cases, such use is essential. The exceptional strength of capitalism arises from the fact that it most effectively extracts value from direct producers.

If we agree that labor is an essential factor in capitalist accumulation, we can go forward to ask to what extent is the right to life incompatible with this process of accumulation. Moreover, the same question can be posed in relation to direct producers within other systems of accumulation. We shall, not surprisingly, find that decreasing the resources to be received by such producers is to the advantage of those who make use of them, increasing the rate at which the wealth-asset can be accumulated. However, we cannot find support for the notion that the right to life is incompatible with accumulation, per se. The issue of labor regulation is reduced to the determination of shares of economic resources that are to accrue to labor and the owners of capital. A social policy that aims to maximize the rate of accumulation on the backs of dehumanized workers may be politically unstoppable, but it is not logically necessary.

Characteristics of Capitalism

Which brings us back to capitalism. The industrial means of production is not like cattle; it has no natural tendency to reproduce and become wealth. In order for the means of production to become capital, it must be embedded in a set of social institutions and rules that allow it to grow—thereby becoming a wealth-asset. We cannot begin to understand capitalism as a general form of social organization unless we focus on capital as a form of wealth and hence on capital accumulation. Capitalism is *one of the sets* of institutions that facilitates the growth of industrial capital, and wages (rather than shares of the product) are central to its effectiveness. During the period of its embryonic development and during the period of "primitive accumulation," it would appear that no system of social organization could compete with capitalism as a mode of accumulation. Surely, the grinding down of the workers' living standards that one finds in that period is not consistent with worker control.

Historically, the state has been organized collectivity within which the growth of capital is articulated. Land as wealth has also required a state formation; but in the case of land, subsidiary corporate structures are common and strongly encouraged, especially patrilateral structures. Capital, however, greets traditional wealth-holding groups with hostility while accepting the state as an ideologically illegitimate but functionally necessary entity. Indeed, Polanyi's conception of capitalism as a self-regulating market implies the irrelevance of the state. His discussion is directed, then, to explaining why a state is necessary for the regulation of money, land, and labor in an otherwise unregulated terrain.

All too often, scholars are able to recognize the cultural context of behavior in other societies, while denying culture as an arbiter of their own behavior. *They* have culture, while we are rational. *They* are embedded in social relations, while we are free to act. *They* have duties, while we have freedom of choice. And by accepting the ideology of an ascendant European bourgeoisie, one can be led to believe that "free enterprise" has no need for superordinate authority. Perhaps, labor, the weak, and the poor have a need for government, but not free enterprise. This, of course, is the argument of Polanyi, who does not notice that for every line of legal code produced in support of labor there are one thousand written in support of some section of capital. It is these many lines of legal code and public administration that are the foundation of "free enterprise." And given the fact that the industrial means of production cannot grow by intrinsic or natural forces, state machinery provides the necessary context for growth.

Capitalism is necessarily embedded in a nest of rules, defined at the level of the state (and increasingly at the transnational level). So while capitalism systematically destroys most forms of social relations common to precapitalist formations, such as lineages, village communities, and a wide range of other associations, it remains embedded in social relations. *The state is to capital as the patrilineage is to cattle and as the matrilineage is to female reproductivity.* In a world system of capitalism, with many state systems in competition, conflict, and cooperation, it is precisely the state, whose role Polanyi believes to be extrinsic, that acts as the manager of systems of capital accumulation.

There is a multiplicity of institutional frameworks for the management of capital, but "self-regulating markets" is not one of them. Which brings us back to Speenhamland. What was Polanyi's point in attacking this policy? He argues that capitalism is inconsistent with the right to life, so that the steady movement toward free markets is met by a countermovement of restrictions by the state for the protection of labor. Polanyi would have us believe that the capitalist state exists for the benefit of workers, and in the last pages of *The Great Transformation*, in an appendix on Speenhamland, he joins with the enemies of labor in an attack on social policy in general:

> The utter incompatibility of Speenhamland with the wage system was permanently remembered only in the tradition of the economic liberals. They alone realized that, in a broad sense, every form of the protection of labor implied something of the Speenhamland principle in interventionism. (Polanyi 1944)

An astounding statement: "Every form of the protection of labor" is, by implication, misguided and counterproductive. Capitalism is a tragedy for workers, but Speenhamland proves that it is better to leave them to their fate.

Yet, on closer inspection any policy analyst would see immediately that the problem with Speenhamland was specific to the details of its provisions and implied nothing about "every form of the protection." In particular, Speenhamland proposed an income subsidy that guaranteed a specific minimum level of income, *with a 100 percent tax on increased earnings below this minimum*! If you earned less than a stipulated amount, the state would raise your income to the standard, removing the relationship between income and work. This is simply bad public policy; but by focusing on Speenhamland and suggesting that its failure implies a much broader fault of policy, Polanyi falls into the camp of brain-dead neoliberalism. Of course, he is exceptional in that he enters that camp with a heavy heart, in horror, with tears; but he enters nevertheless with a seemingly rational acceptance of the awful necessities of human progress.

Polanyi and Marx

The characterization that we have provided of Polanyi is not the common one. More common is the perception of Rhoda Halperin (1998). In this view, Polanyi was a socialist whose ideas were largely derived from Marx, and it is suggested by some observers that Polanyi's apparent differences with Marx were the result of a strategic use of terms that promised to be less problematic and more influential during a time of right-wing

McCarthyism. However, our discussion has relied almost entirely on *The Great Transformation* for insight into his views, and that book was published in 1944. In that book, Polanyi makes a number of references to Marx, most of which dismiss him as a follower of David Ricardo.

As I have argued, herein, Marx's model of capitalism is a model of wealth-accumulation and power at the microlevel and of an increasing concentration of capital at the macrolevel. Workers are victims in this process, but so are the many capitalists who bite the dust of atomistic competition. This process can come to an inglorious end only when capital becomes abundant. And much like the overthrow of fertility by the demographic transition, we would have the overthrow of capital by socialist revolution.

While labor is the source of capital and the force behind its continued accumulation in Marxian analysis, workers enter only negatively in the Polanyi model. The struggles of workers are oriented toward securing the "right to life," even when the promotion of that right can only retard the evolution of fully unregulated markets. There seems to be no dynamic in Polanyi, other than the back and forth movement and counter movement between free markets and restriction. The movement toward the free market ideal will never be realized (unfortunately!) because of worker resistance. Some have complained (e.g., Block 1997) that Polanyi appears at times to suggest that the ideal of unregulated markets has been (nearly) realized. My own view is that he does not presume that any major progress toward complete (capitalist) freedom is feasible; there is only a stalemate in which workers seek a better life, even though no better life can be found.

CHAPTER FOUR
BRIDEWEALTH AND THE ARTICULATION OF WEALTH

Subdual by Gyula Derkovits. Dózsa-Series VII. (1928) Woodcut, 440 × 498 mm, Hungarian National Gallery, Budapest.

The most important accomplishment of this chapter will be a further confirmation of the necessary and sufficient characteristics of wealth-assets. Confirmation will be accomplished by reference to a "Parity Principle," with which we begin this discussion. I shall verify the assertion that wealth is a socially realized factor, such that a given resource may act as wealth in one group and as a consumer durable in an adjacent group, depending on the satisfaction or nonsatisfaction of any one of the four necessary criteria of wealth. In chapter 2 we addressed the Exploitation Principle and a formal explication of the power of wealth-assets. This chapter continues the process by which we demonstrate the unique capabilities of wealth, as defined herein. It is a capability that no alternative conception of wealth dares to challenge.

Even if one were interested primarily in capital and in processes of capital accumulation, we may gain considerable insight, I believe, by backing away from the object of direct interest and gaining perspective on "wealth-accumulation" in general. For example, other forms of wealth have seen their day and have been retired in the face of more powerful forms of wealth. So far, this has not happened to capital.

Introduction

We shall begin with a discussion of the Ahaggar Tuareg, which offers us an opportunity to deconstruct wealth as a concept in social structure. Since the Tuareg are matrilineal, marriage does not involve a transfer of fertility, and there is no role for a transfer of wealth at marriage. In an apparent contradiction to this statement, there is a transfer of camels at marriage from the father of the groom to the father of the bride. However, we shall show that camels do not satisfy all of the essential properties of wealth within the social organization of the Tuareg, while doing so among their Arab neighbors, and that this transfer of camels is not bridewealth among the Tuareg.

A clear conception of wealth as a factor in cultural processes can bring valuable insights into the many cases where the presence of bridewealth has been falsely claimed. The Todas, for example, use "buffalo" in securing a wife in a patrilineal setting. However, we can show that these buffalo do not satisfy the necessary characteristics of "wealth-assets" within the culture of the Todas, and we can show that the fertility of Toda brides is not a wealth-asset; therefore, no wealth transfers are associated with patrifiliation in that society. Rather, it is a transfer of buffalo as consumer durables (sources of milk products) in exchange for sexual and other conjugal services of the wife. Both the Tuareg and the Todas demonstrate a cultural universal not heretofore acknowledged:

The Parity Principle. In no society can there be a routine exchange of wealth except in return for countertransfer of wealth.

No resource should be presumed to satisfy the necessary characteristics of a wealth-asset without a careful examination of the social context in which it resides. It is commonly the case, for example, that a group may face a shortage of grazing land for its animals, thus an increase in their number is not sustainable. Given this violation of the Marginal Value Criterion, the fertility of animals loses "wealth-value" and is reduced to the rank of consumer durables. As such, these animals may rationally and legitimately be exchanged for other consumer goods. Yet, an adjacent group of pastoralists, who face no ecological constraints on herd growth, would refuse to offer animal stock in this manner. N. Thomas Hakansson (1994) points out that in east Africa the lowland Luo were often visited by famine, and under conditions of severe food shortage, they would offer cattle to highland Gusii in exchange for grain. In fact, during such times the Luo and Kipsigis even offered *children* for the grain of Gusii women (p. 270).

Since grain deficits were common among people in the region, the Gusii were able to maintain a steady production of "surplus" grain in exchange for "prestige goods." We can say, then, that famine conditions militate against the wealth-value of both human and cattle fertility, making it rational for people to exchange cattle and children for consumption goods. The children and cattle were wealth-assets for the Gusii, but for the Luo they were reduced to the level of consumption goods (given a failure of the Marginal Value Criterion). This example brings forth the essential meaning of the Parity Principle. While one will not offer wealth in exchange for consumption goods, the opposite is certainly not true. The Gusii are quite pleased to offer consumption goods in exchange for wealth.

The Tuareg or *ImûhaR*

Famed for the wearing of veils, they call themselves *AmâheR* or *ImûhaR*, and we shall employ the latter term, herein. The *ImûhaR* of the Ahaggar region have long been famous as the "savage nobles" of the desert, having since antiquity had the practice of "taxing" caravans that traversed their territory.

At first glance one might perceive the *ImûhaR* to be patrilineal. These men organize into agnatic clusters for the nomadic herding of camels, held in common, and it would appear that the social structure exists for constructing camels as wealth-assets. Moreover, marriage is patrilocal; women move to their husband's camp at marriage. However, if a man predeceases his wife, she rejoins her father's camp if her father is alive or to the camp to which her mother has moved after his death (that of her grandmother). Most importantly, her children follow her to those locations and seek those locations independently in the event that she too is deceased.

Camels do not secure patrifiliation among the Ahaggar (Nicolaisen 1963). The patrilocal residence of children is only a source of "work-power"—service or source of consumption goods. Given the fact that a man's son ultimately returns with his camels to his mother's camp, "patrilineal" inheritance of camels emerges as a clever devise for extracting resources from the father's matrilineage. The agnatic assembly that characterizes the camel camp (giving it a patrilineal appearance) is but a fleeting and opportunistic gathering—to be broken asunder by the death of a father—when the man's sons, following their mother, deliver his camels into the herd of their mother's group. Hence, the exploitation of a man's lifework by the kin of his wife becomes evident only with his death.

It is not common to recognize that households are corporate groups, but they can and should be so recognized—as groups in which individuals hold rights to flows of consumption goods. They are consumption-based corporate groups. Since consumption goods do not have an indefinite life, "consumption-groups" cannot be defined by rules of inheritance. Indeed, they always differ in composition from wealth-holding groups of a given society and may vary in composition immediately by the departure or arrival of kin. Among the *ImûhaR* for example, the consumption-group may include a woman, her husband, and their children, even though her husband is an outsider relative to her wealth-holding group. If the Parity Principle is valid, then the *ImûhaR* will not offer wealth-assets as marriage payments. In other words, it must be the case that *ImûhaR* camels do not satisfy the criteria of wealth-assets.

The devolution of Ahaggar camels is bilateral, but it is only from women that there appears to be a rule of inheritance (dividing equally among sons and daughters).

Men transmit camels to their children by bequest, that is, by a measure of individual choice, rather than by inheritance—leaving most of their camels to their sons (Oxby 1986). This is not a system of double descent. There is no evident and fixed rule of devolution from a father to his children, and, as pointed out in the preceding, the assets that he transmits must eventually depart for the mother's camp. Hence, among the ImûhaR, the camels that are found in an agnatic camel camp will eventually disperse into many directions. There is no corporate group associated with the management of camels; thus, there exists no social entity that is able to enjoy rights to the long-term benefits of herd growth. Hence, in the context of ImûhaR social structure, camels fail to satisfy the Indefinite Life Criterion, discussed in chapter 2. They are not wealth-assets. It is for this reason that camels can be offered without a counteroffer of wealth.

Among the Ahaggar ImûhaR, the socially defining wealth-asset, in addition to the fertility of their daughters, is a set of vassal lineages (each enjoying a positive rate of growth), working on land that ImûhaR control. Although ranking lineages are, themselves, nomadic, they control land on which sedentary vassal tribes work and provide tribute. This is particularly important for the Ahaggar, who seem to be more dependent on vassals for food than do some other groups. In addition, women also inherit female slaves from their mothers, while men receive only male slaves from their mother's brothers (Oxby 1986). The matrilineal principle is supreme.

Female slaves are the wealth-asset, producing the next generation of slaves, and slaves are "essential" factors in the maintenance of herds and the household economy. This means that we have bilateral transmission of camels and matrilateral transmission of herding capacity and vassals. The bride's father obtains possession of bridewealth camels, but not their natural increase, while her husband gains rights to her and her children, but not their natural increase. In both cases, the longer-term benefits of accumulation that characterize wealth accrue to the bride's matrilineage.

Bridewealth

I should stress a point indicated earlier, that bridewealth is not transferred in order to make claim on the (agricultural) productivity of women, notwithstanding the correlational logic that appears to sustain the contrary position. Even the most productive woman (in traditional agriculture) is not worth a single cow if she produces no children. It is true that the flows of consumption goods that are derived from women and from cattle are important to the social organization of their utilization. All wealth-assets produce flows of benefits over time. Their ability to do so is one of the defining characteristics of wealth. However, these consumption benefits do not define the power of the asset. The power of an asset resides only in its rate of growth, given the existence of a flow of benefits. The agricultural productivity of African women has affected their effectiveness as wealth-assets only by making a higher level of fertility nutritionally feasible, in much the same way that access to better grazing land facilitates the fertility of the herd. Clearly, the independent viability of mother-child units also broadens the incidence of polygyny. It is in these indirect ways that the horticultural production of women has been a factor in bridewealth.

Although the potential of one form of wealth to dominate another depends on their relative rates of growth, the exchange rate (e.g., the number of cattle/wife) that applies to those assets is not determined by their relative rates of growth. It has been shown (Bell and Song 1990) that a feasible and stable path of wealth-accumulation and demographic growth is consistent with any exchange rate. Indeed, it was common for the level of bridewealth to be established by custom or by chiefly edict in African societies. Such determination has political significance in the following way: If groups want to be able to use cattle powerfully as a basis for extracting women from outsiders, bridewealth levels must be low. If cattle are to express the power of (internal) groups with marriageable daughters, the level of bridewealth should be high. The level of bridewealth, then, is an expression of the relative power of groups that are relatively rich in cattle versus groups that are relatively rich in daughters. In no way does it measure the relative value of human reproductivity versus that of other species. It is purely nominal. There are rather special conditions under which one thing can be said to be the market value of something else, and those conditions do no prevail in this case.

For example, the Maasai require perhaps only five cows from their massive herds, making wives cheap (Marris 1962); while the Nuer might require as many as forty from less prodigious herds, making wives almost devastatingly expensive, inducing contributions from the kin of the groom's mother as well as from the kin of his father (Evans-Pritchard 1990 [1951]). These differences are not to be explained by differences in the value of wives, but by the greater prerogatives of Maasai lineages that take wives from their cattle-poor neighbors.

China

Although social relations of reciprocity (exchange) are anathema within Confucian thought and although one was enjoined to make resource transfers to others on the basis of merit and duty, rather than by self-interested calculation of net benefit, the Chinese experienced a very early transformation of ritually required "betrothal gifts" into bridewealth. In A.D. 632, after the founding of the T'ang dynasty (A.D. 618–906), Emperor T'ai-tsung complained about "mercenary marriage arrangements" among the leading families and imposed the requirement that monies received in bridewealth must be returned to the couple as "dowry" (Ebrey 1991: 100).

Patricia Ebrey (1991) describes "shifts in marriage finance" among elite families during the T'ang and Sung dynasties, illustrating how forms of marital resource transfers changed over time in response to changed sociopolitical conditions. Although bridewealth remained a stable feature of marriage, the transfer of resources from the bride's kin varied significantly over time and among social classes. One finds evidence of bridal endowment throughout the long history of China. In reference to the Han period (202 B.C.–A.D. 220), Ebrey (1991: 98) says "how well a bride was equipped depended on how rich they were, how many sons they had, the importance they placed on the match, and probably sometimes the affection they felt for her."

During the T'ang dynasty, there was a significant inflation in the level of bridewealth as newly minted officials sought affinal connections with aristocratic families. However, by the beginning of the Sung dynasty (A.D. 960–1279), the marriage payments that elicited most public comment were not bridewealth but dowry: "(1) complaints about mercenary marriages put more stress on men seeking large dowries; (2) people drew up detailed lists of dowries before concluding marriages" (Ebrey 1991: 102). A transfer to the new domestic unit (which I call *dowry*) had already replaced the traditional gift to the bride. During the Sung dynasty it was altered further to become a negotiated payment to the groom and his kin—*groomwealth*! In part this shift in "marriage finance" was prompted by the desire of aristocratic families to obtain as sons-in-law men who had recently passed the imperial examination (which had increasingly replaced aristocratic background as a basis for administrative position).

Chinese marriage has always been accompanied by bridewealth—a fiercely negotiated "betrothal gift." However, the transfer of resources by the bride's kin has always been highly contingent and variable: "The fact that many, maybe even a majority, of marriages did not involve significant transfers from the bride's side; and the difficulty in characterizing China as either a dowry or a bridewealth society as both co-existed (e.g., McCreery 1976)." (Ebrey 1991: 4).

According to Rubie Watson (1991: 239), "Even among the poor the bride did not enter her husband's house empty-handed. At the very least, she would be accompanied by a few small pieces of jewelry, clothes, a chest, and some household articles." Such items are important in maintaining a separation between primary marriage and secondary marriage (concubinage); but they often have only symbolic significance. On the other hand, Watson found concubinage (secondary wives) to be quite prominent in the Hong Kong region, even among people of fairly humble means. Typically, secondary wives came without dowry and in the Chinese sense of the term, they were "sold." Similarly, when girls who have been sold to wealthy families as "little maids" came of age, they would be sold to their husbands. And, finally, during periods of economic distress, a large percentage of girls would be sold into marriage while still in infancy without the expense and formality of weddings and dowry (Fei 1976 [1939]).

In figure 4.1, bridewealth is drawn from the wealth-assets of patrilineage B and transferred to patrilineage A, after fierce negotiation. Then, in the more prestigious primary marriages there would be a comparable transfer of consumer durables to the new domestic unit. Bridewealth transferred rights to the bride's fertility to B, while a gift of consumer durables established an affinal link between A and B. The common prac-

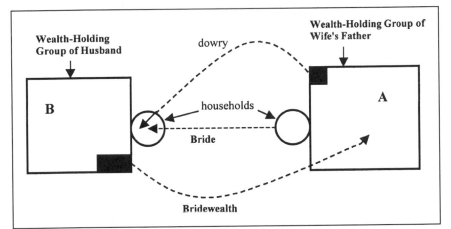

Figure 4.1. Resource Transfers Occasioned by Marriage in Imperial China

tice of referring to marriage-related transfers as "property" (e.g., Goody 1973) leads unavoidably to serious error, making it difficult to identify the nature of the underlying processes of exchange and alliance.

While brides may not always have generated high bridewealth, their fertility was of value to even the poorest groom, since he was ritually obliged to produce at least one surviving son. Given high levels of infant mortality, especially for the poor, a single surviving son became an achievement of uncertain accomplishment. The raising of a large number of children would be a feature reserved to the elite, and it was here that high levels of bridewealth would be transferred. This is what we would expect from the Parity Principle. However, it is also here that the counter-transfer of significant dowry would arise—a dowry that might greatly exceed the level of bridewealth. Hence, the "supply elasticity" of dowry exceeded that of bridewealth.

Yet the code provided by the Standard Sample is simply "dowry." I find this most puzzling. Even if one accepts the practice of coding an entire society by reference to the practices of its privileged upper classes, one should not deny the fact of bridewealth, a transfer of wealth between lineages, simply because the proceeds may be used subsequently for the transfer of consumer durables to the new household. These are separate transfers, each with its own social implications. The code, however, ignores the primary practice in favor of a distorted characterization of the secondary practice.

Equally unfortunate is the concept of "indirect dowry," originated by Jack Goody (1973). Even when applied to those elite Chinese marriages that featured a full conversion of bridewealth into dowry, the depiction of the process in a manner that denies the primacy of bridewealth conflicts directly with obvious ethnographic fact. Even when bridewealth is fully converted, it still serves the function of transferring rights to fertility. This fundamental function of bridewealth does not depend on what the parents of the bride do with it. Similarly, the function of dowry does not depend on where the parents obtained the necessary monies. Why is this not obvious? Consequently, the combining of these two very separate operations produces nonsense.

Much of this confusion is spawned by ideology, of course. Only ideology can induce intelligent anthropologists to abandon very evident fact. In this case, the ideology is rooted in the desire to deny the disinheritance of daughters in Europe and Asia. So, there arises a presumption that in Eurasia daughters receive inheritance in the form of dowry at the time of marriage, even though such inheritance is very rare. The inheritance of land at marriage by the brides in the countryside of Greece as described by Ernestine Friedl (1963) is one of the best-known exceptions. At best, the dowry might be characterized as a bequest, as opposed to inheritance: an important distinction addressed in chapter 2. But even this modification is not allowable, given that the dowry does not belong to the bride, but to the new domestic unit. The fact that the dowry is to be received by the domestic unit is essential to its function as a basis for alliance between groups. Were the dowry a possession of the bride, it would strengthen the relationship between the bride and her parents to the disadvantage of affinal alliance. These are facts of importance that should not suffer avoidance at the hand of ideology. This confusion has also affected analyses of marriage transactions in India and in the Middle East; but that is a discussion for another time and place.

Token Bridewealth

Having thrown a virtual dart against the set of "token bridewealth" societies in the Standard Sample, I have selected the Todas for consideration. As described by the principal ethnographer, William H. R. Rivers (1967 [1906]), the Todas are a people of the hills of South India, made famous because of the practice of fraternal polyandry. They were organized into two endogamous divisions, within which there were five exogamous clans. Sons, only, in a nearly equal division inherit land and animals ("buffalo"), but some land is owned by the clan. The focus of the productive efforts of men is the buffalo—grazing and milking.

Traditionally, the Todas have practiced child marriage, almost always to a mother's brother's daughter or a father's sister's daughter, broadly defined. Once the marriage has been arranged, a boy would twice yearly offer the girl a loincloth (*tadrp*) of little value but offer one of greater value as the marriage date approaches. Formerly, he had also the obligation to offer a buffalo for slaughter at funeral ceremonies of the future in-law's family. Now (1906), he offers a rupee (or less) on such occasions, and at the time for "fetching" the girl for marriage, he would place five rupees into the pocket of her "mantle" (to whose account we are not told). On this occasion, the bride might be given a gift of clothing and ornaments by her parents (*adrparn*).

The elimination of buffalo from the boy's funeral obligation is, I suspect, consistent with the (then) recent general reduction in the "buffalo-cost" of many things mentioned by Rivers, including the fines imposed for renouncing a betrothal. However, the five rupees at marriage, plus the rupees contributed at funerals, may constitute a transfer of some significance for the Todas. Furthermore, the costs escalate with marriage. Once married, a man must offer a rupee to his wife's father whenever his wife places a cloth on the body at the funeral of a clan member—an amount that is not actually transferred until the sum has reached twenty. He must offer a buffalo to the "chief mourner" at the funeral.

These are all costs of affinity that should be placed into the category of "transfers occasioned by marriage." The fact that some of these payments are converted into food does not in this case mean that they do not add to the herd of the bride's family. My impression is that the bride's family has a responsibility to provide meat for the funeral, so that contributions by affines reduce the drain on the bride's family's herd. These payments are ritually imposed and are not child related, as we have come to expect elsewhere. But they are payments, not gifts.

Given what was previously a common practice of female infanticide (indicating strongly a redundancy of fertility due to a shortage of land) and child marriage, there was a shortage of marriageable women. However, a man in search of a desirable woman could offer a substantial number of buffalo to the husband and take the man's wife to be his own (not always, now, with the approval of the married couple). This seems especially likely when the bride is much older than the groom in child marriage and more readily released or when a man seeks a second wife because his current wife is a baby for whom an inordinate delay of sexual relations is necessary.

Of course, the man who lost a wife is likely to repeat this process in order to obtain a replacement, and so on, leading to a rising tide of expensive marriages. If a man who is not the brother of a dead man desires to marry his widow, he must pay twice the number of buffalo that the dead man had paid, the latter having been, perhaps, the cost of taking an already married woman from her husband. Furthermore, a man could obtain marital rights, rights to the sexuality of an already married woman, thereby becoming a (secondary) husband, by offering a large number of buffalo (depending on his own wealth in buffalo).

It should be noted that the "logic" of marriage payments is quite different from that which we associate with most other cultures. This point is clear in the case of the man who seeks only sex and not patrifiliation, yet must offer many more buffalo. And the man who marries the widow of an unrelated man pays twice as much as did the former husband, even if the latter had paid to take her from another. Clearly, the cost of a woman is unrelated to the value of her sexuality or fertility.

To some degree, these facts seem to be explained by a compensation-for-damage principle. By this I mean that sex with a married women may be lacking in social propriety, so that a penalty must be paid for its enjoyment—much like being allowed to continue parking at an expired meter so long as the fine is paid. Such fines must always be higher than the normal cost of parking. Perhaps, the same cultural logic applies to the marrying of a widow, if indeed the Todas believe that widows should not remarry in violation of the levirate, so that a man should be penalized for inducing her transgression. Another principle that operates among the Todas is that costs should vary with the ability to pay, and it is possible that the man who takes a woman only for sex is expected to be relatively rich and should pay accordingly.

The social roles of animals among the Todas are clearly different from those in Africa and the Mediterranean. While I have not yet probed the depths of this issue, one can say the following: In other parts of the world, the number of animals takes on a special significance. One seeks a growing herd as a source of power. However, among the Todas the milk and milk products of buffalo seem to have special significance, to such an extent that it is men who do the milking and any cooking (especially when it involves the use of milk products). Moreover, the Todas have "dairies" for the processing of milk and milk products, making the product of buffalo a significant social product of men. Indeed, some buffalo are sacred and provide milk to sacred dairies under special management. This relatively greater significance to the flow of consumption goods from buffalo, relative to a focus on herd growth, is fundamental to understanding the special roles of buffalo in marital transactions among the Todas.

Two independent factors exclude buffalo among the Todas from the rank of wealth. First, given the lack of land for grazing, the Todas are not able to enjoy the growth of herds. Consequently, the Marginal Value Criterion is not satisfied for buffalo, preventing them from having the character of wealth. Instead, buffalo are eaten on auspicious occasions, rather than offered in exchange, and they are used as a source of milk and milk product. On this basis we know that these buffalo are consumer durables, not wealth-assets. Second, we know that fertility is not a wealth-asset, because of the widespread practice of female infanticide, implying a violation of the Marginal Value Criterion in relation to fertility. Patrifiliation of offspring occurs, to be sure, but the shortage of land prevents a marginal value of fertility from having positive value. Hence, there are no "wealth-transfers" at marriage in either direction, in conformance with the principle that wealth will be transferred only in exchange for wealth (the Parity Principle). If one lacks an analytical characterization of wealth, as distinct from consumption goods, one would be unable to analyze this case correctly. Indeed, the term "token bridewealth" that appears in the *Ethnographic Atlas* is clearly incorrect. A large percentage of marriages are rather expensive (rather than "token"), and they are expensive in consumer durables, not wealth. For cases of this kind, I would use the term *bride-price*.

CHAPTER FIVE
HOUSEHOLDS IN SERVICE TO WEALTH

Peasant Whettering the Scythe *by Gyula Derkovits. Dózsa-Series II. (1928) Woodcut, 486 × 440 mm, Hungarian National Gallery, Budapest.*

The empirical evidence has long pointed to the fact that households are organized and structured to serve the interests of wealth-holding groups in a society. This fact is quite evident in the United States, in China, and in lineage-based tribal societies. However, I had never expected to arrive at a general proof of this proposition. But here it is! We can now say with some confidence that under conditions of scarcity, the allocation of consumption goods at the domestic and broader societal levels will be constructed in the interest of "wealth-accumulation" in any society governed in the interests of a "wealth-asset."

The fact that households serve vital functions for related wealth-holding groups is clearly shown by the services of men to matrilineal wealth in the case of matrilocal residence and by the services of women to patrilineal wealth in the case of patrilocal residence. One of the conspicuous advantages of patriliny over matriliny is that wives can bring wealth in the form of fertility to their husbands' groups while men can bring only work-power to their wives' groups. Getting a man seems to be not such a big deal.

But there are more subtle factors to be addressed in relation to the management of assets by wealth-holding corporate groups. This chapter gives only a glimpse into that domain, but the glimpse is provocative. Not only do wealth holders find a way of exploiting some members of the household in the production of wealth, but they also manage survival rates by designing "customary practices" that differentially determine who lives and who dies in the event of food shortages within households.

I immediately consider an extension of this principle to the contemporary construction of a global economic system. In this world system the Group of Seven, consisting of the United States, Canada, Great Britain, France, Germany, Japan, and Italy, claims priority in the structuring of various international institutions, such as the United Nations, the International Monetary Fund, the World Bank, the World Trade Organization (WHO). These nations establish the rules of the game for all players, regardless of size and resource distribution. It is, I suspect, a law of nature that these rules must differentially determine who dies first.

China manifests gross differences in the power to survive as one moves from the privileged Beijing and Shanghai regions into the provinces. According to the World Health Organization's website (www.who.int/) with data as of September 2001:

[F]or children less than five years of age, the prevalence of underweight ranged from 3% in Beijing to 39% in the province of Hainan while that of stunting ranged from 7% in Beijing to 56% in of Guizhou. The highest prevalence of stunting was observed in the same provinces as those of underweight. According to the WHO classification, the children in the provinces of Fujian, Jianxi, Hunan, Guangxi, Hainan, Sichuan, Guizhou, Yunnan, Qinghai and Xinjiang were found to be highly affected by stunting (>40%) and those in Guanxi and Hainan also showed a prevalence of underweight (>30%).

In Shanghai, Tianjin, and especially in Beijing, overweight and correlated diseases are becoming a public health problem. In fact, in Beijing almost half of the adult population is overweight.

The advantages in consumption that are enjoyed by residents of Beijing and Shanghai are not accidental; they are the results of carefully articulated policies by which the government is attempting to accelerate the accumulation of wealth. These differentials do not imply, of course, that the residents of Beijing are more deserving of food as individuals. Their deservedness arises from their locations within "person-categories" of a wealth-holding corporate group to which all Chinese citizens belong. Nor is it accidental that the reports of being "underweight" refer to children rather than to adults. Differentials in access to food that one finds at the macrosystem levels are reflected within the household. In communities that face chronic scarcity, rights to food and other resources are never equal across categories, and invariably it is children who first die of starvation. These are facts from which most people, even social scientists, tend to shield their eyes. However, the struggle to survive hunger and famine and the socially established rules that regulate the probable outcomes of that struggle are foundational to social structure.

Rights to Domestic Resources

Critical to the ability to sustain life is the right to receive the resources that sustain life, and within the social organization of every mammalian species, there is a corporate group organized for the purpose of providing to its members a share of essential resources. Most commonly it is a form of "domestic" group. This group is centered on the mother-child unit and (perhaps) joined by others who are related by kinship or by affinity to the socially designated mother. Beyond this basic presumption, we make no imputations regarding the specific composition of domestic groups. However, we can say that such groups are essential to life, at least to the lives of the very young and take some form universally. There must be a woman-child unit, and this unit is always embedded into a supporting cast of characters. Among lions, the "pride" constitutes a domestic group, and this role is played by the "pack" among wolves.

Even where a domestic group is available, it cannot be presumed that its resources will be available to a given individual. The data show that mothers care for children if and only if doing so provides more immediate rewards than do the alternative uses of their time. There is certainly no gene that biologically enforces parental care. In the case of the young sexually active Comanche girl, it was often her choice to suffocate her infants rather than submit to the tasks and sexual restrictions of adulthood (Collier 1988). In other instances, an African woman may relinquish the smaller of troublesome twins, and poor women in Brazil may abandon early their efforts to maintain a child, given the deficit in resources (Scheper-Hughes 1985).

Generations of infant girls have perished among the Rajputs of India because the men of their caste seek more profitable relationships with women of lower rank (making their daughters unmarriageable). And boys are more vulnerable to mortality among the Mokugodo of east Africa because their parents prefer to devote available resources to daughters, whose eventual marriage will facilitate the accumulation of bridewealth cattle (Bell and Song 1992–1993). Hence, the care of children is not instinctual, and evolution has depended on the fact that, by and large, children have been the preferred objects of choice within a set of viable alternatives.

The survival of children is structurally at risk, even in the context of domestic groups, because the sharing of consumption goods within domestic groups is affected by a rule that gives considerable advantage to those of higher rank. Although an infant is favored in relation to its mother's milk, given that the mother's own nutrition is sufficient to facilitate lactation, infants may not be advantaged on a broader scale. Rather, individuals have access to food in order of rank, and when food is limited in supply, those at the bottom, including children, may have little or none at all.

It is possible that members of a category will fail to recognize the fairness of their commonly realized share, especially if they are members of the least favored of categories. And in these cases it is essential to the viability of the system that individuals within that category be without an ability to violate social prescription and alter permanently the distribution of benefits to their own advantage by force or deception. A hierarchical system cannot continue without police, jails, and related instruments of social control, required particularly for the control of the least favored of person-categories in the system.

A proposition of considerable significance will be proven: If infrahousehold allocation of scarce resources is a product of cultural rules, then household allocation cannot be oriented by the interests or well-being of any particular category of individuals within the household, nor can it be oriented toward the interests of the group as a whole. It must be driven by interests that are socially external to the household.

The generalization of this finding to community- or state-level allocations is implicit, but not considered directly, herein. Furthermore, it will be demonstrated that food and other benefits will be allocated in percentage shares that vary with the quantity available to the household (in contrast with the allocation of inheritance that is always in nearly fixed percentages).

Varieties of Customary Practice

There is a common tendency for the literature on hunger and famine to focus on the desperate circumstances where food has entirely vanished and where those with sufficient energy begin to rage uncontrollably, even to the point of killing and eating their wives and children. "Starvation mercilessly rips off the 'social' garments from the man and shows him as a naked animal, on the naked earth" (Sorokin 1975 [1922]: 137). We have little difficulty understanding a descent into violence and cannibalism, where constraints of culture and household decorum fall prey to the ravages of complete starvation. However, we often have more difficulty understanding *socially accepted* allocations of food that ultimately grant higher probabilities of survival to some members of a household than to others—circumstances where most individuals accept the legitimacy of their own lower rank.

Some decades ago, there was a movie that began with a caveman scene. It depicted a hairy creature grabbing meat from a carcass and rushing to a corner to eat, cowering in fear that others would attempt to rip it from his hands. While this image may appeal to some as emblematic of the true primitive, it is quite unrepresentative of mammalian behavior. For example, while hyenas may eat rapidly, fearing the arrival of lions, they never need to fear each other. It is more common that there is a recognized rank order among animals, so that those of higher rank eat first and then retire from the carcass to allow others to come forward. Since relative rank is always known, there is little likelihood of conflict.

Among hyenas, females are dominant and nonrelated males are lowest ranking (Kruuk 1972). When most of a carcass has been eaten or when the kill is small, lower-ranking individuals leave the site in order to avoid conflict. Immigrant males are the first to leave, and if the kill is small, they are the last to join. Moreover, if the dominant female leaves the site before the males have eaten, the males leave with her. One can imagine, then, that during periods of food crisis, when food is more likely to be found in smaller magnitudes, the ranking of access to food will be reflected in differential mortality. Comparable processes have been observed among elephants in relation to access to water holes and among lions (Rudnai 1973) and wolves in relation to meat (Pacquet, Bragdon, and McCusk 1979).

Audrey Richards (1948) discusses the allocation of meat among the "southern Bantu." This is a group whose members lived "very near the starvation level, either continually or at certain seasons of the year. Thus the constituents of his daily diet, and his rules and habits of eating, are all linked in one emotional system with the institutions and activities by which food is procured" (p. 87). In the same way that the basic drive for sex is culturally regulated by a host of institutions and practices (the "reproductive system"), so too is the drive for food (the "nutritional system"). Richard's model produces three major insights: First, food is more important than sex, given that it is a precondition for all other things and because the need for it is almost continuous. Second, prestige and social power will be held by those who are *socially perceived to* be most important to the acquisition of food, either through their productive or hunting abilities or through their access to the forces of nature. And, third, those who are socially esteemed will enjoy preferential access to food, the means of survival.

Alice B. Kehoe and Dody H. Giletti (1981: 553) report common manifestations of sumptuary rules affecting women. For example, among the Djerid peoples of Tunisia

> women are restricted from drinking milk, and may drink only water; the men drink goats' milk. These women are not supposed to eat meat or vegetables, their staple food being a spiced fermented paste made from overripe dates fallen from the palm. Djerid men eat good-quality dates picked from the trees as well as meat, wheat, and vegetables when available.

A culturally extensive solution to this food allocation problem has been attributed to the Inuit. Here again, food is the critical resource, the availability of which varies widely during the year and where the threat of starvation is an annual event (Hoebel 1967; Ingold 1980). Male hunters share food among themselves, to the disadvantage of their wives. "Thus the women of the household, who are allowed to eat only after the appetites of their menfolk have been satisfied, may be left in times of want with the merest scraps of food" (Ingold 1980: 149).

Inuit men who are too old to hunt are expected to commit suicide (Hoebel 1967), rather than become a dangerous burden on the family unit. Men who are able to hunt, however, are the sources of community survival, and among them there is a very strict ethic of sharing of all resources, including the sexual comforts of their wives.

The practice of allocating leftovers to women is found extensively. It is common in the Middle East, Bangladesh, India, and China. Evidence from rural Bangladesh indicates that female children receive less than their brothers and that the gender differential tends to increase with age category (reflecting an gerontocratic age bias among males). The problem is particularly acute for pregnant women, whose special dietary needs appear to be overlooked in the food allocation process (Chen, Huq, and D'Souza 1981). L. C. Chen, E. Huq, and S. D'Souza (1981) observed [for Bangladesh] that although it was invariably the wife who

> distributed food at the meals, she gave the choice morsels to her husband, then to her eldest son, and less to herself and her daughters. The practice was a conditioned response requiring no pressure from her husband. (Carloni 1981: 6)

The point is not so much that food is *unequally* divided among house-hold members but that it is *inequitably* divided in relation to the re-quirements of males and females of different ages. This leads to a higher incidence of severe malnutrition among women and girls and excess fe-male infant mortality. (Carloni 1981: 4)

Data from the WHO's website (September 2001) indicate that these difficulties have not abated substantially. While saying nothing about the nutritional status of men, they indicate that

> Malnutrition among women is also extremely prevalent in Bangladesh. More than 50 percent of women suffer from chronic energy deficiency and studies suggest that there has been little improvement in women's nutritional status over the past 20 years.

The WHO data for 2001 on children in Bangladesh do not provide dif-ferences between boys and girls. However, for children of both genders, the data are very disturbing. The facts that would apply to female children can only be imagined.

> Rates of malnutrition in Bangladesh are among the highest in the world. More than 54% of preschool-age children, equivalent to more than 9.5 million children, are stunted, 56% are underweight, and more than 17% are wasted.

It should be emphasized, however, that the processes by which differ-ent categories of individuals obtain differentiated shares of domestic re-sources are never to be constructed specifically for conditions of food deprivation. Women often remain in the kitchen during dinner in many societies, including families in England, other parts of Europe, and many other parts of the world. These practices are followed independently of the volume of food available. The practice in India is described by Una Fruzzetti (1982: 100–101):

> In the evening . . . [r]ice or *rutis* (wheat cakes) have to be prepared and vegetables must be cut and cooked. Once again the men and children are fed first [as was true at the midday meal] followed by the older women, and last the young married women. No *stri* [wife] will eat rice before her husband has finished his meal.

After reading the preceding quotation from Fruzzetti, Huang (James) Cheng-Teh (personal communication) suggested that a similar practice was followed in China "in the old days." Men would eat separately from children, women would eat after the men had finished, and the young daughters-in-law would receive the remainders.

These practices tend not to be noted in ethnographic reports. "To anyone concerned with the study of food supply and famine, the near-blank in the sources on infra-household relations and food allocations is a great drawback" (Vaughan 1987: 120). This curious lacuna in ethnographic reports arises, perhaps, because the subject seems to be of little importance, as indeed it might be in the homes of the prosperous or in the homes of the poor during times of plenty. And it may be due to the use of male informants in the classical texts for whom the question is of no interest. On the other hand, since rules for the access of food are typically discussed in studies of mammalian hunters, the tendency to ignore these issues in ethnographic studies is puzzling. My discussions of these issues with other anthropologists reveal that these questions are very upsetting and treated with denial, in deference to a postindustrial ideology of universal female resistance.

The most ostentatious manifestation of differentiation that I have experienced took place in Saudi Arabia during "feasts" that were arranged to celebrate the arrival from America of my friend and colleague. One of the feasts was given by his widowed mother, hosted by her brother, and attended by about fifteen men, all seated on the floor around a Persian rug. It was a dinner sponsored by a woman to which no women could be present. Theirs would be the leftovers.

Men assumed locations relative to the host that strictly reflected rank and age. The host reached with bare hands into the steaming (whole) lamb and extracted enormous portions of meat for those at the head of the table and continued to offer portions to others in gradually decreasing amounts. For each of his two teenaged sons he offered only a pitiful morsel (to be supplemented later by a second helping).

Every element of this feast has its history in a more uncertain past, when as Bedouin on the desert only the ranking individuals of the stronger tribes could be ensured of survival. As clarified by Tim Ingold (1980), when nomadic peoples face severe deficit, they tend to aggregate in larger numbers, sharing more broadly that which remains. Most men would have nothing, but one man might have an animal to slaughter. He provides a feast. Later, another man is host to a feast, until all of the animal stalls are emptied. In this way feasts were an important aspect of famine, facilitating the broad distribution of very unequally held resources, and, hence, promoting the survival of the group.[1] The cycle of nature will eventually restore the basis of life; but in the meantime there is hunger and, perhaps, death. Hence, the rituals of feasting that were followed and *socially reinforced* in times of plenty emerged as denials of survival for those of lesser rank. And any man who dared challenge the appropriateness of his small portion would only hasten the end of his life.

> When men eat first and women and children what is left over—a feature in some Moslem societies—household eating practices can have a marked effect on the nutritional status of women and children. Furthermore, where males eat in a separate room, they may not be aware of the relative deprivation of the women and children. (Carloni 1981: 6)

I have mentioned these examples of *customary practice* because one might find it difficult to believe that people would accept social practices that decrease their survival probabilities. However, there are three principal factors to consider: First, these customary practices are never presented as stratified survival mechanisms. In every case, the rules of access to food appear as reifications of socially recognized rank. Respect, gratitude, deference and, yes, fear appear to be among the inducements that encourage the yielding of priority to others. Second, the most immediate consequence of an "eating order" is not a drastic reduction in the quantity of food, but a reduction in its quality. Starvation often arises with a full stomach. Studies of animals have shown that death may occur more rapidly from nutritional deficiencies than from reductions in quantity (Sorokin 1975 [1922]). Third, even when the quality is reduced, death by starvation is seldom precipitous; there is hope that more food will arrive, that the deficiencies of the moment will pass, and that the food yielded to those of higher rank will be returned in good measure.

> In a large part the politics of any society always has been and continues to be, first of all, a "bread politics," i.e. a set of measures which are called forth by the nutrition determinant and which are directed toward solving the problem "of the knife and the fork." Similar conditions face ad-

ministrators and rulers in general. The same can be said about the social struggle. (Sorokin 1975 [1922]: 156–57)

A willingness to defer to those of higher rank, to those who are culturally defined as being more important to the viability of the group, need not be imposed by force, nor is it a culturally induced irrationality. In those rather common cases in which men are largely responsible for acquiring the means of survival, household decision making will generally be premised on a presumption of male indispensability. Similarly, men of low rank are encouraged to believe that their welfare depends on the skills and influence of high-ranking individuals. Since the death or illness of a man may predispose the entire family to starvation, it is rational for a woman to experience hunger, allow herself to become ill, and risk her own starvation, in order to preserve the health of her husband. And, similarly, a man of modest social importance may readily yield to those on whom the community depends. Socially constructed indispensability induces an ideology of sacrifice onto part of those of lower rank.

Formal Structure of the Problem

Suppose that each individual within a group belongs to an established social category (such as father, mother, elder son, maternal aunt, grandfather, esteemed visitor, servant), and suppose that for any such category there is a method by which available food (and other resources) will be shared within the group.[2] The most common method of allocation is an "eating order" that allows certain categories of person to gain access to greater quantities or preferred qualities of food in the event that there is a deficit of food. Such eating orders generate a resource division that can be represented by $R = (r_1 + r_2 + \ldots + r_n)$ for the n categories of person. Such a division functions as a set of entitlements and constitutes an *allocation scheme*.

The share of food that accrues to any category will vary with the sufficiency or inadequacy of R. When there is an abundance of food relative to individual capacities, allocations may tend toward equality and the scheme may become irrelevant. As food becomes scarce, differentials in access become more pronounced and the social enforcement of those differentials becomes greater, as in figure 5.1.

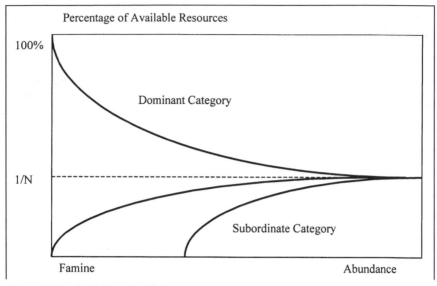

Figure 5.1. An Allocation Scheme

If cultural rules are to reflect meaningful concern regarding consumption levels within a household, they will focus more intensively on augmenting resources for those whose shares are inadequate relative to the social standard. And it can be safely presumed that when individuals are blessed with a socially recognized abundance of resources, there will be little social pressure to increase resources to those persons. The fact that allocation schemes are prompted by the existence of scarcity and that they lose force amidst abundance means that all allocation schemes must manifest, for any individual within any category of person, a decline in the social pressure to increase resources to him or her as the quantity of resources held by that individual increases. This presumption of fact will be labeled the Elementary Principle of allocation schemes.

The Elementary Principle: The strength of social forces oriented toward *increasing* resources to any individual will decrease as that individual's consumption increases.

This principle generates the downward sloping curves in figure 5.2. The downward slope of the curves (but not the specific shapes of the curves) in figure 5.2 is the only implication of the Elementary Principle.[3] This principle of allocation need not apply to a society or social class whose practices are predicated on a presumption of resource sufficiency.

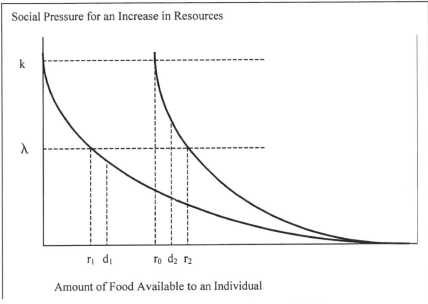

Social Pressure for an Increase in Resources

Amount of Food Available to an Individual

Figure 5.2. Level of Support for Increases in Shares of Food

However, it is, I believe, inconceivable that there could be a society in which hunger, malnutrition, or famine is common that would fail to have adopted an accommodating form of *customary practice*. Having found evidence of such a practice in India, China, the Middle East, and parts of Europe and Africa, this practice can be said to be typical of human societies.

An implicit "equilibrium" arises when social pressure for increases in shares is the same for each individual. Only then is there no effective pressure for a change in relative shares. In figure 5.2 this equilibrium arises for the given level of R when pressure for increased shares is 1 for each. In technical terms, this equilibrium illustrates the principle of *equal marginal social valuation*. To see the validity of this result, look at figure 5.2 and imagine an increase in resources for person One, so that he receives d_1, and as a result person Two must accept a reduction to d_2. We can see that there is substantially more social pressure in favor of increasing the resources to person Two in this event relative to increasing resources for person One, even though Two's share is the larger. This asymmetry implies that the allocation is "unfair" to person Two.

Our discussion presumes that food is available in some magnitude. The case of "total famine," where there is food for no one, cannot be considered by cultural rules. An *allocation scheme,* as such, becomes moot. Yet, it is this extreme case that tends to gain attention. A more common circumstance is one where no one has quite enough food, but where individuals who eat first have access to a relatively greater quantity or a higher nutritional quality or both and, hence, enjoy a greater probability of survival.

Maximizing the Social Value of the Group

In the previous section, a socially generated allocation scheme was assumed to exist, and we were concerned only with the ethical implications of following or not following its prescriptions. We shall now address the problem from the opposite direction: Assume that cultural practices have not been established, and assume that we want to find an allocation scheme that is most strongly induced by the prevailing social ideology. This scheme can be derived analytically.

The literature on infrafamilial resource allocation proceeds invariably from a presumption that allocation is guided by the well-being of the family as a whole (e.g., Dasgupta 1993: 334–36) or the well-being of dominant individuals within the family (e.g., Becker 1991). This chapter proves that both presumptions are false. In order to appreciate the technical results that follow, imagine that there is a force outside of the household—call it culture or the ruling elite or capital—whose interests are to be served by household norms. And suppose that the well-being of this outside force can be described by a mathematical function that is subject to maximization under conditions of food scarcity. Then, it can be proven that the objectives of this outside force are maximized when infrahousehold allocation satisfies the condition of *equal marginal social valuation,* as described in figure 5.2. This being true, the existence of the Elementary Principle implies a set of social objectives defined *outside* of the household—those objectives being accomplished by a set of *customary practices.*

We shall address the very simple problem of allocating a given value of R among family members. The main point to be made here is that we may proceed by positing a very general social preference function. We say nothing about the relative weight of various person-categories to the determination of this function, nor do we indicate its role within the social system. We say, simply: let there be a function $S(r_1 + r_2 + \ldots + r_n)$ for which maximization (given R) can be derived.[4]

The maximization of this function, given that $(r_1 + r_2 + \ldots + r_n) = R$, can be expressed in the calculus of constrained optimization as:

$$H = S(r_1 + r_2 + \ldots + r_n) - \lambda (r_1 + r_2 + \ldots + r_n - R)$$

where λ is a variable that is commonly introduced into problems of constrained optimization. It follows (from the use of calculus) that the social preference function is maximized when

$$S_i(\cdot) = \lambda, \text{ for } i = 1, 2, \ldots, n$$

And where $S_i(\cdot)$ is the amount of social pressure for increased resources to person i, holding constant the level of resources for others in the group. This means that the social preference function reaches its maximum when the pressures for additional resources are the same (equal to 1) for each person. Hence, in order to maximize social preferences for a given value of R, we must satisfy the *principle of marginal social valuation*, as illustrated in figure 5.2.

Embedding Households into the Society

We have just shown that the higher the rank that men commonly have relative to household resources in allocation schemes does not arise for the benefit of men (in their roles as husbands and fathers) but for purposes that are external to the household. Households are always components of larger systems of social action (Richards 1948), and they are important to the reproduction and the viability of those larger systems. This issue is particularly salient in patrilineal systems, where lineage elders commonly approve and finance household formation and are able to claim rights to the children who are the principal social product of households. Since households are important instruments of lineage growth and power, it is to be expected that the interests of lineages would affect the construction of the norms and cultural practices that orient household behavior.

Certainly, those *customary practices* will be to the benefit of men in their roles as lineage members, but they need not favor them as household members. The common failure to recognize, explicitly, the separate groups to which men (and women) might belong has often led to a failure to differentiate between the interests that people have in different domains. It is frequently the case that the interests of an individual are inconsistent across the groups to which he or she belongs.

The practices that favor powerful men may fail to favor weak men. This fact becomes evident in an examination of social structure of the Ahaggar (*ImûhaR*) (Nicolaisen 1963). Given their ownership of camels as an asset around which to build patrilineages, it is peculiar that they retain matrilineal structures. However, powerful men within powerful matrilineages are the ones who have exercised social control. As I see it, they have preferred to retain land-holding matrilineal organizations, exploiting the agricultural work of vassal lineages, thereby retaining their power relative to other men, even though men in general might be better off relative to women with a patrilineal structure. In general, then, the position of men within households is not determined by men in their capacity as household members. The interests of those who have control over central wealth-assets matter, and those wealth-assets always have a social location outside of households.

In the economics literature, M. Manser and M. Brown (1980) and Marjorie McElroy and Mary Horney (1981) provide a bargaining perspective on infrahousehold allocation. A bargaining process would appear to be particularly appropriate to the relatively greater gender equality and role ambiguity found in postindustrial societies. However, bargaining cannot be in reference to psychic utilities, as they presume, since no one really knows what those are, but about fairness, a concept that does not fit well into the atomistic individualism of economics. Unlike utilities, fairness does not live entirely inside of people's heads; it is defined by perceptions of socially normative behavior. Bargaining over shares arises because people often hold different perceptions of those norms. In other words, *cultural practices* are empirically "fuzzy" and subject to competing interpretations.

Among feminists men are often perceived to be egoistic exploiters of household resources with wives who are subversive to their subordination. Culture is believed to affect this battle of the sexes by providing different ideological and material supports to the competing parties, but household allocation itself is relegated to a domain of individualism. However, the household is always among the important sites of social reproduction and, as such, cannot be allowed to operate outside of culture in any society. If this point is granted, then the preceding proof suggests that we should not assume that husbands impose rules and women resist. Rather, *both* parties are faced with the somewhat ambiguous social norms that emerge from the Elementary Principle and *both* may attempt to increase or defend their shares under conditions of scarcity by reference to those norms.

Significance of Customary Practice

Resource allocation within households is shown here to be "embedded in social relations" and in customary social practices that are central to culture and social behavior. Furthermore, we have discovered a previously unknown characteristic of normative systems. Normative systems of allocation are hereby shown to correspond to the maximization of a social preference function whose agents are outside of the household unit. Our findings are culturally uncontaminated in the sense that the implied social preference functions are entirely unspecified beyond the generic Elementary Principle that must apply to any socially supported allocation system. We have argued that the construction of allocation schemes will be related to the objectives of wealth-holding groups that are external (yet connected) to the household. If men prove to be principle beneficiaries of these schemes on most occasions, it is only incidental and by no means inevitable, given that a minority of powerful men are generally not unwilling to permit the subordination of other men.

CHAPTER SIX
ON THE NATURE OF RIGHTFUL
AND IMPOSED CLAIMS

Clash by Gyula Derkovits. Dózsa-Series VI. (1928) Woodcut, 440 × 504 mm, Hungarian National Gallery, Budapest.

At one time the material in this chapter began my narrative. Although it has been delayed in this presentation, it is actually foundational to everything. The distribution of every form of scarce benefit within any form of society can be classified as a mode of sharing or as a mode of exchange, corresponding sociologically to complementarity and reciprocity. In this chapter we look at the two fundamental forms of sharing: rightful and imposed.[1] We can delay until chapter 10 for a fuller discussion of reciprocity.

The received ideology of Western culture implies a strong conceptual separation of rightful claims from those that are affected by force, violence, theft, and deception. However, these forced claims are unambiguously among the methods for gaining access to shares of scarce resources and, hence, are a form of sharing. The discussion herein is shocking for some because I refuse to introduce (Western) cultural valuations into the discussion. Yet, the nation-state itself is usually the product of violently derived and forced claims against the counterclaims of displaced and subjugated peoples, in spite of the popular fantasy that we who inhabit a national territory do so rightfully.

In chapter 2 we presented the four necessary and sufficient criteria by which "wealth-assets" can be identified. Most of those criteria imply the existence of social collectivities that either manage the relevant resources or that benefit from the consumer goods that flow from its accumulation or that benefit from its accumulation (growth). In other words, a resource is wealth only as an element of social structure, and we have argued that it is *always* foundational to the social structure in question. In this chapter we shall continue our examination of the internal operation of social groups within those structures. Our concern here will be the role of forceful appropriation of resources and forceful actions toward specific others.

Claims, Rightful and Imposed

In our last chapter we focused on resource allocations within households. These allocations were presented in the form of "customary practice." One might imagine such practices as the product of force, such that those who have priority in food consumption can exercise that priority only against the active or passive resistance of others. The fact that this is not so is apparently quite disturbing to those who presuppose a world of socially rebellious and culturally nonintegrated individuals, who participate in systems of unequal division only under duress. Given a presumption that every man struggles against the chains of social rank and that every woman rebels against gender roles, it would follow that all prevailing social formations and domestic arrangements exist only through the exercise of brute force.

It was because of this rather extreme ideology that the contents of our last chapter could not be published in a major American journal. The ethnographic facts presented in that chapter were intolerable to some readers, who then asserted that none of it could be true. The claim is that women do not willingly participate in systems of unequal division and that the circumstances uncovered by the research of the World Health Organization in its Bangladesh nutrition study are only "anecdotal" and contrary to fact. As I see it, the social positions of women around the world must be denied in order to advance the ideology of a privileged upper middle class in the postindustrial West.

In popular culture there is the notion that sharing implies an absence of selfishness and egoism. This conception of the matter is conventional within Western cultures—learned by each of us in the context of parental admonitions. However, as an elementary process, we shall see that sharing is often the consequence of forceful acquisition and violence to which the fig leaf of "altruism" may be attached. *Sharing is the process by which various categories of person receive fractions of a given bundle of resources.*

Our task now is to discuss and explain this definition: Certainly, if there is to be some form of sharing, there must be something to share: some form of resource, corporeal or noncorporeal, real or imagined. And this set of shared resources must be exhaustible, subject to being "used up" in some sense, for otherwise there is no need to apportion its distribution among individuals or to prevent access to it by "outsiders." Consequently, sharing implies the existence of a numerically delimited collection of individuals, the "insiders," family members, citizens, or group members, who are allowed to claim a "share" of a finite and exhaustible resource.

The fact that the set of sharers must be finite is obvious when the resource is corporeal in form, such as food or shelter. However, the resource may be behaviorally restricted, as in the case of the affections of a parent, given the limited time and energies of parents by which affections can be made manifest. A more ambiguous form of limitation may apply to the use of a clan or tribal name. Even when there are no concrete resources that are allocated solely on the basis of group identification, an uncontrolled appropriation of identities by individuals will reduce the significance of that identity as a source of benefits for its holders.

Hence, a man's identification as an Ibo (a tribal group in West Africa) is useful as a shared resource only when there is effective restriction on its application. In this case, the shared resource may provide individuals with prestige, preferential access to the friendship and resources of certain others, and in other ways facilitate the acquisition of resources. On the other hand, it cannot be said that individuals have claim to some fractional share of such amorphous resources, notwithstanding the importance of limiting the set of claimants.

There are two basic forms of sharing: There are *rightful divisions* of resources, where the benefits to various claimants are "legitimated" by the support of individuals other than the direct beneficiaries, and there are *imposed divisions* of resources, where allocations are determined by violence, deception, and other extractive methods by the beneficiaries themselves.

Actually, the rightful claims often depend on considerable violence and force. The difference between rightful claims and imposed claims is that rights are defended by categories of person that differ from the direct beneficiary of the right, whereas forced claims are defended (forcefully) by the direct beneficiary. But this difference is "huge." In order to enlist others in the defense of one's claims, there must be provided some rationale of moral substance. It is not enough to say, "I want it." If the resource is scarce, many will want it. Hence, for rightful claims to exist, an ideology must be established, a generally accepted set of ethical propositions (an aspect of culture) must emerge that suggest the appropriateness of the claim.

It is to be expected that the most ardent supporters of the claims of a category of person will include those of another category for whom the existing system of allocation is favorable relative to some imagined or real alternative. For example, the gentry may support the prerogatives of an aristocracy if the security of the latter appears to add to the security of its own very separate and generous claims. Similarly, the aristocracy supports the claims of the gentry since the latter may play a central role in the general process of economic production and political legitimization. In a broad sense of the term, each of these classes has a self-interest in the rights of the other, and the gains of each can be seen to result in a reduction in the shares of a third party—the peasantry. Nevertheless, the rights of the gentry are not those of the aristocracy and vice versa, and in a simple arithmetical sense of the matter, the resources received by one group reduce the potential claims of every other group.

Hence, when we say that the social support that defines a rightful claim must emanate from a nonbeneficiary, we do not imply that the nonbeneficiary is disinterested. That will seldom if ever be the case. There would be no reason for a disinterested category to offer support for a claim, almost by definition. In sum: If there is significant support ("significant" being undefined) for a claim from categories of person that are disjoint from the benefiting category, then we say that the claim is rightful. When the defense of a claim depends almost entirely on the efforts of the benefiting category of person, then we shall say that the claim is forced.

Social support is considered here as a potentially active force that actually defends or protects a certain category in its exercise of right. We may restate our definition of a right: A right is an act of preference or of a course of action by a category of person, the exercise of which is protected by means of negative sanctions or encouraged by others or both.

But suppose that a claim is supported both by imposition by the benefiting category, as well as by social support. How is such a claim to be considered analytically? It is possible that only a few "lackeys support a dominant group," while police forces are arrayed against the great majority. Arguably, the primary support for the claims of such a dominant is force. Yet there is some degree of support from nonbeneficiaries. Is the support of those lackeys sufficient to constitute a rightful claim? To this question there can be no answer.

Certainly, those who support the claim may assert that the beneficiary possesses a right. Those who oppose the claim will certainly deny the existence of a right. It is a political question for which there can be no scientific determination. More importantly, we must recognize that to declare a right is simply to declare one's support for a claim—nothing more. Consequently, it is possible for a number of different individuals to make a "rightful" claim against the same thing. Each such individual may possess social support, and each will possess a right by the definition presented here.

Similarly, when the strength of a claim arises partly from support of a "disjoint" category and partly from force or deception, the character of the claim must be left to the combatants. The real world is not neatly divided into rightful and imposed claims. The strict dichotomy between these two forms is largely formal and analytical, and it abstracts from common fuzziness of real life. Since the beneficiary of a rightful claim is very likely to be an active supporter of the claim—using his or her own force as a supplementary factor in effecting the claim—most "rights" have an element of imposition. On the other hand, claims that are based entirely on force or deception are not uncommon among human and nonhuman animals. Hence, there are claims that are objectively based on force. Rightful claims, on the other hand, are likely to be contested and denied by a class of nonsupporters in a contest of ideologies. Here, we refused to take sides.

One of the more instructive manifestations of imposed claims is that of male lions who have gained control of a pride. This control follows on the forceful ouster of other males and the forced submission of the adult females of the pride from whom the males claim sexual services and a "lion's share" of the food. The claims of such males are clearly imposed. However, once males have taken their share, adult females allocate shares among juveniles, cubs, and themselves. While the shares of females may be claimed by force, their offspring possess rightful claims—given the support of adult females. Hence, with respect to a specific resource, it may be partly allocated by force and partly allocated by social support. But the difference between forceful and rightful claims should not be exaggerated. Both are forms of sharing of a finite resource.

A rightful claim is a claim that is applicable only to a type or category of person. Individuals, as such, cannot have rightful claims except as members of some such categories. Individuals may have desires, physical and mental states, and so forth, but rights they cannot have. In every form of society, human and nonhuman, rights apply to males versus females, older males versus younger males, the progeny of x versus the progeny of y, and so forth. For example, in the United States individuals possess the right to vote on the basis of having been born there, on the basis of the citizenship of one of their parents, or on the basis of a "naturalization" process.

These are categories of eligibility that do not depend on the special qualities of those individuals. Categories of person arise from the needs of the system of accumulation to articulate the set of useful social positions.

However, since any changes in the system of categories will advantage some and disadvantage others, the articulation of categories is seldom fully effective. Hence, it would be a serious error to assume that a given set of rights and customary practices are actually best for the system of accumulation. We can say only that poorly articulated systems are potentially subject to being overwhelmed by more effectively articulated systems.

A good example of an imposed claim is warfare. Most wars are motivated by the effort of one party to seize possessions of another. Land, or land with its population, such as colonies, is a typical prize of warfare. Wars take place when there is no agreement on rightful shares. Hence, the sharing of the relevant resources must follow a different route. Theft is another example. Thieves seek a share of the resources currently in the hands of rights-holders, and if they are successful, the resources will become shared by rightful and imposed claims. The "raiding" of camels among Bedouin is an example of a forced appropriation that is recognized as rightful, but such cases are rare.

Since the supporters of a rightful claim must include predominantly those who are not direct beneficiaries, then, especially in the case of scarce resources, those supporters would often appear to suffer a resource loss as a consequence of that supported claim—they appear to be self-sacrificing. However, those who appear to be the most seriously affected will invariably be among those who are most essential in supporting the claim. There is no paradox. Those who have no claim of their own to a given set of resources are usually in a poor position to support the claims of a particular category of claimants against the claims of other categories within the group. Some would say that it is none of their business! Indeed, there can be no self-righteousness in supporting a division of resources unless one appears to be suffering a personal loss.

The Effectiveness of Claims

We now know that resource claims may be rightful or imposed. And we know that a rightful claim can exist only to the extent that nonbeneficiaries are willing to make efforts to ensure the provision of the relevant resources. However, even when there is a consensus on the validity of a claim, seemingly elementary rights can be violated. Neither rightful nor imposed claims are absolute, and we must recognize their effectiveness as an essential dimension: A claim is *effective* to the degree that any individual incumbent of the relevant category of person, chosen at random, will be able to realize his or her claim.

Notice that there are two components of this definition. There may be variations in the percentage of individuals who are ensured full access to the resource in question, and there may be variations in the amount of the resource effectively claimed by particular individuals within the relevant category of person. Hence, the simplest measure of effectiveness would be the percentage of the claimed resource that is realized by individuals within the relevant person-category. (Such a measure focuses on the ability of the average member of the category to realize a claim, ignoring other moments of the statistical distribution.)

Unless the effectiveness of a claim is 100 percent for members of the relevant category, there may be occasions when particular individuals suffer a denial of their rightful claims. Even though people may have rights to their bicycles, some individuals may have them stolen. These victims might reasonably assert that the effectiveness of their claim to bicycle ownership has fallen to zero. However, the effectiveness with which a claim is held cannot be evaluated relative to the experience of select individuals, but only by reference to an individual chosen at random—the "representative" or typical individual. The appropriate issue then is the extent to which members of this category of person can be secure in their claims. A gang of thugs may overwhelm particular individuals; but so long as the forces of social control limit the degree of gang victimization, its victims possess a right with some degree of effectiveness.

We are accustomed to thinking of rights as a feature of nation-states, where rights are usually codified into "law." However, it is possible that a law, passed in Beijing, is contrary to the strongly held values of a distant province. When this occurs, there will be the assertion of contradictory sets of claims, and it is possible that each set of claims has sufficient social support to qualify as rightful. This possibility exists so long as we do not require a very high minimal threshold of social support as the necessary condition for the existence of a right. As a result, it is possible for a right to be illegal, and it is possible for a "law" to be in violation of a person's rights (in the opinion of some people). In general, there may be competing rightful claims over the same resource. Our theoretical view of the matter does not take sides. We cannot do so without imposing a particular ideology on the issue.

When the forceful appropriation of resources violates the rules established by socially dominant classes, it is called theft. However, P. J. Proudhon (1840), attempted to express a subaltern ideology when he claimed that "property is theft." His idea was that land (and he was most interested in land) is a resource that rightfully belongs (as a use-right) to those who make direct productive use of it, and that this resource has been seized illegitimately by the avaricious and unproductive few. Furthermore, he felt that the state power that supported the claims of the few was an illegitimate agent of the few—an instrumentality for the enforcement of imposed claims. It is for this reason that he favored an elimination of the state—anarchism.

Even if he is correct in asserting that land was initially taken from the peasants (and there is a good foundation for that view), we can see readily that this appropriation has been largely legitimated by the production of an elaborate set of ideologies, by the recruitment of support from other person-categories, and by a system of political and social repression. If the abrogation of the rights of peasants and others has been legitimated, then the very fact of the appropriation can be denied.

In an argument that is similar to that of Proudhon, Karl Marx questioned the legitimacy of appropriation by capitalists of the product of labor. While Proudhon made use of a traditional notion that land should belong to the direct producer, Marx developed the parallel idea that the output of capitalist production belongs rightfully to the worker. And, indeed, if a powerful movement to promote the workers' claims on their productivity were to arise, then the "surplus" appropriated by capitalists would become increasingly recognized as theft, and capitalism could come to an end.

We see, then, that theft is not a particular kind of action, it is an ideological characterization of an action or process. "Theft" is a form of resource appropriation that is deemed to be illegitimate (not supported) by the individual who uses the term. It is not theft to those for whom that appropriation is legitimate. The difference between imposed and rightful claims is potentially reducible to the status of perspective.

The Attendant Responsibilities

There is the nearly ubiquitous expression, "reciprocal rights and responsibilities." Endless confusion has been spawned by this expression and, indeed, it is probably the product of confusion. If we recognize the fact that there are social ("status") positions to which rights and responsibilities are socially designated, it would appear unreasonable to presume that one individual's rights are another's responsibility. Clearly, this expression does not have reference to real reciprocity, whatever that means.

If we can avoid the "norm of reciprocity" trap for the moment, it should be clear that rights are not obtained *in exchange* for responsibilities. Yet, we all know that rights are in some way contingent. That contingency can be expressed by

The Eligibility Criterion: An individual establishes and/or maintains membership in a social category by performing the duties that define eligibility into that category or by possessing particular personal characteristics based on birth, sex, or age, or by a combination of these factors.

Shares of corporate resources are socially generated either by prescription (e.g., entitlement or inheritance) or by "customary practice" (recognition of rank). But how does an individual qualify for a given entitlement or rank? The Eligibility Criterion suggests two distinct methods of gaining eligibility into a person-category. The first method is by the performance of duty, and the other is by virtue of personal, inherent, or biological characteristics that are defined along particular dimensions, or some combinations of these two methods.

Force in Gender Relations

The roles of force and "domestic violence" have been strongly promoted as factors in gender relations, especially by many contemporary feminists. For many women the circumstances seem obvious. Since men often possess an overwhelming advantage in size and strength, they are able to commit great harm to their domestic partners when they become angry, frustrated, or humiliated—these being states of mind to which the male mentality is strongly inclined. Furthermore and most importantly, in the context of isolated nuclear families that has been constructed to serve the purposes of capitalist accumulation, women are isolated from potential sources of protection and made vulnerable to brutality.

Without diminishing the importance of this environment for many unfortunate women, we shall be able to characterize the violent and dangerous brute as a weak man. While he may not be physically weak relative to his wife, he is most likely to be socially weak relative to other men. And while his violence may serve the interests of others, those interests relate to the accumulation of capital and at best only incidentally the preservation of gender roles. In other words, the allocation of resources within households under capitalism is governed by "customary practices," and these practices may involve violence for those (weak men) who suffer a severe deficit in resources. But the violence of weak men is not relevant to the gender dominance of strong men.

In characterizing the violent man as socially weak, I am clearly advancing a characterization for which there are innumerable counterexamples. There are, after all, many ways of being weak or strong, not all of which relate to social position. And some of these other, more idiosyncratic personal and psychological manifestations of weakness are distributed widely across the range of social position. Our discussion, here, is focused on social position as a factor that induces violence, notwithstanding the occurrence of intrafamilial violence and, indeed, homicide among the rich.

We will find that dominance relations by sex depend on differences in corporate holdings of wealth-assets by sex. Although particular males or females may attempt to claim food by force in violation of social rules, those rules will be a function of outside forces that manage the system of "wealth-accumulation."

There appear to be three subspecies of baboon: hamadryas, gelada, and a set of subtypes called savanna. All baboons appear to be a potentially interbreeding species whose phenotypical and social differences are plausibly associated with differences in the ecological conditions in which they live, much like "races" among humans (Smuts et al. 1985). The different basic structures observed among baboons are related to differences in the three ecological conditions in which they are found. In particular, we find hamadryas baboons under conditions of limited food availability and relatively low predation pressure; gelada baboons are found under conditions of greater food availability and low predation pressure; and savanna baboons enjoy a most abundant food supply but relatively high predation pressure. The hamadryas and the gelada are remarkable for having complex, multilevel social structures, and it is on them that we shall focus attention.

Hamadryas Baboons

Hamadryas baboons maintain a trilevel organizational structure. At the lowest level there are "one-male units" that include a set of females, their offspring, and a "harem holder." At the next level there is the "band," consisting of a set of related harem holders (but not members of the harem). And finally, there is the "troop" that is constituted of bands and their harems that assemble for safety on sleeping cliffs in the evenings.

One-male units among the hamadryas feature a male who claims exclusive sexual right/privilege over a set (one to nine) of adult females (Kummer 1968). A harem holder maintains a coercive control over the females in his unit, "herding" them vigorously, as they have a tendency to stray, by biting them on the neck with considerable frequency. Each female is likely to have been "kidnapped" from a different unit of the same band when they were subadults and protected until maturity. Having originated from a given band, females are likely to be genetically related in many ways (Sigg et al. 1982; from Dunbar 1984).

In addition to harem holders, a band may contain one or more subordinate males, usually subadult or fairly old males who are nonreproductive. Consequently, there is differentiation into person-categories among males. Male members of a band move their units across a given "home range" in which they forage during the day, and they tend to occupy a common area of the "sleeping cliff" during the evenings. Furthermore, since band members retain the benefits of female fertility (in terms of female offspring), fertility becomes a wealth-asset of the band. Hence, the band is the principal wealth-holding collectivity—holding a home range and female fertility.

Although it is the responsibility of each hamadryas male to control his females, other members of the band also provide protection to those females from capture by other males. Band members fight as a unit against predators and agonistic conspecifics and manifest restraint and avoidance of the females of fellow band members. Since all males in a band, including those who have no females of their own, offer this restraint and protection, there is clearly an element of rightfulness (social support) in sexual possession. The importance of the band is illustrated by an experiment conducted by Kummer (1970): A one-male unit was extracted from its band and deposited into an alien troop. The result was an immediate attack on its leader by others as they stripped him of his females. Lacking support of kin, he was made to limp away—leaving his divided harem behind.

The hamadryas live in the Kalahari desert where resources are quite scarce and where special knowledge of the ecology of an area may be essential to survival. Hence, a home range is worth fighting for. Survival of the fittest has depended on the ability of individuals and their kin to establish by active force their access to a particular home range. Since males are larger and stronger than females, they have an advantage in securing this resource.

As we find among human groups, males are able to gain control over the *sexuality* of females through hard work, displays of courage, and other manifestations of charisma. But they can gain rights in the *fertility* of females only by having control over some other form of wealth. Forced claims to a home range constitute the wealth-asset around which a group of males may coalesce as a wealth-holding corporate group.

Gelada Baboons

Gelada baboons are quite differently structured, even though their structure is falsely claimed to feature "one-male units." The domain of the gelada baboon provides greater food availability, making the control of a home range and specialized knowledge of food locations unavailable as bases of power for males, and, hence, males are unable to claim land as a wealth-asset by which to gain control over females. In this case, it is the "wealth-value" of female fertility that triumphs, and males struggle among themselves to gain access to the flow of benefits generated by that fertility. Females constitute the foundation of social structure in the form of ranked groups of matrilaterally related individuals.

One "alpha" adult male is attached to these females as the sire of their offspring. Adult males are associated with a matriline only as members of the consumption group. "In a very real sense, the male is a social supernumerary whose role in the group is merely that of breeder. He is virtually excluded from interactions with his females because the latter prefer to interact with their immediate female relatives" (Dunbar 1983: 300). For this reason it is quite inappropriate to use the term "one-male unit" for the gelada. This is not the male's unit; it is more accurate to suggest that he belongs to the unit as its breeder. However, the gelada females are closely related to each other and function as a wealth-holding group.

In addition to the alpha male, units may include one or more male "followers." A follower is unlikely to challenge the alpha male; rather, he will wait for a time when subordinate females of the unit attempt to form a new group, at which time the departing group may adopt him as their breeder. However, most bachelor males reject the "follower" option and join with all-male groups, waiting for a period of peak physical capacity, at which time they may challenge an alpha male for access to females.

Members of a gelada matriline are ranked in a dominance relation that is manifested in an "eating order," as discussed in chapter 5. This is another example of "customary practice." In this way the alpha male and female are ensured the physical superiority required to maintain their positions. The alpha male, in order to serve his purposes for the matriline, must be allowed to eat first. He would otherwise become an easily vanquished weakling. He eats first in service to the wealth of the matriline! Lower-ranking males and females, however, will be smaller, and lower-ranking females will be less reproductive because of relative resource deprivation, not because of inherent or genetic differences.

Access to resources is both the purpose and measure of rank, and as a matriline increases in size, lower-ranking members suffer increasingly from the greater number of superordinate members. They have more limited access to food and water, and while the frequency of copulation may not be reduced, the stress of subordination tends to reduce fertility. Females transmit their rank to female offspring by threats and attacks against lower-ranking females and their offspring, and mother-daughter teams work together to maintain or achieve higher rank. Hence, the lower fertility of subordinate females further reduces the set of allies by which rank is achieved, further threatening their status. For these reasons, lower-ranking females and their female offspring have an incentive to depart as the matriline increases in size. They do so often by recruiting, as their leader, a male who has been a nonreproductive follower of the matriline.

We see here the importance of recognizing fertility as an organizing wealth-asset and as a basis of matrilineal organization in any species. We see also that the male gelada does not achieve dominance through violence, although he possesses the same physical advantage over females as the hamadyras. On the other hand, the gelada males are quite violent among themselves for access to the matriline. It cannot be argued, then, that the basis of power for the hamadryas derives from "biting on the neck."

Subordinate Men

For reasons that I find mysterious, anthropologists commonly believe that there are no societies featuring female dominance. I say, mysterious, because the ethnographic fact of such dominance is evident in the literature. In addition to the admittedly strong example of matriarchy presented by Rembau (see chapter 2) and discussed by C. W. C. Parr and W. H. Mackray (1910), there are other less dramatic cases. For example, Terence S. Turner (1979) in his discussion of Ge-Bororo social organization presents an example of a matrilineal structure where males are distinctly subordinate. These are societies in central Brazil that have access to an abundance of land for subsistence production and access to forest and rivers for a wide variety of other food products.

Agricultural production and the gathering of local items are the primary sources of nutrition, and these processes are under the control of women, supplemented by the hunting, gathering, and fishing of men. Warfare is not a factor in threatening the power of fertility, and men own no countervailing wealth-assets. Hence, this is a society for which a matrilineal-matrilocal form of household organization is to be expected. Men circulate in search of wives and subsequently become the tools of dominant parents-in-law, especially the mother-in-law:

> With the marriage of her daughters and the removal of her sons to other households, the woman exchanges her functional authority as mother over her children and adolescent daughters for the prestigious role of mother-in-law. Now, she has sons-in-law to pay her deference, do her bidding, and submit, if she pleases, to her scolding beyond anything her own sons would be expected tolerate from her. Her relations with her daughters, however, remain open, relaxed, and free. (Turner 1979: 164)

This is a classic pattern in which the power of fertility and its control by a matrilateral group become the basis for female dominance. Clearly, the warm relationships between mothers and daughters yield to daughters a power over their husbands that they can exercise directly or indirectly through the agency of their mothers.

As I see it, this is an "evident" case of female dominance. However, the evidence is insufficient to overwhelm contemporary ideology. Turner presupposes male dominance, in line with a widely held presumption that male dominance is universal. Of course, he has been there and I have not. So, he could be right. But nothing in his discussion supports his conclusion. He justifies his presumption of male dominance with the observation that men have control over an extrafamilial social organization that he then presumes has dominance over households. In fact, he tells us nothing that would suggest the dominance of these interfamilial organizations. Rather, he appears to be making inferences drawn from the study of societies with patrilineal structures, where lineages clearly have possession of and control over households.

Patrilineages are able to do this because they are wealth-holding corporate groups and because the roles of wives and household organization are predicated on the provision of lineage-held wealth. However, the social organizations of Ge-Bororo men control no wealth. They have only symbolic power and provide men only with "symbolic dominance" (Sanday 1981) *by the exclusion of women from their proceedings*. Moreover, in these external organizations of men, young men—men whose daughters have not yet attracted sons-in-law—are powerless and made to remain silent while their elders blather presumptuously. In spite of Turner's claims about male dominance, young men are clearly the most "oppressed" category of person. Young men have no voice among men and, as a condition for access to the sexuality of women, must grovel before their in-laws. They are weak, both at home and abroad.

For those who have studied the cultures of hunter-gatherers around the world, a most revealing fact about the position of Ge-Bororo men is that young men must present the product of hunting to their wives! It is their wives who gain social recognition by distributing the products of hunting, making it clear that the activities of men are derivative of the powers of women. Tim Ingold (1980) discusses a variety of kill-distribution rules, pointing out that it is often the leader of the hunting party, a senior male relative, or a chief who gains prestige from the work of hunters. When this is the case, men are not free to develop a rank among themselves based on hunting ability. Instead, they are subaltern elements of a hierarchy, forced to contribute to the prestige of others. Among the Ge-Bororo, it is the wife of the hunter and, inferentially, her matrilateral kin who gain this advantage. Turner (1979: 156–57) provides this argument for male dominance:

> The tendency for women to be charged with the responsibility for early child care, and thus to be allotted such tasks as are compatible with the socialization role, may doubtless be considered a basic infrastructural input into the shaping of this pattern . . . and must be accounted for as the results of the imposition of a superordinate set of social values. The central value of this set is what I have called male dominance.

However, a lack of power associated with mothering in our contemporary period does not imply a similar lack in a culture for which fertility is the only form of wealth. Mothering joins with biology to produce effective fertility, and effective fertility can be a basis of power. Hence, the dominance of women is reinforced by their essential role in the provision of food, because food helps to ensure the vitality of offspring and hence raises the effective fertility of women.

While the disadvantaged position of young men is patent, that of mature men is left undefined by the material presented by Turner. With the aging and death of the in-laws, a woman loses her powerful domestic allies, and her husband gains the possibility of moderating his subordination. Moreover, men gain a voice among men after the marriage of their daughters. For men the marriage of daughters represents a rite of passage into "maturity," and as mature men, they are allowed to speak fully in ritualistic associations. It is not clear what, if any, indirect benefits accrue to men from the exercise of this new prerogative; but even if there are none, these associations imply a ranking of men relative to each other in the public domain. And as men with married daughters, they gain sons-in-law whom they may control and humiliate. These changes in the structural position of a man relative to other men are likely to have some effect on the relationship of that man to his wife. More respect, perhaps, but certainly not dominance.

The position of mature men in the external associations is the foundation of Turner's belief that men rank above their wives. However, rather than locating power in wealth-assets, as we do here, he locates it in a value system. Quite possibly, the system of valuations that are expressed within male associations implies that men are better than women. However, the expression of such values cannot be a source of power. On the contrary, the purpose of these groups is to present an image of male strength as a conterweight to the fact of male powerlessness. Given the thorough subordination of men in the household domain, a public ideology of male power might be essential as an integrative factor in social organization.

We are dealing here with symbolic dominance, as Peggy Sanday (1981) would call it, a phenomenon that resides in the value domain but lacks a material foundation. It is not unlike the macho posturing of lower-class males in contemporary societies, which often functions as a cover for powerlessness and subordination in the world at large. I might add that this discussion points to the danger inherent in characterizing a society by reference to the statements of informants. It is quite possible that even the women of Ge-Bororo will support the cultural pretensions of male dominance. Value systems are subject to a general internalization, and it is useful to know about the expressed worldview of a society. However, that information can only confuse the ethnographer in the absence of an understanding of social structure and process. That structure exists independently of the expressed values of informants.

The Weakness of Violence

Evidence from the United States suggests that while violence against women can arise in any quarter, it is more likely to play a systematic and significant role when the male perpetrator is poorly placed within the hierarchy of male-male competition. While criminals are outcasts of the system, those who must use violence against women belong to its lowest ranks. It is the man who is, or who feels, socially inadequate that must be feared as violent, and this violence may be visited on other men and on women. Powerful men—men who have advantaged access to society's resources—tend not to be violent men. And if violence is deemed to be essential in accomplishing the goals of successful men, its performance tends to be delegated to men of lesser rank, men of little power—the foot soldier, the cop on the beat, and the men in white sheets.

According to Karen Pyke (1996), upper-middle and upper-class men are able to gain social support (including the support of their wives) for their claims against domestic resources. A husband's success in market work—his success in male-male competition—provides imminence and command within the household. The power of successful men lies in their possession of capital, in its human and/or physical (financial) form. And under capitalism, the position of one person relative to another is defined largely by the position of each person in relation to capital. Hence, by serving more effectively the interests of capital, an individual wins in male-male competition.

Furthermore, fertility suffers a loss of social value by a process commonly called the demographic transition. This transition is characterized by a shift from fertility as a central form of wealth to capital. And it is manifested by a radical reduction in the level of actual reproduction below its unconstrained or "natural" level (which implies that its marginal valuation is zero) and a focus on increasing human and physical capital. Hence, if men are able to claim access to capital and deny similar claims by women, they can monopolize a strong and increasingly powerful form of wealth, leaving women with an asset that suddenly has no value.

On the other hand, there are men who are lacking in capital or become attached to capital at a more humble level of service. Axiomatically, these men are subordinate of more successful men, becoming subject to the dictates thereof. They lose face among men and lose the respect of their wives to the extent that they fail to protect the domestic unit from privation. They also lose position in the market for (extramarital) sexual access, in spite of the sexual braggadocio that is common in the subcultures of the lower classes in the United States. The data suggest that lower-class men are more sexually active and have a larger number of partners than those of higher classes, but only when they are young. By age forty, the consequences of subordination are fully revealed. While all men tend to decline in sexual activity with age, those who are successful decline more slowly, so that by age forty, they are sexually the more active group, and it is they who are likely to have the larger number of sexual partners (Kemper 1990).

The wives of unsuccessful men have reason to be unhappy because their own social position among women has been marked by the position of a loser. And often, they must engage in market work of an undistinguished kind in order to hold the household together. Indeed, it is often the wife whose income is more dependable. The data show that it is among these men that violence is most prevalent. Those without social imminence as a basis of power utilize violence as a tool for enforcing their demands. As with the Ge-Bororo, a position of structural weakness is obscured by the symbols of dominance.

A Contrary Argument

Marvin Harris (1993) has argued forcefully that male domination can be the product of male strength and military prowess as a weapon of use against wives. He provides details on the mutilation of wives, but he fails to consider the weakness of the men who perpetrate it:

> Extreme among extremists are the Sambia, a highland Papuan group whose males are obsessed with acquiring semen through fellatio practiced between junior and senior men. . . . Sambia men faced a multiplicity of physical dangers. A man could be ambushed, cut down in battle, or axed to death in his gardens; his own defense was lifelong training for physical strength, stamina, and phallic mastery. Women were his primary victims. (Harris 1993)

There is a problem with this argument. We see here that men are continually in the midst of warfare. Their enemies are not women; their enemies are the men of other groups. And, yet, we are expected to believe that their principal victims are their own wives. For this to be the case, Sambia men would have to be singularly unsuccessful in their conflicts with enemy groups. The Sambia environment is one in which some men are vulnerable to failure relative to other men and vulnerable to criticism from their wives as a result of such failure. It is unsuccessful Sambia men who can be expected to victimize their wives.

Harris goes on to discuss "external warfare" as exemplified by the Iroquois who would send as many as five hundred men to distant battles. He points out that this form of warfare does not lead to a challenge of the prerogatives of women who, among the Iroquois, managed the production and storage of crops and other matters. This is as our discussion would anticipate because these expeditions did not involve raiding for women and slaves. In other words, the case of long-distant warfare does not provide men with a source of wealth by which to overwhelm matriliny, nor was it associated with humiliation and the loss of power that would arise had they been unable to defend their communities from aggression. External warfare among the Iroquois would have had dramatic consequences for gender relations had its purpose been the capture of women, since those captives would compete with Iroquois women in the production of daughters, allowing men to have higher rates of (indirect) fertility than women.

Gender and Global Accumulation

Violence against women is never an entirely private matter, even when it takes place in the privacy of a domestic unit. The macrosocial system to which successful men owe their eminence manifests its interests in systems maintenance either by vigorous intrusion or by a carefully constructed blind eye. In the United States during the period from 1900 to 1960, a period of mature industrial capitalism, social policy encouraged the establishment of families that featured a woman at home and a male income provider. In this structure, the man was on the front line of capital accumulation, and it was deemed important that he maintain sufficient authority at home in order to maximize his economic effectiveness. Male authority was important, not because it made men feel good, but because it was arguably a positive factor in their economic productivity outside of the home.

Some would say that women were relegated to the private sector (e.g., Sanday 1981). However, the private sector was the vital backbone of the system to which considerable ideological sanctification was devoted. And, indeed, given the then current technology of parenting, the social reproduction of various categories of labor would not have been possible without the placement of mothering in that vital center.

The production and maintenance of male authority have been difficult to achieve among unsuccessful men, as Pyke's (1996) data suggest. Women whose needs are left unsatisfied are more likely to be "disobedient," and violence has been an unfortunate, yet socially necessary method of keeping them in line. Violence in poorer households was perceived to be socially necessary because it helped to ensure that wives attended to their husbands' needs, given that those men had important, albeit poorly paying, roles in the system of capitalist expansion. The police would attempt to keep their distance; the courts would find fault with the wife, and so forth.

However, the growth of the feminist movement has been coincident with the period during which the needs of capital have changed fundamentally in relation to the domestic unit. Capitalism has abandoned the wife-as-complement strategy as a necessary artifact of global accumulation. Global capitalism is not concerned with maintaining families; it is concerned with strengthening its control over each (increasingly isolated) individual agent, and, hence, the importance of *methodological individualism*. There are many manifestations of this new perspective: in the United States the general movement against "welfare" is more fundamentally an attack on mothering as a legitimate social role. The easing of divorce laws and the campaign against domestic abuse are forceful denials of male authority in a world in which his position is increasingly likely to be challenged (given the increased labor market attachment of women). These are changes in the rules of access to resources formulated in the service of wealth-accumulation.

While we certainly rejoice in this newly found enlightenment, it would be a mistake to associate this or any other manifestation of enlightenment with progress in human integrity. Violence against women would have continued to be acceptable if women had remained in a secondary relationship to capital and in a family role that was complementary to the efforts of men. Enlightenment is a function of social structure, and with women now being recruited to be primary producers, violence against them has become contrary to the general interest.

MARRIAGE AND LEGITIMACY

Verbőczy by Gyula Derkovits. Dózsa-Series X. (1928) Woodcut, 516 × 438 mm, Hungarian National Gallery, Budapest.

Those who have read much of the material in the preceding six chapters will understand that "marriage" is an institution that creates special "person-categories" into domestic groups. As in other such institutions, those person-categories are identifiable by reference to rights and responsibilities in an array of complementarity.

This chapter presents marriage as the construction of dominant groups that manage access of men to the sexuality of women. Marriage is defined as an institution that grants rights to men under conditions that men accommodate the demands of those dominants. In some cases the dominants are matrilineages, so that they include women; in other cases they are patrilineages, and in yet other cases they are states. Furthermore, the sex rights granted to men are identified as a minimal criterion by which the institution of marriage can be identified, where each manifestation of marriage must possess some common characteristic. In most instances, however, other rights may be allocated to men and to women.

The second part of the chapter breaks entirely new ground for social analysis, identifying "legitimacy" as being determined by eligibility for membership in relevant wealth-holding corporate groups. This characterization has not been evident to social theorists in the past since they have lacked a conception of "wealth-assets" by which to understand the issue.

Introduction

A cross-culturally valid conception of marriage must begin with a definition of husband-wife and with a distinction between spouses and lovers. From this perspective we find that marriage is an institution by which men are provided (socially supported) rights to women. Typically, this institution is embedded within a domestic group wherein a multiplicity of other rights and responsibilities are assigned. Hence, the definition of marriage attributable to E. R. Leach (1955) confounds domestic rights (which may exist in the absence of marriage) with marital rights.

"Marriage is a union between a man and a woman such that children born to the woman are recognized legitimate offspring of both parents" (quoted in Gough 1959: 49). This definition is consistent with vernacular usage in that a child is said to be illegitimate if its mother is not married. However, we are provided with no independent definition of legitimacy, and in the absence of such a definition, the statement that marriage is required to produce legitimate children is a tautology; as P. G. Rivière (1971: 62) indicates, "the argument is purely circular."

It is generally accepted that the illegitimacy of a child is indicated by some form of damage to its social position because of improprieties of its parentage, and an individual's social position is determined by rights to membership within relevant households, lineages, tribes, nation-states, and similar collectivities. The consequence of illegitimacy, then, must always be a loss of access to the resources that rightful membership in one or more of these collectivities would confer. Moreover, the illegitimacy of a child should be identifiable as a characteristic of the child itself, so that the social basis of that characteristic may be determined empirically. We might find that the improprieties that disturb an individual's social placement and produce illegitimate children within a given culture do not relate to the marital status of its mother. Some other aspect of the mother's (or father's) social position may be the source of the problem.

The data demonstrate conclusively that marriage is neither necessary nor sufficient to define the social position of children in many cultures. In the United States the children of never-married mothers are "illegitimate" in customary speech, but the citizenship rights of children, their rights to the support of their father (and to his legacy if he dies intestate), and other rights do not require marriage to the mother. Legal fatherhood, with its attendant rights and responsibilities, exists without modification in the absence of a relationship between the father and the mother. While it is clear that a child may suffer a disadvantage when the father is unknown or unreachable, the marriage of the father with the mother has no consequence for the formal social position of a child in American society, notwithstanding conventional terminology. It is vital, then, that the confusions and imprecisions of contemporary Western usage not be allowed to control and distort our understandings of a concept whose significance goes far beyond contemporary Western cultures.

Many societies provide a sharp differentiation between marriage and socially recognized parenthood. The Nuer, for example, distinguish legal fatherhood and marriage by the levirate and by ghost marriage (Evans-Pritchard 1990 [1951]). In these cases legal fatherhood and the social placement of children are determined by the person in whose name bridewealth has been paid, even if that person is no longer alive and the mother of the children is married to someone else. And there is the common

African solution to the absence of an heir, the filiation of the sons of an un-married daughter, and there are the legitimate offspring of the *epikleroi* of ancient Athens, who delayed marriage in order to produce a child for her heirless father with the seed of a patrilateral kinsman (Lacey 1968). There is hardly any culture area of the world that has not violated the *Notes and Queries* definition of marriage.

Many anthropologists consider it essential for the definition of mar-riage to impute a marital construct to all societies, in line with Ward Goodenough's (1970) declaration that the definition of marriage must ac-commodate a presupposition of its ethnographic universality. It is in def-erence to this objective that E. Kathleen Gough (1959) revises the *Notes and Queries* definition, suggesting that "marriage is a relationship estab-lished between a woman and one or more other persons, which provides that a child born to the woman under circumstances not prohibited by the rules of the relationship, is accorded full birth-status common to normal members of his society or social stratum."

Once again, the marital relation is defined by reference to the social position of children born to a woman—their "legitimacy"—but it is a def-inition that tells us nothing about the relationship that defines husband-wife. What kind of "relationship established *between a woman and one or more other persons*" constitutes marriage? Defining this relationship should be quite separate from identifying the functions that this relationship, once defined, may serve for other relationships, such as the relationship of a woman's children to the social structure. We simply cannot say that mar-riage is necessary to the legitimacy of children unless we can define mar-riage independently of legitimacy.

Marriage

Among the Nuer, a woman's children are legally assigned to the man for whom bridewealth has been paid (usually her first husband). Indeed, with "ghost marriage," the Nuer allow bridewealth to be paid in the name of a dead man, allowing one of his brothers (or sisters!) to produce children in his name.[1] In this way, a woman may never be married to the person who provides her children their social position. If the husband is a sister of the legal father, a low-status man is employed to act as genitor (a role that may be sought for an impotent male husband as well). In this event, genitor, father, and (female) husband turn out to be three different people. Of these three, it is the husband that is relevant to the definition of marriage.

The Nuer case is clarifying. We know the husband uniquely as the individual who can demand restitution in the event of unauthorized sexual access. The husband is the only person with the right to control the sexuality of a given woman, and this role need not be held by the person who defines the social position of the children born to that woman. Other men may have access to a woman by stealth or by permission, but only a husband has an institutionalized, socially supported *right* to control her sexuality.

Having introduced the term "right," we must spend a bit of time clarifying its meaning. Regardless of the form of society, the existence of a right implies a socially supported claim on scarce resources for some category of person—such as the claim of a child for essential consumption goods from its parents or the claim of a young man for bridewealth cattle. An individual, standing alone, can never have a right to a thing. Even when an individual is strong enough or fierce enough or both to gain possession of a desired benefit, individual effort alone does not define a right. *Rights are conferred by the actions of others on a category of person.* A right or "demand-right" exists only to the extent that there are other individuals who will cooperate in securing access to the thing or benefit in question.

In most contemporary societies rights tend to be primarily state originated and state supported. However, the appropriate cross-cultural generalization of the rights concept would include less bureaucratic mechanisms, including particularly the claims on resources that are ascribed to individuals by community-level associations and kin groups. Indeed, even in state societies, many rights remain to be enforced only informally, although the loosening of kin ties and the increased size and anonymity of residential groupings have reduced the significance of these informal mechanisms.

Rights are more readily claimed than effectively conferred. Even when there is social consensus on the validity of a claim, seemingly elementary rights can be violated. Rights are not absolute, and we must recognize *effectiveness* as an essential dimension of any claim. A claim is effective to the degree that any individual incumbent of the relevant category of person, chosen at random, will be able to realize it during some time period.

115

The efforts of males to make claims against the services of females have roots that are ancestral to the evolution of Homo sapiens. However, in the absence of rightful claims individuals commonly must attempt to realize claims by means of their own personal abilities. This reliance on personal abilities characterizes *lovers*. As a lover, a man or woman can retain sexual access to a desired partner only to the degree that he or she is able to remain more desirable than others who may seek access to that partner. The relationship between lovers is a form of friendship relation, because the continuation of a relationship depends on the attractiveness of an individual's attributes and resources relative to those offered to that partner by interested others. That is, it is a dyadic relation in which each individual earns resources from the other by giving resources more highly valued than those to be gained by similar efforts from alternative relationships. Instead of relying on some significant extent on pressures from others, each person must induce a supply of the resources of the other independently and noncoercively, and whenever a more appealing partner comes along the old one risks losing out.

Few contemporary human societies rely entirely on this competitive method for allocating female sexuality. Beyond a period of free adolescent experimentation, it is likely to be a most unsatisfactory arrangement. Given the importance of sex as a staple of human life, the independent efforts of men to secure access to women often lead to social disruption and social instability. One reads of the common incidence of homicide among the !Kung, the Inuit, and other groups in which competition for women is the singular cause. Therefore, it is not surprising that in almost all societies access to women becomes institutionalized in some way so as to moderate the intensity of this competition.

However, the solution that is embodied in marriage is by no means oriented primarily toward regulating sexual access and moderating the violence of competition. Certainly, if those who tend to be winners of such conflict were to develop an institutionalized process, the attributes of "winners" would remain unchanged. They would find a way of making the competition more systematic and less prone to fatalities without significantly affecting its outcome. That, however, is not generally true of marriage. In most cases, the criteria by which men are evaluated for acceptance into the category of "husband" are different from those that would be used independently by the woman whose services are sought. In the structurally simplest case, marriage involves the entry of a man into a woman's domestic unit. As a member of that unit, he must obtain the support of her kin in claiming access to the domestic resources that accrue to members of that group, and as a husband, he requires their support in the disposition of a woman's sexual services. Moreover, these individuals may assist him in barring the entrance of others who might seek access to the same woman.

A man's qualifications for joining a domestic unit may differ markedly from those that qualify a lover. It is to be expected that the characteristics of husbands will differ from those of desired lovers to the degree to which members of the group other than the woman of choice are important to the decision. Indeed, the woman of choice may be entirely excluded from the choice process, and in the most complex case both parties to the relationship become tangential to its arrangement, the matter being taken over by two or more groups of individuals whose interests are unrelated to the provision of sexual services.

What we find, then, is that the social support that a man obtains for his claim on a woman becomes contingent on demands from the groups that provide the support. In particular, socially powerful individuals other than the sexually linked pair exploit (youthful) sexual energies for their own purposes in constructing the rights and responsibilities that will apply to any cultural articulation of marriage. Quite possibly, a man may gain rights to a woman only if he is willing to become a member of her domestic unit and accept stipulated responsibilities therein. When these broader social groups are not heavily involved in placing demands on husbands, the level of support for his claims tends to be weak.

In fact, a lover may have greater security of effective sexual access than a husband in the event that the attractiveness of the lover is great relative to the social sanctions embedded in the institution of marriage. The lover is distinguished from the husband not by the strength of the claim of access but by the source of it. The source of the lover's claim is personal influence and attractiveness; for the husband it is a socially recognized and supported demand-right within an institution. When this social support is strong and compelling, even physically weak, elderly, and incompetent men can control access to the sexuality of women in the face of physically more fearsome, more powerful, and more attractive adversaries, thereby reversing the natural order that gave rise to the evident dimorphism between the sexes.

The Sharanahua (Siskind 1973) present an example of structurally weak marriage, in which the husband's claims may be openly challenged by lovers (he is expected to avoid jealousy). In this case the institutional advantage of the husband is small, forcing him into competition with lovers with little leverage. We find a stronger set of marital rights among the Comanche. E. Adamson Hoebel's (1967) discussion of rights enforcement among the Comanche depicts social mechanisms that combine the protocultural importance of fierce individualism with the systematic sanctions of the social group. The husband from whom a wife has been taken is presumed to be the weaker party, but he is allowed to augment his strength by involving his kin while the interloper must stand alone. In most cases this arrangement tilts the playing field in favor of the "rights-holder" so that restitution can be forced from the rights violator while preserving the presumption of the latter's greater strength.

In the Inuit case (Hoebel 1967), there is no presumption that brothers will stand together against wife stealing. Rather, the husband himself must stand alone to challenge his rival to a nonviolent song contest or to mortal combat with vengeance potentially devolving on his son (when the latter comes of age). An example of institutionally strong marriage is the Rwala Bedouin, among whom the husband, whose wife is believed to be his property, has the right to slay, with full deliberation and without fear of vengeance, the "thief" who has trespassed on that property (Musil 1978 [1928]). A husband's control becomes ostentatiously complete in those societies in which he is able to lend his wife to friends and "age-mates" while exacting severe economic sanctions in the event of unsolicited access (e.g., Maasai).

If women are to gain rights through marriage, they must do so by reference to the idiosyncratic cultural articulations of the institution. Wives may have rights of sexual satisfaction, but their sex rights rarely include a right of access control. In the Trobriand Islands (Weiner 1976), there are strong sanctions against adultery for both husband and wife. In some African (Evans-Pritchard 1990 [1951]) and Middle Eastern societies (Musil 1978 [1928]), women have well-defined sex rights. A wife may also gain the security of economic support for herself and her children (Giesen 1994). This view of the matter is supported by observation of those (hierarchical) societies in which women are prevented from or severely limited in engaging in independent economic activity. However, we know that in many horticultural societies women are important direct producers and may have a primary role in subsistence production (Burton and White 1984). In many matrilocal systems, the basic economic security of women is gained from the groups to which they belonged prior to marriage, in which case it is the husband who gains the security of economic support.

The possibility that women may gain nothing from marriage is a source of concern for Jane Collier (1988) in her discussion of the Comanche. For the Comanche woman, marriage meant a loss of sexual freedom and the onset of domestic obligations with no apparent benefits. However, in the event of matrilocality, the domestic group to which she belonged gained a productive member, and the band hoped to end the violence among her lovers and the disquiet between those lovers and their wives, because an unattached nubile woman became increasingly troublesome as she matured. It was to these social benefits that a woman was sacrificed.

Whenever a system of marriage is stronger, it should be inferred that the sexual control rights of husbands are more effectively held. However, effectiveness is not the only dimension by which to consider marital institutions. Marriage systems may differ in their degrees of institutionalization—the extent to which rights and responsibilities have accumulated within the institution. The increased institutionalization of the husband-wife relation implies a reduction in the arbitrariness of the husband's behavior toward his wife. The husband's freedom of action is limited as a precondition for social support of his claims. The Maasai have a strongly institutionalized marital system, and men have considerable authority over their wives. However, this authority is limited to well-defined rules of behavior.

Men who chronically overstep their prerogatives are subject to being beaten by an assembled mob of angry women. The rightful subordination of women is great but limited. Not only is marriage institutionalized, but also the importance of women in subsistence production tends to be high. This is a characteristic that seems to hold for a number of African societies, and one may argue that the importance of women as producers of goods and children is a factor in promoting a more complete institutionalization of marriage. A middle position applies to Bedouin wives. Here we find husbands with considerable arbitrary power, even though there is great support from kin for their sexual access rights. The critical factor in this case is the subordinate economic position of women in a culture oriented around the camel. Hence, it is possible for social support to apply only to a rather narrow spectrum of issues in the marital relation, allowing marriage to be "strong" and husbands to be arbitrary simultaneously.

Marriage defines for both men and women a place within the social structure; it implies that they are members of some group or groups from which they may gain access to certain resources and to which they may bear socially recognized responsibilities. Hence, to say that a man is married or that a child is legitimate is to say that the individual has a particular placement in social space. The dimensions of this social space consist of the rights to various resources that apply to that position and the responsibilities that must be fulfilled in order to validate one's continued placement. In any society that maintains a marital institution, the location of the marital tie within the space of social relations is defined by a particular configuration of rights. It is this configuration that constitutes marriage in that society.

However, in order for marriage to be *marriage*, it is both necessary and sufficient that it contain the rights-obligation linkage that defines husband-wife:

Definition of marriage: Marriage is a relationship between one or more men (male or female) to one or more women that provides those men with a right of sexual access within a domestic group and identifies women who bear sexual and other domestic obligations.

Within domestic groups there are rights that accrue to children, to members of older generations, and perhaps to genetically unrelated individuals, and, of course, rights that apply to wives (Leach 1955). Many of the rights that are conferred on particular categories of person within domestic groups exist independently of marriage.

In the most elementary form of marriage, a man attaches himself as a worker for the kin of the desired woman. The woman retains her rights as a member of her natal household and gains no additional rights. However, the man gains a right of access as the reward for his economic subordination. *Only he gains rights, but his status is likely to be distinctly inferior.* Even though marriage is identified by reference to asymmetrical criteria, the social status and powers of the husband may be less than those of his wife.

The Na, a small minority group in the south of China, illustrates this possibility. Cai Hua (2001) finds the full spectrum of relationships, ranging from an institutionalization of a lover relation to virilocal marriage. The modal and most esteemed form of relation between the sexes among the Na is the "furtive visit," an often spontaneous and always free and flexible arrangement of late-night sexual encounters. There is no pretense of marriage, as we find among the Nayar. The difference is that the man who visits is enjoined to avoid detection—climbing into her window unseen by others. Older persons who may have chosen to reduce the variety and frequency of visits might chose to abandon the "furtive" scene and become "conspicuous" visitors, an arrangement that promises no greater fidelity, but which allows the man to enter more conveniently through the front door.

From our point of view, and theirs, we are still fully in the domain of lovers. However, some men may choose to "cohabit." In this case a man offers his work time to the matrilineage of a woman in return for the right to live in the house with more direct sexual access, a practice that is consistent with our "elementary" form of marriage. Apparently, such a man is often, but not always, free to displace or discourage a furtive visitor who has arrived before him. To the extent that he achieves priority over lovers, the cohabitant assumes the appearance of a husband, by the preceding definition, although he shares his partner with lovers with fairly small advantage. It is a weak form of marriage in the house of the woman.

Then, there is *marriage* among the Na. By this, I mean a relationship that has the trappings of the surrounding culture (a simple ceremony involving both lineages) and the blessings of the state, so that it is called marriage by the Na and others. And indeed this relationship offers to a man a presumption of monopolized access as well as virilocality. The allure of the surrounding culture often induces a wife to continue furtive visits, but now the consequences are sometimes severe.

A principal reason for marriage among the Na is the filiation of her children to the husband's matrilineage. High infertility among the Na often places the continuation of a matrilineage at risk. Moreover, the Chinese state required the tribal administrator (*zhifu*) to be married and practice patrilineal succession into his position. However, as soon as the state abolished this traditional position in 1956, the family of the former *zhifu* immediately reverted to the visit modality. Hence, the Na provide a spectrum of relationships along the "sexual rights" dimension. "Cohabitants" have rights to take some of the children when the relationship is terminated, and married men may claim all of them. In this context marriage preserves best the social position of a man. Cai (2001) indicates that the conspicuous visitor, if he arrives early, may be expected to wait quietly and unnoticed in a dark corner until the family completes its evening. The status of the sex seeker is, I believe, well marked by this observation. The status of the furtive visitor is yet lower.

The commentaries on my paper in *Current Anthropology* seem invariably to presuppose that an asymmetrical conception of marriage implies husband dominance, in spite of the fact that I introduced the right of sexual access as being contingent on subordination to the demands of the wife's kin. Students of the Trobriand Islands commonly fail to recognize the inferiority of husbands. Branislaw Malinowski (1922) and Annette B. Weiner (1976) perceive a relationship of equality. I will neither affirm nor deny that characterization since, in the context of a gender-based division of labor, it is difficult to know what equality really means. On the other hand, there are indications that brothers have control over sisters, and wives have control over husbands. Sex rights of husbands are a basis of subordination. It is also true, in this case, that wives have exclusive rights to the sexuality of husbands. This symmetry is, I suspect, yet another manifestation of the subordinate status of husbands, relative to the circumstances that are common to patrilineal systems.

The (typical?) strategy of matrilineal organization is to offer rights to a woman only on the condition that a man accepts a role of the *matrilineage's* design within a system of complementary relations. In this Trobriand case, the man is an outsider (as Malinowski points out) to his own nuclear family. He is only the husband (read: sex partner) of his children's mother. This fact is made more significant by the observation that a husband does not provide the family's food supply (yams); this is the responsibility of his brother-in-law. And when a matrilineal kinsman of his wife (brother-in-law) dies, a husband must assemble "women's wealth" (bundles of banana leaves and piles of skirts) from among the women ("sisters") whom he supports with yams. These sisters of the husband will then march behind his wife in a public demonstration of the "work-power" of *the brother-in-law*! And if a man is not sufficiently successful in helping his wife assemble women's wealth, a brother-in-law will powerfully question the value of his sister's marriage and may threaten to discontinue the supply of yams.

The problem facing the brother-in-law is the public perception of his matrilineage as a source of work-power. For example, when a chief seeks a wife (or an additional wife) he takes into account the demonstrated strength of the men who will be providing him and his wife with yams (the brothers-in-law). Although having a sister become wife of a chief requires much hard work, it presents opportunities for upward mobility. The advancement of a group, in this very competitive environment, depends in part on the extent to which women can force out of their husbands the goods that will make their brothers look good. This is the price of sexual access. Clearly, husbands are subordinated; as we expect from the Exploitation Principle, they must work to advance the wealth-position of a group to which they do not belong. Brothers, however, must exercise control over sisters whose relationship with husbands may induce them to be soft in their demands. Hence, the power of brothers. This means that "gender relations" are ambiguous. The world is not always defined by gender, but often by the more specific roles of sibling and spouse.

The sexual-access right that identifies the marital tie may not be culturally defined as the most important aspect of marriage in a given society, but we are not concerned with the salience of given rights within the institution. It is not surprising that as the breadth of the institution expands, those who construct the ideological presentation of the institution will tend to focus greater attention and concern on supplementary rights and responsibilities. There is, however, a more difficult problem: The characteristics of marriage that are evolving in contemporary Western societies not only are broad but also involve weak support of sexual-access rights. Hence, contemporary Western marriage is a poor vantage point from which to consider the ethnographic universe of marriage.

We have seen that marriage is commonly exploited by dominants within the social system for purposes other than the provision of sexual access, and that a woman's kin may capture the work effort of a man in this context. However, in more complex tribal societies, marriage has been seized on as an occasion to seek advantages in rights to wealth. In particular, men *who are linked by inheritance to wealth* have used portions of their wealth as a means of capturing the reproductivity of women. Agnatic groups, by offering rights in cattle (and other forms of wealth), have been able to use their wealth as a powerful tool for gaining access to women. However, their use of cattle has not been for securing sexual services.

Marriage is often feasible without a transfer of wealth, perhaps through a matrilocal option to which men from poor groups are relegated by necessity. Moreover, since sexual access is a consumption good, it would be unwise for any wealth-holding group to expend its wealth routinely for this purpose. Rather, wealth is used to gain rights in female reproductivity[2]— it is an exchange of material wealth for the wealth that is inherent in female fertility.

When land is not a scarce resource, the power of a group tends to be a linear function of group size, and the fertility of women is the wealth resource with which a group may realize an advantage in demographic growth. By means of bridewealth, a wealth-holding group can secure a net transfer of fertility from groups that are relatively lacking in such wealth— taking more wives than they give to others (Bell and Song 1994). So there are two very separate operations, one providing a man with rights to control the sexuality of a woman within a domestic group (which is marriage), and the other involves transferring rights to the reproductivity of that woman to a wealth-holding agnatic group.

However, under contemporary conditions, we no longer have men who are linked by inheritance to wealth. In response to pressures from the church in its bold construction of a feudal system and to the subsequent irrepressible imperatives of capital, systems of inheritance were abandoned in Europe in favor of systems of bequests, so that each individual became an independent corporate entity with the freedom to transfer wealth to another corporate entity of his or her own choice. Consequently, a man who seeks the sexuality of a woman in the role of husband is additionally, by himself, a wealth-holding corporation, and his marriage initiates a merger with the wealth-holding corporation controlled by his wife. Indeed, marriage is identified in industrial societies largely by reference to wealth and property arrangements that define the allocation of resources from the marital estate in the event of divorce.

Rights in corporate wealth issues that are ancillary to marriage have become central to marriage, while the rights that define marriage have diminished in force. A woman's control over her husband's sexuality has always lacked effective social support, but now a man faces the same limitations in relation to his wife. In the United States women continue to experience greater stigma in the event of publicly exposed adultery and may face a disadvantage in the financial and custodial settlement of a divorce if burdened by the scarlet letter. Moreover, a man retains to some degree a plausible claim that the killing of his wife and her lover is a "crime of passion." However, divorce and homicide are both rather primitive mechanisms in relation to the rightful control of a wife's sexuality, and the continual weakening of those controls tends to level the playing field of husbands relative to the actual or potential lovers of their wives—threatening to reduce husbands to the status of lovers.

This weakening of marriage under capitalism is consistent with the weakening and abandonment of other aspects of the institutional legacy of the earlier ("feudal" or "tribal") social formations. The principal goal of institutional development in preindustrial societies had been the construction of *technologies of social relation*, and there has been a radical abandonment of those technologies in favor of the exigencies of the technologies of production. For this reason, we should not be surprised that marriage has become a casualty of capitalist development. Marriage, as defined herein, is an aspect of the traditional social technologies, all of which now appear to sit uncomfortably with the technologies of capitalist production. Under postindustrial capitalism, social relationships of individuals to each other—in marriage and otherwise—are subject to challenge, and they are being replaced systematically by property relations and relations of individuals to capital.

If marriage is reduced to an issue of property arrangements and subsistence support, then it becomes functionally indistinguishable from a cohabitation in which individuals are legally tied to common resources rather than to each other. Recent "palimony" cases have brought attention to this form of association, and many people have been concerned that the rights that are allocated with marriage are little different from those that are attached to these informal associations. This concern is appropriate, because as contemporary marriage rights converge toward those of other communal associations, the institution of marriage is increasingly at risk as a feature of social structure. Like the Nayar, we may be abandoning marriage—they for the sake of prestige via hypergamic ritual,[3] and we for the sake of accommodating the individuation of economic process demanded by the forces of capital. And, like the Nayar, we still have a need to legitimate sexual relations and family formation by reference to something called marriage, even as the substantive character of the relation becomes progressively deficient in ethnographic generality.

In thirty to forty years, we will have accumulated cross-cultural ethnographic data on the postindustrial present. We should have before us a considerable variety of social structures and should be able to construct a definition of marriage that applies to societies of a new and very different kind. In the most extreme manifestation, the system of (traditional) social relations would be entirely vanquished by the forces of capital, to be replaced by the atomistic automaton of neoclassical economic theory. Marriage in such a society might be defined as a relationship of individuals to corporate assets, not a relationship of one person to another. Certainly, there could be considerable cross-cultural variation in the set of property rights that define this institution, and we would be faced with the task of deriving the necessary and sufficient conditions for marriage to exist in this context. We would, then, have two definitions of marriage: the one posited herein for systems of interpersonal relations and another in relation to a system of property relations. However, it is much too early to consider this latter form. Indeed, we cannot be certain that marriage by any connotation will retain its salience.

Legitimacy

The archetype of the contemporary Western ideas of legitimacy is derived from ancient Athens. In 451 B.C., the governing body of Athens passed a law specifying that only the offspring of Athenians could be citizens of Athens. Simultaneously, marriage between Athenians and *xenoi* (noncitizens) became illegal (Lacey 1968), and the offspring of Athenians and *xenoi* became ineligible to inherit from their fathers. Consequently, persons of mixed blood were excluded from three kinds of wealth-holding corporate groups: that of the father, that of the father's clan (*phiateres*), and that of the Athenian state. These exclusions constituted the substantive meaning of illegitimacy; they are exclusions from membership in centrally important corporate groups to which their fathers belonged. It had not always been so, but for reasons not yet established by scholars, the leaders of Athens had developed a strongly aristocratic and "racialist" posture relative to noncitizens, many of whom lived in an unfree status as a servile caste.

The effect of those rules was to increase the size of the *xenoi* and restrict access to wealth to the smaller group. Marriage was fundamentally irrelevant to the fact of illegitimacy in Athens. It is only because marriage between Athenians and *xenoi* was illegal that legitimacy became related to marriage. Even if the parents had been allowed to marry, the offspring would have been illegitimate. Legitimacy required that the father be Athenian and that he be able and willing to go before his *phrateres* and claim that his was the child of an Athenian mother.

In contemporary Western societies, there is no direct analog of the Athenian case, but there is a close parallel with "racial" structures in the United States (and other places). In the United States the offspring of a white-nonwhite union is illegitimate. That is, such offspring is nonwhite and cannot inherit the rights associated with white skin. These special rights have been considerable, including until recently the right to vote in many states, to compete for occupational opportunities in a caste-structured labor force, to enjoy access to housing, and so forth. Much of this structure remains to this day. Thus, just as the offspring of Athenians and *xenoi* were *xenoi*, the offspring of Anglos and non-Anglos are non-Anglo. Anglo fathers are thereby prevented from fully claiming their own children for the corporate groups to which they belong.

A salient alternative to the Athenian or American rules is for children to belong to the "race" (*phiateres*, clan, tribe) of the father regardless of the origin of the mother. This is the rule that has traditionally governed filiation among Arabs and many other patrilineal cultures. The rule of the Arabs arises from an eagerness to capture the fertility not only of their own daughters but also of other women, including that of female slaves (of any ethnicity). Larger group size was advantageous to Bedouins in their efforts to claim privileged access to scarce desert resources. We see a parallel process in patrilineal African societies under conditions where the strength of a group tends to be linearly related to its size. A more inclusive case is offered by the Catholic Church, which insists that children be raised as Catholic if either the father or the mother is Catholic. And the most inclusive criterion of legitimacy is suggested by contemporary rules of citizenship, whereby a child may choose the citizenship of either parent or of the nation-state on whose soil she or he was born.

Jewish law contains a matrilineal rule that defines the tribal membership of offspring by reference only to the mother. However, in the ancient patriarchal setting this rule effectively required both parties to be Jewish, not unlike the Athenian rule for which this result was explicit. Caste-based requirements that *both* parents be members of a dominant group, as in the case of "races" in the United States, place greater stress on the monopolization of privilege for a small group than on the desirability of filiation and greater group size.

Since the purpose of legitimacy is to determine the eligibility of individuals to enjoy certain benefits and advantages, only a dominant or higher-ranking group can declare the illegitimacy of a child, since only the dominant group can effectively restrict that child's access to valued resources. Hence, it would have been absurd for the *xenoi* to declare the offspring of a *xenoi* and an Athenian to be *xenoi*. This would have been no cause for celebration, since the child was *xenoi* by default. Similarly, the offspring of a Brahman and a Nayar woman is illegitimate, while the offspring of this Nayar woman and a man of lower caste is also illegitimate. The suggestion that the Nayar can announce the legitimacy of the offspring of a Brahman and Nayar is absurd, at least when the genitor is known. Yet, Gough (1959: 72) attempts to have it both ways:

> There seems to me no reason why we should not regard these latter unions [of Brahmans with Nayar women] as concubinage from the point of view of the Brahmans and (since they fulfilled the conditions of Nayar marriage) marriage from the point of view of the Nayar. . . . But the Nayar wife and her children traditionally had no rights of patrilineal descent or inheritance whatsoever, might not enter the kitchen of the Brahman house and might not touch its inhabitants.

These limitations on the rights of Nayar children with Brahman fathers are among the objective factors that define their illegitimacy. The point of view of the Nayar is irrelevant. It is common to the character of illegitimacy that the lower group accepts the child. As mentioned earlier, the illegitimacy of the Athenian and the *xenoi* was not contradicted by its acceptance by the *xenoi*.

A similar problem of caste rank and legitimacy has been faced by the Devadasis (Marglin 1985). These Hindu temple dancers and prostitutes are available to Brahman temple servants (among others). They are not really supposed to have children. Rather, they are expected to adopt the children of their brothers or those of other people who can afford no better disposition for their daughters. If the Devadasis have children from their association with Brahman temple servants or others of high caste, they are (politely) to deny it, pretending that those children are adopted, whereas if they have children by certain lower-ranked individuals they are subject to a severe limitation of their duties. Since the offspring of Devadasis are not members of a recognized caste, those children would be illegitimate whenever the father is known to be Brahman.

By contrast, the Basavi are women who have been appointed to produce heirs for their fathers' lines (Dumont 1983). The ritual given to Nayar and Devadasis (the tying of the *tali*) is performed also for the Basavi, who are then free to produce children with lovers of the appropriate caste. These children are legitimate, given the purpose to which the Basavi woman has been appointed, even if the genitor is Brahman. This, however, is a special case where the genitor is acting as a surrogate for the woman's father in preserving a male line, somewhat parallel to ghost marriage among the Nuer.

Conclusion

The nature of marriage as an institution is of fundamental importance to the study of culture. However, in order to understand marriage at the level of generality required for ethnographic analysis, we must examine it as a construction in a social space whose dimensions are defined by an articulation of rights and responsibilities, and for the purposes of cross-cultural analysis, it is essential that we define the minimal set of rights-responsibilities that may constitute a marital tie. We may then inquire into the factors that influence the structure of this institution, its "strength," and its "breadth," and the factors that may explain its absence.

Even within a given society there may be various categories of husband and wife. For example, the position of concubine within the social technology of imperial China differed from that of the number-one wife. We know that she is a wife (for the purposes of cross-cultural analysis) even if she is not so labeled within that society. However, she is lacking in rightful claims relative to the number-one wife, suffering a disability that is homologous to that of an illegitimate child. In this case, the father's lineage has not made a material offering to the new domestic unit and, thereby, fails to establish an alliance with the lineage of the groom.

We recognize legitimacy as a rule by which membership in *wealth-holding* corporate groups is screened on the basis of a person's parentage.

We find it as a social feature of societies in which the wealth value of female fertility has been superseded by the value of wealth conferred on men—allowing men in general to take a dominant position relative to women and men with privileged corporate memberships to dominate other men. Both marriage and legitimacy are institutions that relate to the appropriation of scarce resources. The essential goal of marriage is to produce social order through a specific method of allocating conjugal services, while legitimacy is constructed in order to facilitate the monopolization of wealth.

Since marriage is an institution for the production of a certain form of social order, it is to be expected that it would become connected with legitimacy in the construction of order. The inclination to support structures of legitimacy with marriage appears to be particularly strong in societies dominated by lineages, clans, and similar kin associations. These kin structures have been marginalized or destroyed or both by the forces of industrial capital in Western cultures, and it is for that reason that the continued caste character of American society is no longer buttressed by formal rules against intermarriage. Elements of strategy were evident in Athens as well (Lacey 1968: 113):

> During the Peloponnesian Wars, after the Sicilian disaster in 413, we are told that the Athenians temporarily abandoned their rules about requiring a child's father and mother to be formally married because of the shortage of men, and citizens were allowed to marry one wife, and breed children (that is legitimate children) from another. . . . After the battle of Chaeroneia (338) foreigners also were enrolled, and those who had been deprived of citizenship were restored.

So, even at the center of our archetypical connection of marriage with legitimacy, we find a strategic break. Legitimacy is revealed as a political strategy of dominant groups, and in relation to legitimacy, marriage is sometimes useful and sometimes not.

CHAPTER EIGHT
RIGHTS: THE SHARED AND THE PRIVATE

Battering at the Gate by Gyula Derkovits. Dózsa-Series III. (1928) Woodcut, 441 × 494 mm, Hungarian National Gallery, Budapest.

This chapter takes a look into the peculiarities of Western economic theory. In particular we examine a theoretical discussion by which to justify a denial of customary rights as though they do not exist. The theory of private prerogatives considered here relates most directly to the early interests of the peasantry against the private property claims of the bourgeoisie.[1]

Introduction

There can hardly be any word more fraught with meaning than "property." The linguistic history of this term indicates that its current connotation developed rather recently, during the period of an ascendant mercantile and industrial capitalism. Its basic and original meaning had been in reference to a *characteristic* of a person, so that when first applied to land during the 1700s, it was understood that property in land was indicative of the social position of the individual who owned it. On this basis, it was quite natural for property to be ascribed later to productive capital and industrial establishments because those possessions became the more essential indicators of social position.

According to C. B. McPherson (1985: 81–82), the meaning of property narrowed over time to emphasize exclusive use rights to material things

> and then with the rise of the capitalist market economy, the bulk of actual property shifted from often nontransferable rights to a revenue from land, charters, monopolies, and offices, to transferable rights in freehold land, saleable leases, physical plant, and money. Property became predominantly a right to things.

Consequently, property rights came to be associated with the right to effect voluntarily the transfer of resources from one person (or group) to another: the right of alienation.

It is difficult in this day to recognize the revolutionary and culturally peculiar nature of the right of alienation in relation to land ("real property"). As P. E. Peters (1994) indicates so powerfully, the customary view of land was as a place to which persons and groups belonged; people were of a place. It was only with the gradual domination of commercial and capitalist interests during the eighteenth and nineteenth centuries that full supremacy could be gained for the notion that place was a thing that belonged to the person.

The "people of a place" had been those who by virtue of birth and social station shared with others rights to the use and revenue of some set of resources. Hence, "place" was more than geography; it included quintessentially the corporate group that had use rights to the resources therein. Hence, people and place were, each, both "people and place," neither being definable without the other.

The concept of the "place of a person" divests the place of its people to become a thing—a thing to be transferred among persons, together with its use rights and revenue rights: it becomes property. Clearly, the people of the place must be ousted as a precondition for this transformation; only then can land devolve from its use as a commons to become an alienable thing of its owner. During the feudal period, the granting of property rights in land (and serfs) would have been destabilizing since it would have enabled an ambitious noble to begin a process of land aggregation and consolidation that could eventually challenge royal power itself. However, the Church wanted alienation to be facilitated, at least in the form of a bequest, in order to accumulate the wealth of parishioners at the expense of heirs:

> The Church discouraged intestacy, protected alienations for its own benefit, enforced written contracts, supported creditors of the dead. To it, more probably than to any other agency, was due the decay of communal society. (Jeudwine 1975 [1918]: 160)

Property rights in estates emerged only slowly during the Middle Ages, experiencing accelerated development with the revolutionary change in laws associated with the Enclosure Acts. While it is true that there are alienable things in almost every society, those things do not deserve the term "property" unless social position is determined by reference to things. However, in traditional systems, things are not themselves the basis for the determination of social rank; rather, social position tends to be the basis for making claims against things. For example, in Imperial China a wealthy peasant could realize prestige from his skill, hard work, and intelligence, but he was still a peasant. Transforming that wealth into social position involved using it for the education of a son and that son's passing of competitive examinations. As for wealthy Chinese merchants, they were largely subject to condemnation *no matter how great their wealth in things*, unless their resources became the basis for entry into administrative positions.

Property is peculiar to specific social contexts (Peters 1994; Strathern 1988). In the more formally structured post-Neolithic societies, social position was not defined directly by "goods-accumulation." In these societies, things were not property. In order for a thing to become property, it must be possible for social position to be established by processes of goods-accumulation rather than by ascription. Hence, the casual use of that term in ethnographic investigations creates a severe risk of superimposing on other cultures the shadowy fragments of a contemporary Western *Weltanschauung*. Rather than gloss over a wide range of phenomena under the mantle of property and property rights, we should effectively deconstruct property into the essential elements that distinguish specific forms of rights in relation to resources.

Categories of Rights

One may delineate many categories of rights: rights of person, use rights, rights in property, rights in private property, rights in the commons, and rights in common property. The list seems endless; for example, L. De Allessi (1980) refers to job-access rights and job-termination rights, and there are the rights to make certain types of "deductions" on income tax forms and countless other rights that are the focus daily of development and amendment in state and federal legislatures. Some of these rights are alienable, some are inalienable, and some have greater consequence for some persons than for others. Out of this melange of rights, one may be able to discern a "structure of rights" that is defined in terms of the categories of rights and their incidence among categories of person within the social formation. In looking at possible structures of this kind, I will focus special attention on the significance of inalienable rights, to be called *rights of person*, in the context of a social system dominated by rights in private property.

There are hardly any rights that cannot be abrogated or violated by the force of superior authority. However, there is a meaning of inalienable that is verifiably a distinguishing characteristic of certain rights: some rights cannot be alienated voluntarily by means of sale. Most notable among these rights are those of citizenship—the rights to vote and to receive a passport and a number of unspectacular entitlements, such as eligibility to apply for Fulbright Scholarships. These rights are inalienably attached to the person because of some intrinsic characteristics of that person, and they can be called *rights of person*.

There are other rights for which alienation is fully expected and socially facilitated. They can be called *property rights*. We shall say that if some *characteristic* of a resource is subject to legitimate and legally protected voluntary alienation, then there is a property right in that characteristic. For example, a person may have the right to reside in a hotel with an annual lease; this is a *use right*. But if this person has the right to sell this lease, then there is a property right in the lease (characteristic) of the hotel (resource). Furthermore, when one alienates some characteristic of a resource, one sells the property rights that adhere to the characteristic. So, when the right to use a thing or to receive revenue from it is sold, the right to sell it is also sold. For this reason, we may say that property rights generate *rights in property*.

For example, a hotel is a resource with a multiplicity of characteristics, each of which may bear use and property rights, and each of which is subject to a decoupling from the set of other characteristics. Hence, its occupants may have alienable use rights to their apartments, and some business firm may have *alienable rights* to manage it, while someone else may hold *alienable rights* to receive revenue. Finally, the right to destroy or alter the hotel may be controlled by the state in terms of statutes concerning historical preservation. However, the contemporary implication of "owning the resource (or property)" is essentially that one holds alienable rights to the revenue generated by that resource and that the market value of this resource depends (perhaps in a complex manner) on its expected future stream of revenue. Selling the resource usually means selling the rights to this future stream, notwithstanding the existence of other parties who own other valuable characteristics of the resource and whose presence will generally negatively affect its market value. The property will be sold together with the various encumbrances imposed by others.

In many societies, it would appear that women have been transferred among groups in exchange for some form of wealth. There is hardly any part of the globe that has not seen this practice. However, it was seldom the case that all rights in those women were exchanged. Rather, rights in only a limited number of the characteristics in those women have been exchanged for wealth—those characteristics being related most prominently to fertility. Only rarely has the right of alienation been transferred to the wife takers; hence, it could be claimed that neither she nor any of her characteristics were property.

Some theorists (e.g., Gregory 1982; following Mauss 1990) claim that a defining feature of gifts in lineage-based ("tribal") societies is that the gifts are not alienated. Rather, gifts are offered as a means of creating social bonds between individuals and groups, and this function of gifts requires that they remain attached to the giver. Bartered goods, on the other hand, are seen to be fully alienated. However, in order for a gift to be inalienable, it must be the case that the receiver has no right to give it to another without the permission of the original giver. This form of inalienability is observed in the case of major marriage in Imperial China; a bride who came with a dowry was not transferred together with a right of alienation. Those rights had not been purchased by her husband (or her in-laws). She could be sold only with the permission of her parents (usually after the death of her husband). A concubine, on the other hand, had only a "minor marriage" (without ceremony and dowry), and she was said to be "sold" to her husband; no residual authority in relation to her was retained by her parents, allowing her to be subject to resale.

Harold Demsetz (1967) tells the story of how property rights developed among the Montagnais in the regions around Québec during the seventeenth and eighteenth centuries. This Native American group became involved in the fur trade and sought to protect the exploitation of fur resources in its immediate domain from others. It did so by securing privileged use rights for each agnatic group to specific blocks of land. In the absence of these rights, there might have been a tendency for some people to exploit aggressively those common resources for personal gain to the disadvantage of all: a "tragedy of the commons."

This is a rather commonplace situation. However, Demsetz is wrong to say that this is a story about rights in property. E. Leacock (1954) informs us that these groups could not alienate their holdings in land to other agnatic groups or to persons in other tribes:

> Nor is there any prestige attached to holding a sizable territory or any emphasis on building up and preserving the paternal inheritance. Nei-

ther can land be bought or sold. In other words, land has no value as "real estate" apart from its products. What is involved is more properly a form of usufruct than "true" ownership. (pp. 1–2)

The story of the Montagnais is one about the conversion of an *open-access resource* (to which no one holds any rights whatsoever) into a *commons* (to which only members of the agnatic group have rights of use). This basic confusion has been strongly attacked by Daniel Bromley (1989), Bonnie McCay and James Acheson (1987), and others. There is an unfortunate tendency to attribute to the commons the potential weaknesses of open access. This error is implicit in Demsetz' discussion of the Montagnais: he fails to recognize that the benefits of restricted use can be realized with the commons, having conflated the commons with open access, and he is forced to attribute these benefits to private property.

Private Property

The meaning of "private property" has been widely confused. "Private" is often thought to imply "personal" or individual ownership, perhaps because there must be some agency—some legal person—who has the capacity to own or to effect the alienation of resource characteristics. However, this entity can be a group of individuals of any enumeration: a business corporation or even a nation-state (consider the Louisiana Purchase).

Nevertheless, private property rights are rights of a particular form. As a technical term, private property rights are embodied in a specific rule for the allocation of rights to revenue from a production process involving human and nonhuman resources. In particular, this rule specifies that *all* of the revenue generated by a process of cooperative production belongs to the owner of capital (and/or natural resources). In the same way that enclosures removed the use rights of peasants, private property rules remove from workers the rights to shares of the product (as in the "putting out" system and other forms of piecework).

Lacking membership in the group that holds rights to revenue, the owners of human resources receive *wages* in exchange for the alienation of "work-effort." While it is conventional to claim that the wages constitute a share of the product, that is not the case. Even if the market value of the product suddenly falls to zero, the earned reward to labor remains unchanged. Given private property, the market value of the product becomes independent of the exchange value of productive effort. Hence, private property (as a subset of property) is characterized by the right to receive the *total returns* from cooperative production, together with the right of productive agents to receive market-clearing side payments.

By contrast, De Allessi (1980) says that private property means that

> the owner has the exclusive authority to choose how the resource he owns will be used, as long as the selection does not affect the physical attributes of goods owned by others. Moreover, he has the exclusive right to receive the income generated by the use of his resources and to exchange his property rights with those of other individuals at mutually agreeable prices. (p. 4)

In this definition, De Allessi clearly indicates alienability as a characteristic of property and the exclusive right to revenue as the characteristic *of private* property. But he adds to this definition the *unconstrained* right to manage this resource. This additional right is complementary to the right to receive revenue and much beloved by the holders of property rights. However, it is not a necessary attribute of private property; more importantly, it very rarely occurs. One of the salient issues of public policy is determining the socially appropriate limitations to be applied to the right to manage privately held resources. But more critically, by omitting any reference to workers in his definition of property, De Allessi obfuscates the distributional implications inherent in the structure of private property.

We cannot really understand the meaning of private property unless it is positioned in relation to a set of alternatives. The system of private property, as a method for determining the distribution of benefits among factors of production, is unique and revolutionary relative to traditional systems. In the latter systems, rights to resources are most commonly defined by shares of the total product, as in sharecropping (sharing the output) or demands for shares of work-effort (as in some forms of the feudal system). Or benefits may be allocated on a communal or household principle within families, lineages, tribes, and tribal states. In these systems, work-effort is rarely drawn from a market based on an exchange principle; hence, work-effort has no socially defined exchange value.

In the absence of that exchange value, there is no way to define the social cost of production in real terms. Instead, the validity of any allocation of work or reward is determined not in terms of the logic associated with rights in property but by reference to an ideological construct that defines the responsibilities of various categories of person to the corporate group (Bell 1987–1988). The development of systems of private property involves the general suppression of such preexisting systems in favor of a system in which direct producers receive side payments rather than shares, and work-effort becomes the property basis of consumption, consumption being no longer a right of person.

Many economists blanch at the suggestion that capitalism is a system of distribution that ousts workers from ownership of their product. Apparently, only a Marxist, or someone of similarly malevolent temperament, would refer to this fact—inducing a denunciation of capitalism for its "alienation" of workers from their product and announcing socialist revolution as the ineluctable solution. It is for this reason that discussions of rights of person tend to be suppressed. However, we should not allow these political concerns to interfere with our understanding and analysis of social systems.

Rights of Person

Many rights cannot be alienated by the person who holds them; they can be transmitted only to heirs. Furthermore, these heirs qualify for ownership by virtue of age, sex, and parentage; that is, by birth not by achievement. In the context of contemporary capitalism, we find that a person's right to vote, to be free from slavery, or to have freedom of speech, cannot be sold. Nor can one sell the responsibility-cum-liability to serve in the military. These are rights and liabilities that reside with the person by some principle of *entitlement* rather than in the resources to which a person is entitled. They are *rights of person*.

However, contemporary ideology is quite uncomfortable with *categories of person* as factors in the structuring of a social system. The good (bourgeois) society is thought to be constructed, at least metaphorically, through a social contract among socially equivalent individuals. People may differ in their "wealth-accumulations," but not in their right to accumulate; they may differ in their innate capacities, but they do not differ in

139

the right to express and develop fully those capacities. We have here the idea of society as a collection of individuals who lack intrinsic differentiation. Categories of person, on the other hand, recall the too slowly weakening legacy of a feudal past, where a person's ultimate social placement and achievements were largely a function of sex and parentage.

It was against such feudal ideologies that the bourgeoisie required a philosophical alternative on the dawn of its ascendancy. The alternative adopted—rights in property—was revolutionary in form and consequence. However, the displacement of rights of person by rights in property has always been quite selective. Most prominently, citizenship has been preserved as the basis of "person-categories," with rights being sharply curtailed for the noncitizen. Age, too, remains an unchallenged basis for formal differentiation, so that legal differentiations apply to those under the ages of 18 or 21 and to those over the ages of 55, 62, or 65. Gender and racial classifications also have been traditional bases of person-category, but often under conditions of questionable legitimacy. The purposes for which rights of person are derived and ideologically justified vary widely. The social history of a group, its current and past forms of social organization and technology, and its class structure and power relations all conspire to give specific form to its system of rights.

Although Demsetz (1967) does not argue explicitly against all rights of person, his use of the exchange paradigm in attacking selected rights and responsibilities could be applied quite broadly. Demsetz (1967) argues for the displacement of rights of person by rights in property—for example, suggesting that military service should be induced by means of higher wages instead of the draft. And if the draft must continue, he favors allowing those who are subject to it to offer a cash payment for exemption. That is, he opposes this basic responsibility of citizenship unless it can be converted into a property that is subject to purchase by the state.

One way of accommodating the concern of Demsetz would be to confer full rights of alienation on draft status, allowing it to be sold to the highest bidder in an *international* market for military personnel. The person who seeks military exemption must be replaced. If a military obligation were converted into a lien-encumbered property, its replacement could become the responsibility of the original owner.

The fundamental premise of the argument in favor of granting rights in a military obligation is that we can maximize the aggregate social product by permitting the execution of mutually beneficial exchanges. Since the sellers and purchasers of a right or obligation are all better off, the society must be better off—given a conception of society as a simple collection of such individuals. Demsetz is concerned about the lack of property rights in other situations: He insists that "freedom" should be property, so that its optimal allocation among persons can be achieved:

> A law which gives the firm or the taxpayer clear title to slave labor would necessitate that the slave owners take into account the sums that slaves are willing to pay for their freedom. . . . It is the prohibition of a property right adjustment, the prohibition of the establishment of an ownership title that can thenceforth be exchanged, that precludes the internalization of external costs and benefits. (p. 349)

While this argument may represent a fine example of hardheaded economic reasoning, it reflects an unawareness of rights that rest on principles other than the logic of property. The price-theoretic form of that logic assures us that no right can be optimally allocated among persons unless it is placed on the open market. For example, by converting the right to vote into property, the state would allow those rights to accumulate in the hands of those for whom they can be more instrumental and allow the previous owners of those rights to receive preferred alternatives—making both parties better off. Even the right to free speech may find a limited market. Presumably, the purchaser, while enjoying no greater freedom, would benefit from the silencing of specific others (as in legal proceedings).

However, we understand from history that the nature of a society—the structure of social classes, the central dynamic forces shaping the growth in population, technology, and wealth—depends on how rights are allocated among groups and individuals. For example, we prefer that the economically powerful not be able to purchase votes. The general social consequences are thought to overwhelm the benefits of isolated dyadic exchanges in property rights. Similarly, the decision to abolish slavery did not rest on some arcane observation on the benefits of mutual and voluntary exchange processes. It was a choice between two fundamentally incompatible ruling elites, such that the social infrastructure and public policies of one group could not coexist with those of the other. It was a choice between rural slavery and its associated mercantile underpinnings versus an urban industrial capitalism based on free labor. These are metasocietal matters that cannot be addressed by the algebra of indifference curves.

The Right of Prior Possession

There has, perhaps, never been any right more fundamental to the development of social relations and social systems than the *right of prior possession*. However, few of us are aware of it. It is not part of the set of rights enshrined in the Constitution or in the noble speech of the politicians of recent times. Yet no right can be more fundamental. It is because of this traditional right that a person can claim indefinite use to land that he or she clears for cultivation, so long as he or she continues to make effective use of it. It is the basis of the transmissible use rights of serfs and peasants to their share of the arable in the absence of formal or state codification. The right of prior possession has been essential to the social order.

The right of prior possession suggests that the initial occupant of a resource should be allowed to use it without undue compromise from the actions of others. The continued operation of the right of prior possession can be seen daily in the form of "Do Not Trespass" signs along roadways. Without the presence of such signs, a person could covertly make "conventional use" of the unoccupied resource, either as a walking path or as a place of permanent residence. It then becomes feasible that these conventional uses take precedence, by right of prior possession, over alternative uses subsequently sought by the owner of property rights.

If a residential community exists prior to the planned construction of a polluting factory, the liability for that pollution (in health losses or housing values) must be incident entirely on the factory. By the right of prior possession, the community should not be faulted for having located itself in the lovely valley that subsequently and unpredictably became the potential site of a belching factory. Yet the analytical edifice constructed by Ronald Coase (1960) rests critically on a casual denial of the right of prior possession. He refers to this right as the *doctrine of lost grant*.

This doctrine states that "if a legal right is proved to have existed and been exercised for a number of years the law ought to presume that it had a legal origin" (Coase 1960: 14). In reference to this doctrine, Coase says that "the reasoning employed by the courts in determining legal rights will often seem strange to an economist," for whom, he believes, maximal economic production is the only relevant criterion (p. 15). The inscrutability of judges on these matters arises from that fact that the doctrine of lost grant is a right that cannot readily be converted into a property right, since it adheres necessarily to *the person* whose situation was prior. (A person who purchases a house from an original owner, after the construction of the factory, has no claim for damages.)

Coase presents the case of a physician who builds an examination room whose walls adjoin that of the neighborhood baker, only to find that the noise of the baker's machines is disturbing to his business. The physician then files suit against the baker. The court decided in favor of the physician! Coase supports this judgment on the grounds that the baker and the physician are *equally at fault*, arguing that the noise of the baker's machinery caused no nuisance until the building of the room by the physician. He is indifferent to the distinction between two circumstances: 1) the baker has the option of paying for the right to continue operations, or 2) the physician has the option of paying for him to stop, because they differ only in the consequences for the distribution of income, not the level of total production.

But the right of prior possession is not designed to determine the optimal distribution of income. It is related, instead, to the maintenance of orderly social processes, much the same way that the rules of rights of way are useful in various modes of transportation. A person who possesses rights of way, or who holds rights of prior possession, may be willing to compromise those rights when provided adequate compensation. A person hurrying to the hospital could (in the absence of transaction costs) purchase rights of way from their "natural owners" (say, those with green lights). But when a violation of rights of way leads to an accident, the two parties are not equally at fault, even though both cars are necessary to the accident.

Hence, a more balanced solution to the baker–physician problem would be to allow the alienation of rights of prior possession, when appropriate. In this case, the physician could pay the baker for any compromise of his rights of prior possession. This option is technically superior to that chosen by Coase, who favors the judicial destruction of a valuable asset, the asset inherent in the right of prior possession, and the creation of stronger rights in property to the advantage of the gentry. This does not constitute a Pareto-optimal change—that is, we have no basis for claiming that society is better off. Furthermore, one cannot argue effectively for measures that increase output (the efficiency criterion) if those measures involve the massive destruction of valuable assets.

The abrogation of the baker's rights of prior possession in favor of the property interests of the politically dominant gentry, in the case discussed by Coase, was part of a more general process by which the traditional rights of the peasantry gave way to the demands of mercantile and industrial interests. Coase is certainly free to support the special interests of the gentry; however, he is not plausibly indifferent to the distribution of income when he denies the baker's right of prior possession in favor of rights in property.

Property Rights, Efficiency, and Distribution

One of the most exciting aspects of anthropological information is the great variety of forms that resources and rights may take and have taken among the cultures of the world. Social systems are structured by the set of rights of person and rights in property that are enforced and by the attributes of available resources. These systems of rights orient direct demands for shares in social resources and have implications for the probable distribution of those resources. For example, the system of private property grants revenue rights to individuals and implicitly removes revenue rights from other persons. However, in the management of the social system, wage earners may be given "rights to organize" into bargaining units, and those units may be allowed certain prerogatives in asserting their claims.

The activities of these bargaining units may negatively affect the opportunities of wage earners who lack bargaining power, as well as affecting the net revenue of employers. Hence, the right to organize generates a particular division of the *social product* among owners of private property, unionized wage workers, and nonunionized wage workers. On the other hand, there are capitalist states, such as Taiwan and South Korea, whose political structures facilitate the denial of workers' demands for organized representation, minimum wages, and other benefits, with the consequence that a larger share of the social product may accrue to the owners of capital.

Some social systems enjoy the reinforcement offered by ideologies that assert the natural character of their system of rights and responsibilities. A natural character is claimed in order to deflect discontent from those who would be outraged by the obvious fact of human intervention. In traditional systems, the natural differences among people, by sex, age, and parentage are most common as bases of "natural differences" in rights to resources. Although this form of rationalization has long been under attack by the ideologists of capitalism, capitalism has its own form of the natural; it is expressed by the *ideology of economic efficiency*.

Economic efficiency is achieved when it is not possible to produce a particular combination of goods at a lower cost of "inputs." Since inputs include the providers of labor, the fact that their rewards are minimized has no obvious objective merit. However, it is easily shown that a reduction in the unit cost of inputs will commonly lead to a higher level of production, provided that the level of demand for the product is not adversely affected by the reduced cost of inputs. Hence, if we use as an "objective" criterion of social benefit, the value of total output, it would appear that a society organized for efficient production is preferred, provided that we are indifferent to the distribution of income. This is precisely the Coasian principle of optimality.

However, the doctrine of economic efficiency cannot possibly be indifferent to the distribution of income, since efficiency is an ideology for the rationalization of a particular form of distribution. This fact is more readily seen when we place private property against its historical predecessor, the feudal regime of common nonproperty resources. Many societies have made the transition from systems of nonproperty resource management to systems of private property. In every case that I have examined, this transition has been predicated on an increase in the size of the rural population that placed unacceptable pressure on the system of corporate shares. That is, as the population of serfs grows, they become redundant at the margin.

At the same time, their increasing population induces pressure for a larger share of the common resources, at the expense of the elite. In this way, population pressure becomes inconsistent with the maintenance of traditional corporate shares and prompts a search within the elite for an alternative social formation. In England, this situation was reached by the seventeenth century; it was reached in Russia by the beginning of the nineteenth century, in the Philippines by the early part of the twentieth century, and so forth. In each case, the broader social, technological, and political contexts were particular to time and place, but in each case it is clear that the norms of corporate shares became unsustainable on account of demographic forces.

In contrast to traditional criteria of allocation, the doctrine of efficiency thrives on a redundancy of hands, and the immediate consequence of abandoning traditional forms has been to reduce the share of the social product allocated to the direct producer. There is found in the system of private property a means of increasing economic efficiency—increasing the share of the social product to the upper classes—by means of a rule that grants all rights to revenue to the owners of land and abolishing the traditional use rights (rights to revenue) of the common people. Private property in land in the face of an excessive rural population provides the conditions for the subjugation of the peasantry and working classes to the standards of economic efficiency.

Daniel Bromley (1989) expresses concern over the way in which the set of rights embodied in the status quo influences judgments regarding the economic efficiency of a planned institutional transaction. His example is of safety for mineworkers who, in the absence of any socially defined rights to safety on the job, may demand additional compensation for working in unsafe conditions as a condition of employment. Alternatively, the workers could be offered an annuity that covers the full cost of accidents and internalizes the cost of unsafe conditions to the firm. The equilibrium amount of safety under these two regimes is likely to differ. How much you will pay for safety is different from how much you demand in compensation for giving it up. So argues Bromley, there is a significant wealth (or income) effect that differentiates the desirability of these two regimes from the perspective of the worker. Hence, characteristics of the status quo make a difference in the final outcomes, in contrast to the implications of the standard Coasian analysis.

A discussion by Bromley (1989) explicitly presupposes that workers have the option of actually taking a safe versus an unsafe job, so that they can demonstrate an aversion to a lack of safety by rejecting unsafe jobs that lack adequate wage differentials. However, if there is a "redundancy of hands" in the relevant labor market, due to chance or to governmental policies that facilitate labor mobility to the job site, the optimal price of safety will be zero in either case. Some workers will avoid mining on this account, but many others will find no alternative. Indeed, if the latter suffer an occupational disability because of ethnicity or geographic location, the wages paid in unsafe mining jobs may be below those of comparable safe jobs.

For Bromley (1989: 115): "The issue is one of how to define efficiency, and which point—the status quo or some alternative institutional arrangement—will provide the basis for the efficiency calculation. Who will speak for the miners?" However, there is no contest here. If the annuity increases production costs to any extent, it will almost certainly be output-reducing in equilibrium and, hence, be inferior to the status quo ante by efficiency criteria, even if it constitutes only a minor nuisance to the employer and a great benefit to the workers. Efficiency does not depend on the relative gains of mine owners and miners. It is at least formally, the gain of an abstract consumer that matters—a consumer who is neither a miner nor a mine owner.

The annuity for safety proposed by Bromley (1989) implies that rights to safety are alienable—they have property rights. Were he to consider the right to safety as a right of person, a conflict with the efficiency criterion would be immediate. As we have seen in our discussion of Demsetz, the logic of indifference curves contests such claims. But we know that if the right to safety were established by the Congress of the United States, it would be inalienable. Congress would certainly combine a mandated annuity scheme with regulations of safety standards. Congress will choose this solution because the set of workers is not unitary in character. Any subset of workers who lacks a concern for safety or that is desperately in search of employment can frustrate the "entitlement" of others.

The same argument can be made about the entitlement to be free from enslavement: Unless those who are *least advantaged* by this right hold it as a right of person, society as an institution will suffer the consequences. The law against slavery (or lack of safety) is likely to disadvantage the hapless and desperate individual who has only his freedom (or life) to offer. It is for the sake of others that he is restrained.

Conclusion

The arguments of economic theory suggest that the consumer is sovereign in a perfectly competitive, efficient, productive system. It is in relation to

147

this theory that rights in property have their fullest rationalization. Rights of person, on the other hand, depend on political determinations of appropriateness in relation to defined person-categories. The contemporary rationalization of these determinations is associated with theories about the sovereignty of independent citizens within a republican form of representative government. These theories share with the neoclassical model a conception of people as independent, perhaps atomized, and self-interested—people whose elected representatives are expected to realize the social optimum through public choice.

Even if these two forms of sovereignty operated perfectly in accordance with the norms relevant to each, the development of a properly articulated combination of rights of person and rights in property would be difficult to achieve. However, under the rubric of public choice, many economists have launched a wide-ranging attack on government as decision maker, demonstrating the inefficiency of government and the potential increases in efficiency achievable from unfettered market operation. It is a pity that so many good minds have been committed to this task. It would be senseless to judge a new consumer product on the basis of a congressional vote, and it is equally senseless to evaluate rights of person based on efficiency criteria. Bromley's attempt to mold an efficiency argument in support of occupational safety could only lead to error. As I have shown, the logic of efficiency is properly imposed on only a very narrow domain. Outside of that domain, it becomes an elephant among the petunias, crushing all within its path. Not even a (nonalienable) right to vote is defendable on efficiency grounds, nor is the obligation to forswear one's own personal enslavement.

Amitai Etzioni (1988) has suggested the desirability of expanding the neoclassical code to include moral dimensions. The moral imperatives that he posits are precisely those that support and rationalize rights of person. However, rights of person cannot be advanced by adding new arguments to utility functions. The necessary "new economics" cannot be a thematic variation on the old. The task of socioeconomics is to determine the attributes that characterize the socially optimal configuration of rights of person and rights in property, given that the ideologies that support the former are disjoint from the ideologies that support the latter.

CHAPTER NINE
CHARITY

Priest Lõrincz *by Gyula Derkovits. Dózsa-Series XI. (1928) Woodcut, 439 × 512 mm,
Hungarian National Gallery, Budapest.*

I suspect that any society that has something called charity must have a mythology about it, and there will be almost no one who does not subscribe to that ideology. Hence, the discussion here will disturb and confound some of you. But there is a simple test that may contribute to your acceptance of the arguments presented here. Imagine that everyone who is now the recipient of charity in your society has been lovingly accepted and protected by matrilineal or patrilineal kin. In this case the beggar would receive nothing because we all know that he need only return home to be housed and fed. He could not plausibly be *deserving* of charity.

Having imagined a society without charity, let us try to understand how and why our own society is not structured in this way. Clearly, it is a matter of social structure, not simply at the lineage level, but also at the macrolevel. Charity thereby becomes an aspect of customary practice that is exercised at a community or national level.

Beggars

It is often noted that many families in the United States are only a few weeks from "homelessness." The loss of a job, a serious illness, or some other event of readily conceivable occurrence could reduce a family to total desperation, making its members subject to moral inconstancy and lower life expectancy. Many other families are only marginally better off, while many others enjoy a reservoir of resources from which to escape the effects of unexpected events. Hence, American families could be ranked in relation to the probability of reduced viability. We could also rank American families relative to families in other societies in terms of a similar index. Such indexes are measures of power—the most elementary form of power—the power to survive.

When kin groups prove to be unable to support the needs of their members, traditionally the case has been that informal community-level corporate groups emerge to sustain individuals. These forms of supplementation are commonly called charity. Unlike income redistribution through a system of governmental taxation, charity is an individually volitional transfer of essentials from one set of strangers to another. Many of those who are capable of providing assistance refuse to do so, having failed to internalize an ethic of responsibility or having decided that a particular individual is not eligible to receive a rightful claim. However, the subset of potential donors who actually transfer shares to beggars do so on the basis of the presumed deservedness of the beneficiary. Hence, they are doing that which they "ought to do."

The man who seeks handouts from strangers is presumed to lack an effective domestic group. Presumably, the household from which he is normatively to receive life's essentials does not exist or has failed him rather miserably. And if he is ineligible for a substantial distribution from a government agency, he may seek his basic essentials from among individuals to whom his well-being is of relatively little consequence and within which his rights are only tenuously held. For this reason, begging is not such a fine way of maintaining one's life. Even though there may be a large population in the broader community to which the beggar may appeal, he or she tends to live less well than do those who depend successfully on the support of a few within a domestic group. Indeed, if one could live a better life by begging than by returning to a domestic group, a larger number of individuals would desert the domestic hearth in favor of the streets. And eventually the number of individuals seeking alms would overwhelm the supply of donors who are willing to recognize their claim, thereby ensuring the relatively greater efficacy of domestic groups.

The beggar, like the recipient of governmental assistance, is able to gain resources from other categories of person through validating procedures that attest to his deservedness. I noticed a particularly powerful practice on the streets of Beijing. While on their knees, people would rapidly raise their heads up and down only inches from the ground in supplication. These and other indications of deservedness imply eligibility for membership into an amorphous collectivity of "have-nots" whose claims on resources define them as a category of person within the community. As a category of person, they deserve a share. However, it is the very rare beggar whose appeals are recognized universally. There will always be those who question his deservedness: Does he really have only one leg? What does he plan to do with the money, buy wine? Why does he not get a job? These questions challenge the eligibility of the particular mendicant for a handout from the particular nonmendicant. Almost every individual who is blessed with a reasonable adequacy of resources is willing to transfer resources to a qualifying other; people differ widely, however, in the stringency of those qualifications.

Beggars must be recognized as a category of person in order to receive resources, and in some cases their category is formally established. For example, there have been groups of Friars in Europe whose way of life required begging and poverty as an oath to God, and there have been beggars quite prominently in India among Brahman priests. These are cases where criteria of eligibility are institutionalized. However, beggars are seldom in control of an ideology by which their claims are legitimated. And lacking a central position within the ideology of distribution, their claims are likely to be rejected altogether by many individuals, and most of those who support those claims will make only the most modest of contributions. Yet to the degree that beggars are able to survive as beggars, we can say that they are the beneficiaries of socially supported claims against the resources of the community. A share of community resources rightfully belongs to them.

It is likely that people who offer resources to beggars have the belief that they are acting as individuals in a relationship with a particular individual in need. However, there is in fact no such relationship. The beggar and the donor are strangers, having no rights or responsibilities to each other *as individuals*. Only as a presumed member of a category of deserving Others is the beggar recognized. The actual relation is between two categories of person within a community, such that some of the money in the pockets of the "haves" is rightfully to be received by the "have-nots."

One of my undergraduate students at UCI, Marilyn Calderon, who by now must be a medical student, introduced to me the thoughts of St. Thomas Aquinas on the nature of charity (Gilby 1960). St. Thomas addressed issues previously raised by Aristotle's Nicomachean Ethics (McKeon 1980). Whereas Aristotle had argued that a good man would love the good in another, given that he loves the good in himself, St. Thomas asserted that man should love the God in others and that charity toward others was a means of showing love toward God. Furthermore, since love of God provides credit toward the afterlife, there is also a personal reward to charity. This conception of charity is powerful in promoting its provision.

My interest in charity was prompted by the sudden appearance in Southern California of men standing at the roadsides with crudely written signs announcing: "Will work for food." I was often inclined to engage in an ethnographic inquiry into the histories and motivations of these men. After all, they looked healthy and unemployment was low. Why were they there? Although these men with signs posed a puzzle for me, they seemed to offer no puzzlement to the typical passersby. The immediate response of some individuals is to stop, place a dollar bill into the hand of this "worker," and drive away. Since there has been no request for alms, this typical response is anomalous. He had announced an intention to earn his daily bread, and he is explicitly denying eligibility for membership in the category of beggar. This raises two questions: 1) Why doesn't someone ever take him up on his offer to work for food? And 2) Why does he pretend to be a nonbeggar?

Let us understand that working for food, while almost unknown in wage economies, is a common feature within traditional paternalistic systems, like the "jajmani system," a caste-structured, feudalistic organization of production that was once common in the countryside of India. However, it was only the lowest category of worker that was remunerated in this way. For example, latrine cleaners were often paid with a few chapatis (flat breads). The implication of this form of payment is that the recipients can expect no more than survival as their appropriate shares of corporate resources. Its functional equivalent in the United States would be "welfare" payments in the form of vouchers for food and lodging. However, while a payment in chapatis may constitute a very meager reward, it is different from charity (or welfare). At least the latrine cleaner had a service of value to offer in return. Furthermore, this service was obviously a very important one. One gives little to the latrine cleaner because the work is so defiling and because he (and his assisting wife) is of such low caste that he deserves little as a category of person. A payment in the form of chapatis is not a wage, set by the supply and demand for latrine cleaners; rather, it is a corporate share that is appropriate to the deservedness of the recipient.[1]

When one contemplates hiring the man on the street and "paying" him in food, there is an implication that most of us would find alarming: Were he to work and receive the food from our table, he would become (for a limited time) a "person-category" within the household. Although his membership would be transitory, his work represents his "ability" and constitutes eligibility for a corporate share that satisfies his "need."[2] Paying a wage does not have this implication at all. Wages are determined by the market valuation of a service, not by the needs of the recipient. So even though food costs money, the direct provision of food instead of money places the process into the domain of "complementarity," or sharing, rather than reciprocity.[3]

Returning to the man on the roadside: Were we to take him home to cut the grass and provide him with a take-out pizza, we would be inducting this man into our own domestic group for a period of time and awarding him with a share that is appropriate to his miserable status. Such an action is fundamentally different from simply dropping currency into his hands. In either case it is our intention to facilitate his survival, and hence, we are still acting as a surrogate for the kind of domestic group from which one normatively obtains basic essentials. However, by placing money into his hands and by not allowing him to join our family household for an afternoon, we will have relegated him to a more amorphous and more distant (community-level) consumption corporation—the consumption group to which beggars generally belong. For most of us, there is greater comfort in maintaining him in this broader consumption group of "have-nots" than in allowing him to join our family, albeit briefly.

Before leaving this particular case of charity, let us ask: Given the improbability of a successful request, why does the man offer to work for food? The answer is immediate. He is more deserving of alms as a nonbeggar than as a beggar. This statement may appear to contradict our earlier assertions about eligibility. But not really. Earlier we had been concerned with the eligibility of a begging man for membership in a category of beggars. What we know is that eligibility implies a rightful claim, but we also know that it is a rightful claim to something quite small. Beggars deserve to live, but their lives are expected to be rather lousy. Moreover, we can expect a beggar to remain a beggar, no matter how much money is transferred to him. And given that he is a beggar, we have reason to be completely ignorant of his lifestyle and the manner in which our transferred resources will be utilized. The unemployed worker, on the other hand, is like us. Indeed, as mentioned at the beginning of this chapter, many of us are only a few paychecks away from utter destitution. "Except for the grace of God, there go I." Hence, the reflection of oneself in the face of this disheveled stranger carries with it the terrifying message that the person by the side of the road is identical to the person driving by. Surely, such a person is deserving of a life with greater comfort than the life appropriate to beggars.

Begging Peasants

A cultural feature of peasants in Czarist Russia is yet another case of the begging of nonbeggars. In many areas of the country their soils were of poor quality and the rains unpredictable. Famine was a visitor to most homes at some time or another. As described by Stepniak (1888), most peasants lived in fear of the day when their pantries would fall empty. Their last morsel of bread might be consumed long before the next harvest. Some people even consuming the seed required for next year's planting, thereby mortgaging their futures to the outrageous usury of a local merchant. In the words of Stepniak (1888: 180–83):

[T]hen, when all other means have been exhausted, and the last bread has been eaten, the children and the old people swing the sacks over their shoulders and tramp to the neighboring villages asking help. . . . A young man or girl feels reluctant and ashamed to beg, but there is no help for it. There is nothing, literally nothing to eat at home. Today they have eaten the last loaf of bread, from which they yesterday cut "morsels" for those who knocked at their door. No bread, no work. Everybody would be happy to work for bare food; but work? why, there is none. A man who seeks for "morsels" and a regular "beggar" belong to two entirely different types of people. A beggar is a professional man; begging is his trade. A beggar has no land, no house, no permanent abiding place, for he is constantly wandering from one place to another, collecting bread, eggs, and money: he straightaway converts everything he receives in kind—corn, eggs, flour, etc.—into money. He is generally a cripple, a sickly man incapable of work, a feeble old man, or a fool: he is clad in rags, and begs in a loud voice, sometimes in an importunate way, and is not ashamed of his calling. . . .

A man, however, who asks for "morsels" is of quite another class. He is a peasant from the neighborhood. He is clothed like all his brother peasants, sometimes in a new armiak; a linen sack slung over his shoulders is his only distinguishing mark. If he belongs to the immediate neighborhood even the sack will be missing, for he is ashamed to wear it. He enters the house as if by accident, and on no particular business beyond warming himself a little, and the mistress of the house, so as not to offend his modesty, will give him the "morsel" incidentally, and "unawares." If the man comes at dinner-time he is invited to table. The moujik is very delicate in the management of such matters, because he knows that some day he, too, may perhaps have to seek "morsels" on his own account.

"No man can forswear either the prison or the sack," say the peasants. The man who calls for a "morsel" is ashamed to beg. On entering the izba he makes the sign of the cross and stops on the threshold in silence or mutters, in a low voice, "Give in Christ's name." Nobody pays any attention to him; all go on with their business and chat or laugh as if nobody were there. Only the mistress approaches the table, picks up a piece of bread from three to four square inches in size, and gives it to her visitor. He makes the sign of the cross and goes.

It is not as beggars that these men sought alms, but as peasants whose pantries had emptied somewhat earlier than those of their benefactors. Hence, their right to life and their rights to consumption goods greatly exceed those of beggars. We see here the possibility of a *system of ranking* in relation to those who live by extending the hand.

"Your Wallet or Your Life"

Robbers are different from beggars. The robber says, following Peter Blau (1964), "Give me your wallet or I'll take your life." Students of the "exchange theory" have puzzled over this interaction and have attempted to understand robbery as a dyadic exchange relation between two individuals. Of special interest to them was the question of "power." Their focus on the substance of the particular interaction led them to suggest that the robber had the greater power in an exchange of money for forbearance. However, at this point I would hope that you know that there is no exchange problem here. The robber is not in a position to offer "life" to the victim in exchange for his wallet. The victim's life is not alienable; it cannot be sold, given as a gift, or destroyed without a violation of law. In other words, "life" cannot be given; it can be taken, but not taken in exchange.

The appropriate analysis of this problem is much the same as an analysis of a theft that involves no face-to-face interaction. The face-to-face issue may be important to the experience of the victim, but it does not change the fact that there is no personal relationship between the victim and the robber. Rather, their *relationship* is one between two *categories* of person, not between individuals. Structurally, it differs little from that of the beggar and the donor. In both cases there is a *sharing* of resources between categories, notwithstanding the difference in the means. There are rightful claims (to shares) and imposed claims, and the robber shares by imposition. But each form of claim is a division of community resources among categories.

The other dimension on which the beggar and the robber are similar is the "power" dimension. Our sociological friends have perceived the robber to have power over the victim. Indeed, that would seem to be the case if this were a social relationship between two individuals. However, since this is an interaction between strangers, to be characterized as a relation between two categories of person, it is clear that the victim is socially advantaged and the robber is a social inferior. To be sure, the victim loses his wallet, but given a suitable flow of legitimate income, he purchases another and returns to his warm bed. The robber, on the other hand, is likely to live less comfortably, experience periodic imprisonment, and die an unpleasant death among unpleasant people. The reason is simple. The victim and others like him have constructed a system of law, courts, jails, and police that limits the freedom of the robber. In most cases a "system of justice" (that is financed and controlled by the victims) overwhelms the weapons of robbers, thereby limiting the share of community resources that they can enjoy. In this way, the robber's share is regulated by the system of "wealth-accumulation" and his right to life delimited.

A Theory of Charity

Mary Douglas (1990) in her foreword to a more recent edition of *The Gift* by Marcel Mauss (1990 [1950]), points out that the recipient of charity is not happy with his benefactor. "It wounds," she says. How can this be if charity consists of gifts that express solidarity? And how is it that a social security system financed by taxes, which Professor Douglas called "redistribution," does not "obligate persons in a contest of honor," as would be the case in the classic potlatch.

Douglas follows a conventional but invalid paradigm here, by accepting the notion that all transfers constitute a form of reciprocity. In this way, she also follows Mauss. However, a destruction of goods (the product of much work) in an agonistic display of relative powers in a potlatch can hardly be said to be a system of gift giving. Nor is a redistribution of consumption goods to the poor from the self-conscious rich or to the old from the statutory young a form of gift giving. Mauss (1990 [1950]: 18) suggests that

> [g]enerosity is an obligation, because Nemesis avenges the poor and the gods for the superabundance of happiness and wealth of certain people who should rid themselves of it. This is the ancient morality of the gift, which has become a principle of justice. The gods and the spirits accept that the share of wealth and happiness that has been offered to them.

In this way Mauss has beautifully expressed a demand for the rightful distribution of *shares to those who deserve them*. However, he should not claim to be talking about gifts. *First, a person cannot give* (transfer rights to) *something to someone if that thing already rightfully belongs to that person.* I say, "clearly," but of course it is not so clear. The mind simply rebels at the idea, given its roots in common understandings. To be sure, a thing that belongs rightfully to another can be *transferred as a physical object* to its rightful possessor, but that is a very different meaning of "to give." Unfortunately, and perhaps not accidentally, the English language is ambiguous in the use of the verb "to give" by using the same term for two fundamentally different forms of transfer—the transfer of rights and the transfer of the physical object. This confusion serves the interest of the myth of reciprocity. *Second, people cannot give* (transfer rights to) *something that they do not deserve to have*. A simple analogy would be making a gift of stolen goods.

Hence, we have two independent reasons for denying the possibility of *giving* as an act of charity. Of course, various charitable organizations promote the idea of giving as an act of "generosity." The clearly contradictory notion that the donor can rightfully possess something that is deserved by (and already the rightful possession of) a needy recipient serves well their desire to stimulate a false pride of generosity.

To repeat: One cannot give that which belongs *already* to, or is deserved to be possessed by, the recipient, and one cannot give that which one does not deserve to have. It is on this basis that I insist Mauss' statement (in the preceding) is nonsensical. Yet it is a statement with which few would argue. Such is the power of the "norm of reciprocity." By speaking of gifts, we maintain a myth of reciprocity.

The transfer of a thing to those who deserve it is not a transfer of rights, since that right is presumed already to be theirs by the presumption of deservedness. A voluntary transfer of rights can take place only in an exchange process. The receiver of a commodity gains a right to it through an actual or promised reciprocal action (payment), not by being a deserving category of person. It is a reciprocal transfer of rights over things. The purchaser of a loaf of bread has a rightful claim on his money that is not compromised by a rightful claim by the grocer. And the grocer has a rightful claim on the loaf. It is only by an exchange that rights are transferred. Similarly, in the offering of a gift, there is no *social* obligation to offer the benefit in question (only a *privately* constructed obligation borne of the desire to maintain a relationship). Hence, the recipient has no right to it. One is "obliged" only when one desires to maintain the relationship with a particular Other—which is a personal matter, not an issue of socially recognized categories of person.

With charity, however, the recipients must be recognized as deserving independently of any reciprocal action. And in the absence of any required action, they are deserving of a transfer prior to any action on the part of the donor, as well. But here is the problem: Why do people believe that a beggar is deserving of something that is deservedly held by the donor? What, I ask, is the alchemy that produces this logically inadmissible simultaneity? We know that it is easily feasible to possess something that belongs to another. We know that you can physically possess something to which you do now hold a rightful claim. The fact that something happens to be in your pocket does not make it yours. The "generous" woman does not deserve to have the thing that she transfers and must "rid [herself] of it." However, having no moral right to have it, obviously she cannot give (transfer rights to) it. And if she cannot give it, she loses the opportunity of claiming generosity. But if a charitable donation is reduced to the level of social or moral obligation, it will be stripped of its potential of providing to the donor the joys of virtue.

In the face of this terrible moral contradiction, there is a curious tribal belief—the norm of reciprocity—that converts, fleetingly and unannounced, a thing that should be transferred (since it already belongs to someone else) into something that one may generously give. In reference to the distribution of meat by Inuit hunters, Tim Ingold (1980: 160) asserts that

It is a necessary condition for the functioning of a hunting society that men be motivated to produce the means for their material reproduction by an ideal of generosity and a desire for prestige. But there can be no generosity without a conception of property: to give away, one must first have, and others must not. A pretense of appropriation has therefore to be constructed ideologically, in order that it may be canceled out socially.

The primary function of the norm of reciprocity is to provide a mantel of grandeur to the performance of ethical obligations. Unfortunately, the acceptance of this norm is intellectually crippling for social scientists since it hopelessly confounds the most fundamental of social processes—sharing within groups and reciprocity between groups or individuals.

Since there is perhaps no contemporary society that denies generosity as a possible basis of donations, there must be some rationalization. And perhaps it is this: Even though a donor recognizes that she has an obligation to "rid herself of it," there are others of lesser virtue who lack this perception. These others do not and will not make a donation; they deny rightful claims of beggars. By implication they do not agree that the donor should rid herself of it. For the nondonor, a donation takes the form of a nonreciprocated gift—a "free gift"—that of course he (the nondonor) *justifiably* refuses to give. It is the existence of this nondonor who is critical to the "generosity" of the donor. First, in the absence of nondonors, no donor can boast of generosity. There can be no pride in the performance of a universally performed activity. And second, the donor must adopt a nondonor's perspective, so that the satisfaction of a moral obligation can be transformed into a free gift. So you ask, should an individual be thankful when he is the beneficiary of someone's obligation? And should the donor feel pride of generosity? I would answer yes, to both questions. It is the nondonor who we can thank for that.

CHAPTER TEN
THE LOGIC OF RECIPROCITY

Stakes by Gyula Derkovits. Dózsa-Series VIII. (1928) Woodcut, 439 × 512 mm, Hungarian National Gallery, Budapest.

Whe have now presented a wide-ranging exposition on complementarity (sharing). We have considered rightful and forced
claims on a given set of resources, both of which lead to a
sharing thereof. And forceful claims have included theft and warfare,
which are undeniably methods of dividing a resource among claimants.
The remaining allocation process is exchange. Since we have recognized
sharing as a distinct form of allocation, we may now proceed with an
analysis of exchange.

So long as we were burdened with a concept of reciprocity that included everything from communal sharing to market exchange, no
progress could be made. Anthropologists and sociologists have for some
time desired, and dismissed the feasibility of, a precise conception of balanced exchange for all forms of exchange relation. That task was always
dismissed as the responsibility of an unnameable Other, like the Jewish
prophet, Elijah, for whom a place is always prepared at the Passover seder,
but who never seems to appear. However, without having to present the
credentials of an Elijah, I propose to present this long-awaited characterization of exchange. The feasibility of so doing arises, not from other-
worldly inspiration, but from a complete unshackling from the norm of
reciprocity. Moreover, we shall present this model in the form of a formal
proof, so if it is not correct, an observable error should lurk within.

Defining the Problem

Alvin Gouldner (1960) complains that Talcott Parsons (1951) devotes all
of his time discussing "complementarity," which is Parsons' characterization of sharing within groups, and that Parsons ignores reciprocity. However, Parsons is concerned with the nature of social institutions and the
organizational foundations of social systems; he therefore has no need to
consider reciprocity. Gouldner attempts to present reciprocity as an important, but fundamentally different, form of allocation. But in spite of his
clear and powerful differentiation of reciprocity from sharing (complementarity), Gouldner asserts, later in his paper, the universality of an internalized "norm of reciprocity." And in his examples of relationships to
which the norm of reciprocity applies, he makes reference to parent–child
relations, even though it is precisely these forms of relation that he had
earlier recognized to be defined by socially recognized status positions,

that is, as complementarity. It is by this surprising conflation that Gouldner is able to posit the plausibility of reciprocity as an internalized and
universal norm by which all forms of allocation are to be considered.

Marshall Sahlins (1972) makes an effort to relate the theoretical issues presented by Gouldner to ethnographic fact. He begins with an apparent acknowledgment of the fundamental distinction between sharing
("pooling") and reciprocity that is comparable to the difference between
complementarity and reciprocity: "Pooling is socially a *within* relation, the
collective action of a group. Reciprocity is a *between* relation, the action
and reaction of two parties" (p.188). However, he abandons the distinction
stressed by Parsons and Gouldner when he characterizes sharing as a system of reciprocities, "generalized reciprocity." In doing so, he is following
a suggestion offered by Bronislaw Malinowski (1922: 191) who suggested
that "it will be therefore interesting to draw up a scheme of exchanges,
classified according to the social relationship to which they correspond."

And Gouldner (1960) explicitly influenced Sahlins. Both influences
led him into the snares of individualism and into the Western mythology
that posits reciprocity as a rationalization for all forms of social process.
That is, rather than recognize the household, for example, as a locus of
joint, cooperative production to which various individuals hold rightful
shares, Sahlins (1972: 194) describes it as a set of interpersonal transfers,
as a set of nonreciprocal relations of reciprocity:

> It usually works out that the time and worth of reciprocation are not
> alone conditional on what was given by the donor, but also upon what
> he will need and when, and likewise what the recipient can afford and
> when. Receiving goods lays on a diffuse obligation to reciprocate when
> necessary to the donor and/or possible for the recipient. The requital
> thus may be soon, but again it may be never. There are people who even
> in the fullness of time are incapable of helping themselves or others. *A
> good pragmatic indication of generalized reciprocity is a sustained one-way
> flow.* Failure to reciprocate does not cause the giver of stuff to stop giv-
> ing: the goods move one way, in favor of the have-not, for a very long
> period. (italics added)

This is a truly remarkable manifestation of the universalizing of a norm of
reciprocity. And it is similarly remarkable that generalized reciprocity is
among the standard concepts used by American anthropologists. The

problem is not a problem of terminology. Since there are two fundamentally different forms of allocation, it is impossible to understand either when that understanding must accommodate a conflation of the two.

This conflation arises in the works of Marcel Mauss (1990) in the form of what I would call the "gift and return-gift" fantasy. Mauss presents exchange as an initial gift followed by a corresponding "return-gift" between two individuals or groups. This presentation could be defended as a simplification of an obviously more complex process, but it is more than that. If we can pretend to be watching the initial exchange of benefits between Ego and Alter, the familiar language of debt can apply. That is, we can say that the receiver is now indebted to the giver, having willingly accepted something.

I shall ignore at this point the possibility that the receiver does not recognize his indebtedness. Rather, I would like to challenge the construction of the relation as a gift and return-gift. The ethnographic fact is that we are invariably observing transfers that are elements of an indefinitely long series of exchanges between the parties, a series stretching indefinitely into the past and future. Within this history, a history that defines a *social relation* between the parties, the momentarily observed "gift and return-gift" shrink in significance. Against the backdrop of many transfers in each direction, not much "imbalance" can be attributed to a given transfer. In fact, we are unable to identify any gift as having the property of being "initial" or of any gift carrying the label "return." Perhaps the initially observed gift is a return-gift, or maybe every gift is a return for the gift transferred earlier. However, it is entirely presumptuous for an ethnographer to claim that his or her arrival on the scene was the occasion of a gift and return-gift. But that being the case, the notion of "debt" vanishes.

This problem is most evident with Mauss' (1990) discussion of the *kula*, he describes the *vaga* offered by an arriving partner as an "opening gift" that is followed by a reciprocating gift, the *yotile* from the resident partner that Mauss claims to be equal in value to the *vaga*.

> [The relationship] begins with a first gift, the *vaga*, that is solicited with all one's might by means of "inducements." For this first gift the future partner, still a free agent, can be wooed, and he is rewarded, so to speak, by a preliminary series of gifts. (p. 27)

There is much that reads incorrectly here. But the problem to which I bring attention is the idea of a gift and the equivalent counter gift. In fact, there is no basis for assuming that this is the initial encounter of these two men. By referring to one party as a "future partner," Mauss introduces a false picture of the relationship for which there is no ethnographic justification. Almost certainly, these men have been exchanging valuables for years (and perhaps their fathers before them). But recognizing this fact frustrates the indebtedness argument by which the gift becomes the embodiment of a soul that desires to return, and so forth. We should immediately abandon any theoretical concept that leads to a denial of the underlying ethnographic facts.

Moreover, if there is in actuality an ongoing exchange relation of many years' duration, it takes not much thought to understand why one gift follows another. There is no need for a flight to the exotic, to the mystification of the Other. It should be clear that there exists a mutually beneficial relationship that each has preferred to maintain. And we should like to discover what these benefits are and why they are sought with the particular partner. But those essential questions are lost in the confusion of gift and return gift.

Another problem with the conventional consideration of this matter is the reduction of the data to a dyadic relation. We have two partners and by intensively observing them, we hope to understand their actions. But after positing a false Ego and Alter, we *must* fall into error and suffer allusions about the strangeness of the Other. We are led into a comfortable and fashionable myth of the "savage mind."

Upon encountering the *kula*, Europeans have been mystified and amazed. And having discerned that this was an institution very unlike any found within their own societies, they have concluded that they must operate by means of a peculiar mentality. It is, however, the mentality of Ego/Alter and gift/return gift that displays the fundamental peculiarity. The important myths reside with the observers, not with the observed.

The Equal Benefits Criterion

In the context of a many-person world, suppose that we select two individuals at random and challenge them to consider the desirability of having an exchange relationship of some kind, for example, a friendship relation.[1] Our task is to determine the conditions under which these two individuals should be willing to build a relationship. Without a doubt each of them would like a relationship that is rewarding and beneficial in some way, but as free individuals they might prefer to establish a relationship with someone else or reject all comers in favor of an untroubled solitude.

Most scholars presume that a mutually acceptable exchange relation must provide (roughly) equal benefits to each party. Sahlins (1972: 194–95) suggests that

> "[b]alanced reciprocity" refers to direct exchange. In precise balance, the reciprocation is the customary equivalent of the thing received and is without delay. Perfectly balanced reciprocity, the simultaneous exchange of the same types of goods to the same amounts, is not only conceivable but ethnographically attested in certain marital transactions. . . . Balanced reciprocity may be more loosely applied to transactions which stipulate returns of commensurate worth or utility within a finite and narrow period. . . . Balanced reciprocity is less "personal" than generalized reciprocity. From our own vantage-point it is "more economic."

We see here that Sahlins (1972) cannot imagine a conception of balanced exchange except for "the simultaneous exchange of the same types of goods to the same amounts." However, this form of exchange is balanced only under specific conditions. For example, groups may exchange daughters into marriage. However, such an exchange would hardly be acceptable with any and every group whatsoever. A woman from group A is not automatically the equal to a woman from group B. The question then is, under what conditions would their exchange be consistent with a satisfactory exchange relation? A balanced exchange relation may include the exchange of daughters, but such an exchange will never constitute the totality of the relation. And once we understand this, we can imagine a balanced relation in which women are sent in only one direction (and other things are going in the other direction). The question remains unanswered: What is a balanced relation?

Of special reference at this point is the idea that balanced relations provide "commensurate worth or utility." The term "utility" refers to a measure of happiness or well-being that has a long history among economists, whereas "worth" would be a more objective or culturally customary measure of value. I shall refer to these two criteria as the "equal benefits" criterion. Equal benefit is an important criterion for social scientists, who often identify unequal benefit with exploitation. Since people are presumed to avoid exploitative relationships, unequal relations would not arise in a free environment and would fail to be stable or persistent, except under coercion. But consider the alternatives. If an unequal relation is to be rejected, should it be replaced by a balanced relation that provides even fewer benefits? In other words, if the unequal relation provides great benefit, should it be rejected in order to prevent even greater benefit to the other party? In an Ego and Alter world, the answer is yes. Alter should insist on a "fairer" allocation of benefits as a condition for continuing the relation, and we may pray for some success on his part.

Unfortunately, there can be little hope of success once we leave the dyadic world of Ego and Alter and consider a world of many people. Given a number of alternatives to Alter in the part of Ego, Ego is likely to have alternatives that she prefers to a more equal relation with Alter. The question for Alter, then, is whether an unequal relation with Ego provides more benefits than any of his own alternatives. In this context, a rejection by Alter of his best option (Ego) appears small-minded. There is the old Western proverb: "Don't cut off your nose to spite your face." The expression must sound strange in Chinese translation. But it means that you should not make things worse, simply because they are not as you would desire. As we proceed, we shall adhere to that injunction.

Defining Exchange Value

We shall begin by considering again the conditions under which a relationship should be continued. Consider the two randomly chosen individuals that we mentioned earlier and recognize that the relationship should be stable and mutually acceptable to both parties, if it is true that

1. on the basis of each party's evaluations of this exchange relation, each prefers to maintain that relationship *rather than do without it*; and

2. if each party evaluates all feasible alternative relationships (that they might have within this many-person world) and perceives

that there is no preferred feasible alternative to a particular relation, then, it follows from these *Preference Propositions* that

3. each party *should* prefer to maintain this relationship.

The reader may observe that the conclusion follows unavoidably from
the premises. It is not sufficient that a person prefers a given state of affairs to any feasible alternative; she must also prefer that relationship to
having none at all. Conceivably, none of the people available to her is
worth the trouble. However, if the first Proposition is satisfied, she will
want a relationship with someone. The question at this point is, with
whom? And the answer is, with a particular individual if and only if he is
preferred to all others *with whom she can develop a relationship*. Of course,
there may be wonderful people in this many-person world with whom she
would very strongly desire a relationship. Say, Robert Redford or President
Clinton. But these guys are too busy. Only *feasible* alternatives are considered here. Having sought a relationship with a number of notable individuals and failed, she finally reaches the realm of feasibility. If there are
individuals within this feasible set who are desirable in a relationship, then
she will choose her most preferred of these feasible options.

In the domain of preference, this conclusion is straightforward and
does not constitute an earth-shattering observation. However, we cannot
claim that an individual should be satisfied to maintain a relationship unless those Propositions are sustained—the conclusion implies the premises.
This is not a trivial observation. We see this by considering the consequences of dropping either Proposition. It should be clear that if either is
dropped, the conclusion fails. A person should prefer to abandon a relationship if it prevents the establishment of a preferred relationship, and a
person should have no relationship whatsoever if none of the alternatives is
preferred to having no relationship at all. So if people are free to act in accordance with their preferences, they *should* act in the manner suggested in
the preceding. We conclude that the premises are the necessary and sufficient conditions for justifying the continuation of an exchange relation.

This conclusion seems to depend on an egoistic maximization of preference idea, and it is clear that an egoist will act in accordance with these
Propositions. But suppose that the individual is "altruistic" and wants to select the individual who will be most benefited by the relationship. The al-

truist cannot discern the level of benefit provided to others by any direct reading of a benefit scale. Although the equal benefits idea has lived long in this domain, it is without empirical meaning. There is one and only one method for identifying the seemingly most benefited individual: he must examine the reactions of various individuals to the flow of resources (material and nonmaterial) that he can transfer to them in a friendship relation.

These reactions will come in the form of gifts and from the evident pleasures of time spent together. In other words, a friend will manifest the level of benefits received by means of a reciprocal transfer of "smiles, love, gifts, and the use of time." Hence, in searching altruistically for a friend, one examines the potential reciprocal reactions of all feasible alternatives and selects as a friend the individual whose reactions seem to be the best. But here is the rub. The evaluation of "the best" can be made only by the altruist, whose judgments must be in terms of his own criteria. The evaluations of smiles, love, gifts, and the use of time must be his valuations, which are then to be imputed to the other. Consequently, the valuation of the friend's responses must be computed in relation to the reciprocal benefits received. Which means that the altruist selects the individual whom he most prefers. QED. We have now deduced an equivalence of egoism and altruism in the context of exchange relations.

Later in this discussion, I shall discuss the "mythology of friendship" that constitutes a tribal belief in the West. It is a belief that is held out of a fear that friendship might otherwise be perceived as selfish. It is a belief in "giving without thought of return." Given the proposition that we have just proven, it should be clear that giving with *indifference* to return would be thoughtless and cruel, relative to providing ones gifts to those for whom they seem to matter. Such an act would actually demonstrate an indifference to the happiness of others, since the "return" in its various possible forms is the only measure of that happiness. Fortunately, for Western peoples, the myth does not guide behavior.

Balanced Exchange

We have said nothing yet about balanced relations. The solution to this problem must begin with an identification of the variable that is relevant to a balanced exchange; that variable is exchange value.

The *exchange value* of anything or any relationship is precisely, and by definition, the most preferred thing or relationship that can be obtained in exchange for it within the context of many alternatives.

I shall prove in a moment that exchange value is the necessary focus of a balanced exchange, but you should recognize that we have already proven that if an individual has found a friend whose reciprocal responses constitute the exchange value of her friendship time, she should maintain that relationship. This should be true of her friend, as well.

Here, let us consider an exchange relation, such as friendship between A and B, where the flow of benefits from B is β and the flow of benefits from A is α. Suppose, further, that when B searches for an exchange relation, he can secure no relation that he prefers to a relation with A and vice versa. Then, we may conclude immediately from the definition of exchange value that

$$\text{the exchange value of } \beta \text{ is } \alpha; \text{ and}$$
$$\text{the exchange value of } \alpha \text{ is } \beta.$$

Now, to think through this problem properly, imagine that there is an index of value by which α and β can each be compared, much like money in a commodity market. Like money, this index is entirely arbitrary. It does not matter that some people measure value in rubles, others in pesos or yuan. What does matter is that certain things can be said to have equal values in terms of that index. So rather than exchange β for α in a barter transaction, as would be the case in a friendship relation, we imagine that there is an intermediary transaction into the index, Ω, for each party. Since we already know that the exchange value of β = α, and so forth, we may conclude immediately that

$$\text{the exchange value of } \beta = \Omega = \text{the exchange value of } \alpha,$$
$$\text{where } \Omega \text{ is an arbitrary index.}$$

We do not know whether A and B will be satisfied with their relationship. If they are uncertain of the alternatives available to them, they may continue looking in vain for more satisfactory relationships. However, if we know that no better relation can be found, then we can say that each individual *should be satisfied* with that relationship, and the relationship is *exactly balanced in exchange value.* This may be called the *Fundamental Law of Exchange Value* (FLEV); it provides the conditions under which individuals should be satisfied with an exchange-based social relation.

It is often the case that things exchange at valuations different from their exchange values. For example, an individual could accept an occupational position that is inferior to his or her most preferred option, in terms of wages, working conditions, and so forth. In this case the value of his or her work would be less than its exchange value, as defined by the preference ordering of that individual. This can happen because the set of feasible options is not always known. Hence, when we look at exchange relations as they may exist in the world, we should not assume that they satisfy the Preference Propositions. It is only in a world where people are fully aware of their alternative opportunities that the realization of exchange value can be ensured.

The conception of exchange processes implied by this analysis has revolutionary consequences for our understanding of social relations. First of all, the FLEV applies equally to commercial exchange relations. The difference is that the use of money enables people to provide their gifts to one person and receive their gifts from another. This is flexibility that friendship does not allow. Furthermore, with commercial exchange, the use of money gives us a recognized index of exchange value, rather than the imaginary Ω. Otherwise, on a purely theoretical basis, intimate friendship and gift exchange reside within the same model as commercial exchange. The differences are, I hasten to add, substantial, but those differences lie in the domain of cultural articulation, not in protocultural foundation.

Furthermore, we now have a conception of a balanced exchange that is, in principle, independent of the behavior of real people. We know the conditions under which individuals *should* be satisfied, but observation of behavior only finds the conditions under which people have chosen to be satisfied. We cannot assume that they are aware of their most preferred feasible options. Nor can we know what that option would be, since only their valuations of alternatives can be relevant. On the other hand, there may be many ethnographic domains where the set of alternatives is limited and well defined and where the individuals concerned can be presumed to be aware of those alternatives. And, conversely, there are circumstances wherein one can presume that a lack of sufficient information is a dominating factor. The cost of identifying one's most preferred option is often so high that the net benefits of finding it are negative.

A balanced exchange is not the only relation with which one may be satisfied. But it is the only relation that is objectively deserving of satisfaction. The choice of any other will be acceptable for some and not others. Each of us may chose a different time to end our search process (depending on the opportunity cost of search, the expectation of locating a preferable alternative, aversion to risk, and so forth), and consequently each of us may have different reasonable criteria for accepting the best of the already identified options. However, it is *axiomatically* true that one should be satisfied with the most preferred feasible option. The mutual occurrence of that option defines balanced exchange.

The Mythology of Friendship

I have used the friendship relation as the basic example in the preceding discussion. I have in mind the conception of friendship that is common *outside* of China, particularly in European cultures. Chinese and Europeans both use the term "friendship" these days, but the meanings of the term diverge significantly. Traditionally, the Chinese would not use the term "friendship." Alan Smart (1993) found that Chinese respondents seldom identified people as "friend." Rather, they used such terms (in Chinese) as "fellow-student," "fellow-worker," "fellow-villager," and so forth. We know these terms as indicative of *guanxi*, taking the form of hierarchical relations of responsibility, such as father-son, older brother-younger brother. We shall consider those relations in more detail in the next chapter. However, the ideal European form of friendship is classically the relationship between two very similar, affluent, and highly ethical men. So while the Chinese model finds its best expression in Confucius, the Western form finds its best expression in Aristotle.

In his Nicomachean Ethic, Aristotle presents the image of a good man who has need for nothing save the company of another man of similar merit. These men will love that which is good in each other as they love the goodness within themselves. And they give to each other equivalently in a relationship of balanced reciprocity, each being the most preferred feasible alternative for the other. Aristotle suggests that a good man will give to his friend without thought of a return. But Aristotle shows his wisdom in recognizing that since a nonreciprocal relation is not friendship (i.e., a love for a wine does not produce friendship with the bottle) and since the good man has everything except, perhaps, a friend of equivalent goodness, this relationship must be reciprocal. It is a relationship for which the FLEV would apply. Unlike Confucius, who found the seeking of self-gratification to be inconsistent with virtue and who saw man as a relational being, the Aristotelian man is a detached, individualistic utility-maximizing man, even in his most intimate of social relations.

Western writers are commonly embarrassed by the fact of balanced reciprocity within even the most intimate of friendships. There is an implied manipulative egoism in balanced reciprocity that seems out of place. Yet balanced reciprocity is the criterion that applies to Aristotelian friendship as well as to commercial relations. Hence, it is common for people to stress the notion of "giving without thought of return" and denying reciprocity. Giving without return is the Western mythology of Western friendship. It is the ideological medium by which the relationship can be elevated above all others. It is for this reason that Western scholars must look to exotic places to study gift exchange and imbue it with savage mysticism and magic. It is likely that Christianity produced the Western obfuscation of Aristotelian principles. In our discussion of charity (see chapter 9), we remarked on the struggle that St. Thomas Aquinas had with these issues; he ended with God as the Ultimate Friend—constructing Man as God's most preferred alternative.

Unfortunately, no one seems to notice that "gift giving" in China is almost never gift exchange. The literature from elsewhere is imposed on China. Even Chinese scholars, having been educated into the norm of reciprocity, fail to separate the complementarity of *guanxi* from the reciprocity of friendship. For example, in the context of many ritual occasions in China, individuals are expected to bring gifts of appropriate value. Hence, if two individuals sponsor the same ritual, then each will receive a gift from the other. And there you have it. Gift exchange! The fact that some people sponsor few if any rituals while others sponsor many is not seen as disturbing the model. Myth always overwhelms reality. The presumption is that gift exchange need not balance or have balance as its norm. Given the norm of reciprocity, there can be no other analysis.

GUANXI AND THE LAW OF THE VILLAGE

Dózsa on the Wall by *Gyula Derkovits. Dózsa-Series V. (1928) Woodcut, 497 × 440 mm, Hungarian National Gallery, Budapest.*

W e began these chapters with a characterization of "wealth-assets." That characterization implies that wealth-holding and consumption groups are foundational to culture. The primary mode of within-group resource allocation for both forms of group has been called *sharing*. But in the last chapter, we presented an analysis of the properties of allocations that can arise between independent bundles of resources—that is, *between* consumption groups or wealth-holding groups—reciprocity (exchange).

We are now in a position to focus on a most difficult case: Chinese social relations. Given the confusion spawned by the "norm of reciprocity," it is to be expected that students of Chinese society would impose a gift modality to the particular forms of interpersonal relations that dominate Chinese society. However, unlike the West where between group relations have been based on a friendship model, the Chinese have modeled it on a father-son model—a model drawn from within-group relations. For the analyst this creates a difficult problem. The Chinese organize between group relations by converting them into within-group relations. Instead of converting strangers into friends, they convert them into kin. Consequently, our discussion of sharing comes strongly to the fore.

Introduction

Now that we have discussed reciprocity in its exact manifestation, we are able to clarify the fundamental differences between Western and Chinese modes of interaction. We begin, of course, with the important work of Fei Xiaotung on this issue. Fei (1992 [1947]) presents two analogies, one for China and the other for the West. His analogies are powerful because they give us a distilled essence that stimulates and informs; but as is the common case with analogies, they provide an incomplete characterization.

Fei (1992 [1947]: 61–62) describes Western social organization as small bundles of straw (categories of person) that are bound into larger differentiated bundles (corporate groups) that are then gathered together to make a pile (society):

> In Western society, these separate units are organizations. By making an analogy between organizations in Western societies and the composition of haystacks, I want to indicate that in Western society individuals form

organizations. Each organization has its own boundaries, which clearly define those people who are members and those who are not. That much is always clear. The people in an organization form a group, and their relationship to the organization is usually the same. If there are differences among group members or distinctions among ranks within the organization, these would have been agreed upon earlier as part of the rules of the organization.

However, Chinese society is said to be different:

In Chinese society, the most important relationship—kinship—is similar to the concentric circles formed when a stone is thrown into a lake. Kinship is a social relationship formed through marriage and reproduction. . . . In the traditional structure, every family regards its own household as the center and draws a circle around it. This circle is the neighborhood, which is established to facilitate reciprocation in daily life. A family invites the neighbors to its weddings, sends them red-dyed eggs when a new baby is born, and asks for their help in lifting its dead into coffins and carrying the coffins to the cemetery. (p. 63–64)

Here, we find an "egocentrism" where each individual is the center of a set of relations, beginning with himself, moving on to relations within the family (with family relations as the model), extending out into the village, and finally into the nation. Consequently, the Western structure is one in which each individual possesses a socially designated position relative to others and must interact with those others in terms of a general set of criteria. That is, members of one bundle are expected to interact with every member of another bundle in a socially specified manner. In the Chinese structure, individuals are free to construct their relations with others idiosyncratically, and those relationships determine the social position of a person. So rather than having one's personhood defined by the bundle in which one is located, one is defined by the set of individuals with whom one has been able to construct relations.

When this "model" is presented as a description of Chinese social organization, it seems to be overdrawn. There are groups in the Western sense in Chinese society. The organization of the government can be described as so many bundles of straw piled into a pyramidal structure; similarly, schools, villages, and businesses are organized as

177

complementary structures of "social action." The village was designated by the emperor as a unit for the payment of taxes and the providing of corvée. They often shared a village deity and other corporate assets. Similarly, students in an educational institution face fairly standardized criteria of eligibility, certain rights and restrictions as students, and variations in specific rights as they progress through the curriculum. Hence, it can be said that individuals become incumbents of identifiable "person-categories" within those institutions. They are like straws in a bundle. Insofar as superordinate authority has the power to structure social organization for the management of wealth, there will be corporate groups of the standard form.

However, Fei's discussion is not a description of social organization, it is a cross-cultural comparison of characterizations of "personhood" or of the "self." In the Western cosmology, individuals see themselves as members of groups within which their relationships are largely prescribed. Of course, individuals have specific personal relations within organizations, but these are commonly defined as "informal" relative to defining relationships that are culturally or administratively defined. Furthermore, each individual is a member of a megabundle consisting of all citizens of a nation-state. And in spite of possible profound social differentiation within the nation, each individual is normatively equal in rights and responsibilities. It is equality before the law and before God. This megabundle defines a moral community of equivalent individuals. It is this conception that is identified by "individualism."

Chinese "egoism" is a conception of individuals who are defined by their relations to others, with ego at the center. This means that there cannot be a megabundle of social and moral equivalents. In Chinese tradition morality is situational and conditional on the relations of others to ego. This fact was brought strongly to the fore when I asked students at Peking University a simple question: If a stranger committed an act that you believed to be morally wrong, would not that same action be wrong if performed by your own father? To the Western mind, the answer is an immediate "yes" (reflecting a common moral community), but for my students the question was ridiculous. I received puzzled stares, students looking at each other and back at me as though I had suddenly expressed vulgarity.

Philosophical Issues

According to Confucius, a man of "perfect virtue" (*jen*) is one who is motivated by duty toward others and who suppresses inclinations toward desire and personal gain.[1] And while instrumental "connections" are common to most cultures, they are burdened by a negative valuation in Confucian thought, where individuals are encouraged to develop relationships of respect and responsibility and not use others as instruments toward objects of desire. As pointed out by Gary G. Hamilton and Wang Zheng in an introduction to their translation of Fei (1992: 21–22):

> Each link in a Chinese person's network is defined in terms of a dyadic social tie (*gang*). These interpersonal ties are known in Chinese as *guanxi*.

And in a footnote to this statement, they argue that

> [r]elationship in English, however, does not quite capture the binding quality suggested by the Chinese terms. . . . *Gang* is the term used to define the three closest relationships (*san-gang*): the ties between father and son, emperor and official, and husband and wife.

Hence, *guanxi* refers to relationship in the most profound sense of the term, with implications that are beyond customary English usage—relationships that are modeled by the father-son and the husband-wife relations. In Confucian philosophy there are five *gang* for which broadly significant behavioral rules apply, each of which has its archetypical manifestation within the domestic family. These five cardinal relationships are called the *wu-lun*. Clearly, these relationships are not "connections." A structuring of interpersonal relations based on (intrafamilial) *gang* is very distant from the myopic instrumentalism from which the notion of "connections" arises.

Guanxi emerged from the soil of China, Fei might say. It emerged from the hard and uncertain life of Chinese peasants. A population that increases unrelentingly against a fixed landmass, together with the vagaries of weather, has forced the peasants of China to experience famine and starvation with some regularity. It is this environment that has been the cradle of *guanxi*—where reliance on ones family is often not sufficient, and an extension of familial forms of support has been sought through membership in a village, work group, or kin group. The specifically Chinese method of articulating this extension of familial support beyond the domestic family is *guanxi*.

In most, if not all, cultures there is a counterpart of the *wu-lun* for the guidance of intrafamily behavior. The special characteristic of Chinese culture is that the *wu-lun* are extended beyond the domestic group into other ethically supportable forms of relation, and once the *wu-lun* are expressed in other collectivities, the boundaries of the family become enclosed by a broader quasifamilial structure—a broader structure of duty and responsibility. *Guanxi* is the mechanism within Chinese culture by which the *wu-lun* are exported beyond the family setting.[2]

In the West personal relationships outside of the family are not constructed on the *wu-lun* or any other model of complementarity. The family is not the ethical frame for other relationships. In the West most nonfamily personal relations are modeled on the friendship relation of independent individuals, as defined in our last chapter. Yet the "norm of reciprocity" befuddles Western and Western-trained scholars. For them, all relationships can be described by reference to the exchange relationships of independent individuals—the Western conception of reciprocity. Although Western sociology understands the difference between complementarity and reciprocity, it does not know how to deal with this difference. In the absence of the appropriate model, all processes are described as balanced, negative, or imbalanced forms of reciprocity. It is from this fogbank that the "norm of reciprocity" emerges as an obscuring mindset.

The Structure of *Guanxi*

In his discussion of *guanxi*, Fei (1992) admits the existence of groups in Chinese culture, patrilineages being a salient example. Chinese patrilineages are wealth-holding corporate groups of a rather common form. The fact that this is so suggests the enormous importance of wealth-assets as determinants of social organization. The domestic family is also a particular cultural articulation of a general social form. In both cases, these are obviously relations of complementarity. However, outside of organizations of kin, the personal relations of individuals in China are, as Fei indicates, "ego-centered."

Nevertheless, since these external relationships are constructed on the *wu-lun* of intrafamilial relations, there must be a collectivity, *liminal* and implicit, that springs forth from the set of individuals with whom an individual possesses those relationships. The traditional village offers a good example of this liminal collectivity. The genius of the Chinese form is that properties of a group, as implied by complementarity, can exist without a corporate structure to support it. Or, more correctly, the relationships within groups can be defined from below, by ego, and are not defined culturally or by superiors.

The ego-centered Chinese system of relations allows an individual to have, or not have, a relationship with others who live in his village. Hence, for any Ego, the active set of complementary relations is not the village as a whole (as it would be in the Western form) but a subset thereof. We shall refer to those of the village with whom an individual has relationships as his "village association." There is a single village, but potentially there are as many village associations as there are individual families. However, every "village association" consists of families within the village.

Membership in the village is a necessary but insufficient condition for membership in a particular association. Similarly, there are coworkers with whom one is related and other people who work in the same place with whom one is not related. But all coworkers work in the same place. My teaching assistant, Liang Yongjia, often refers to fellow students as "my academic brother, my academic sister." In doing so he is clearly imposing a *wu-lun* on those relationships in which he must ultimately appear in a more specific role, that is, as older brother or younger brother, since these are the categories in which *wu-lun* are specified. I could easily imagine reference to brother-worker or sister-villager. And, of course, the teacher–student relation commonly assumes the role of father-son.

The structure of relations becomes more complex, however, when two individuals are related through one or more third parties. For example, they may not be fellow villagers, but share relatives who are comembers of a village association. And if they each have warm feelings about those relatives, then a good relationship can develop between them. Or there may be a single individual with whom each possesses some relationship, each such relationship being, perhaps, different from the other. In these ways individuals may become members of a village association, in liminality, without ever having seen the village itself. For this reason, two individuals who have no known "basis" for a relationship will search for one by means of conversation and will be delighted on discovering one.

Liwu in the Village

We have defined a "village association" as a subset of families within a village whose members have met ritual obligations in relation to a particular Ego. In the typical case, these associations are largely overlapping, and in the best of cases, everyone is related to every other person in the village, so there is a single such group in the village. As is the case with other groups outside of the domestic family, membership is by achievement, not by ascription, and only members of the association have rights to the benefits thereof. For example, in the event that a constituent family announces the wedding of a daughter, members of the association are expected to contribute to a pool of resources (the dowry) that can be devoted to the launching of the marriage.

Some individuals sponsor more events than others, even to the point of being accused of exploiting the process (and losing respect). However, there is, normally, the presumption that contributions are made to those who have need, and needs are unevenly distributed among contributors. In the special case of a dowry, the pool of resources endows the bride but does not belong to her. It is a ritually required contribution to the household of the groom (or of his father) and assists the groom's father in his provisioning of that household (without implying that the father-in-law is unable to perform this task without assistance). These contributions are *liwu*, where *li* refers to the ritual or customary obligation of a virtuous man, and *liwu* is a "thing" that in some way represents or accomplishes *li*.

Yan Yunxiang (1996) points out that in times of severe economic distress and famine, one's patrilineal relatives or affinal relatives, from a neighboring village (where famine conditions may be less severe), may be called on for an offering of grain. Many families have been able to survive crises only because of such assistance, and lacking such relationships, others have perished:

> Mr. Guo recalled that his younger sister fainted several times owing to food deprivation and he too fell seriously ill during the famine. However,

his family did not suffer as much as many others, because his elder sister, who had married into a village four miles north of Xiajia, gave them a great deal of help. Despite a similar threat of famine, his sister's family lent Guo's family 180 *jin* of grain. Guo said: "I still remember clearly the evening my sister's husband came to our house and carried a sack of maize on his bicycle. That saved our whole family." (Yan 1992: 92)

Furthermore, the benefits of protection that are gained by the family of the bride also accrue to some extent to all members of the village association. The subordinate village becomes eligible to incorporation as a member of the virtual household of the dominant village. For this reason members of the village association (people on good terms with the bride's family) may receive shares of resources held by the dominant village in times of need. This sharing is *zhanguang*, the sharing of (relative) good fortune. Hence, the benefits to be gained from *liwu* are not reciprocal *liwu*, but the possibility of *zhanguang*, a nonritual, nonroutine share under unpredictable circumstances (that may not ever arise).

Unfortunately, *liwu* is translated as *gift* by all of the most prominent students of Chinese culture, and the overall process is generally labeled *gift exchange* by those who discuss these issues in the English language (e.g., Yang 1994; Yan 1996; Smart 1993; Wank 1996; Kipnis 1997; Gold 1985; Pye 1995). Let us be clear on this point: A translation of *liwu* as "gift" is not erroneous in itself. It creates no problem for the Chinese where the term applies to ritually appropriate transfers (to superiors, to children, to lovers, etc.). However, in the context of anthropological literature, the concept of the gift is associated with voluminous literature on exchange and, hence, with Marcel Mauss (1990), Bronislaw Malinowski (1922), Marshall Sahlins (1972), and others. Hence, "gift" carries a host of theoretical entailments that do not apply to *liwu*.

In the village studied by Yan, families differ in the number of children and other factors that might prompt a ceremony, so the number of ceremonies sponsored by families varies widely, and conceivably some families would retain membership in the association in the absence of any potential sponsorship:

The costs of remaining in the association are unrelated to probable benefit. Propriety dictates the kinds of gifts [that are] suitable for which categories of relatives or friends (*dui shenme ren, sui shenme li*). I discovered this rule first by transcribing the gift lists, for I noticed that relatives in the same category usually present similar gifts in a ritualized situation. . . . They told me there were indeed standards for gift giving and that everyone knows the code. For instance, in 1990–1991, the standard gift to attend one's wife's younger brother's wedding was 50 yuan, while that for a fellow villager (*tunqin*) was a maximum of 10 yuan. (Yan 1996: 125)

Clearly, in the presence of this code, we are observing complementarity, not (balanced) reciprocity. The contribution to the wedding of a wife's younger brother might be different from the donation that would be offered by the brother for the marriage of his older sister. Social ethics are defined relative to categories of person: father and son, husband and wife, older brother and younger brother, and brother and sister in relations of complementarity. This logic of relationships carries over into the village association, so that the donations from individuals who share a given relationship to the recipient are likely to be very similar. *Li* (propriety) implies a contribution of the right magnitude, and it is improper to make contributions that might shame other donors.[3] According to Yan, everyone in the village has learned the complex formulas that define *liwu*.

From the Perspective of Superiors

Confucius has been credited with the codification and elaboration of the interpersonal conduct that constitutes the *wu-lun*, but it is most unlikely that they are his invention. Confucius was a product of his culture and could only make more effective the processes that he perceived around him. This codification and the training of officials into their intricacies were highly valued by the emperors of the time. Hence, we know that *guanxi* has value, not only as a source of support for the weak in times of difficulty or opportunity but also as a source of empowerment for the strong. Indeed, the latter's property must be the basis for its adoption as a basic cultural characteristic.

Understanding the manner in which *guanxi* profits the well positioned is still rather illusive for me, given the very different perspective taken by most of the literature. Within the literature, the superior is simply the victim of a responsibility, having received from the subordinate some rather ordinary things. However, consider the residential fire insurance company. It, too, is the recipient of routine and unspectacular contributions from clients, and on rather exceptional occasions, it may offer grand and very significant assistance.

Like *guanxi*, this is not an exchange relation; it is pooling or sharing among the clients, with the fire insurance company receiving a share for having assembled and managed the pool. But clearly the insurance company is in the driver's seat because they are able to set "rates" of annual payment on the basis of estimations of the probabilities of fire. The rates actually chosen will accommodate an estimated surplus for the company, but there may be many insurance companies competing for scarce clients, thereby reducing the level of company surplus. For the outsider, the benefits of having insurance are readily seen, but not the surplus. It would appear that *guanxi* is similar. The client faces ritually fixed contributions while the superior has discretion. Moreover, clients are unlikely to have multiple sources of a given form of assistance. The superiors available to a given individual have a near monopoly position. Hence, within their discretion comes power.[4]

And another factor favors the superior. The superior is most often able to provide a favor with a very modest expenditure of his own time. The man coming on a bicycle with a sack of grain is not the only depiction. Indeed, it may be the exception. The advantage offered by the superior may actually cost the superior nothing, or the cost of one client's advantage may be no more than a loss of opportunity for another client, it may be a loss suffered by the provincial or state government, or it may be a loss to no one. The superior is in a position to garner the greater gain because he seeks nothing. It is the client who initiates and maintains the relationship with a flow of *liwu*, and it is the client who seeks the favor. The superior sits, accumulates, and waits. So we may conclude that *guanxi* generates an upward flow of things to those who have the advantage of social position.

Finally, the state has been a major determinant of the flow of potential favors by which men of social and administrative position may maintain clients. The manner in which this is done is well illustrated by the current reform process. From a fairly early point in the history of the People's Republic of China, there has been a tendency toward decentralization of policy implementation, so that family and village could emerge as significant actors in public policy. Mao Zedong "pioneered" this strategy in his policy of delivering prerogatives to the provinces during the Great Leap Forward (1958) and the Cultural Revolution (1966–1969). "Mao sought to overcome the resistance of stodgy central bureaucrats to his vision of accelerated growth and revolutionary collectivism and egalitarianism by appealing to provincial officials and building up their power with the Central Committee" (Shirk 1993: 151).

A comparable strategy of decentralization has enabled Deng Xiaoping to gain support of "market reforms" in the face of potential objection from a conservative Central Committee. By providing to local officials the ability to control and gain financial advantage for themselves and their communities in the reform process and by augmenting policy-making bodies with representatives from the provinces, Deng was able to push reform forward.

As we observe the current reform program, we see a continuation of Chinese administrative tradition. This has been a tradition in which the Center allocates the responsibility of interpreting and implementing general policy directives to provinces and villages. This allocation of responsibility places into the hands of officials at local and higher levels the necessary favors. So if the "flow of gifts" is large, it is due in large part to a *carefully maintained capacity* of administrators to deliver a flow of favors in a highly competitive environment.

The Linking Individual

In the story told by Yan, the bride was considered a "linking individual." However, we failed to place this link into motion. If the link is the bride discussed in the preceding, she can serve as an emissary of her natal family to the potential sources of assistance. In the tale about lifesaving grain to the family of Mr. Guo, it was a sister who "gave them a great deal of help," although it was the brother-in-law who actually appeared with grain. A bride's family might complain about the costs of raising and marrying a daughter, but if she marries "well," the benefits may be incalculable. Her value will be a function, in part, of the dowry by which her family and its village association introduce her into the new family. While we cannot say that she will have more influence when the dowry is greater in some linear fashion, we can say that a substandard dowry (in the opinion of the groom's family) would spell disaster for her status in the family and for her role as an intermediary.

The use of intermediaries is common to perhaps most instances of *guanxi*. The "intermediary" is a linking individual whose relationship with a potential source of assistance is instrumental in securing it. If the intermediary is subordinate to the potential source, he will have maintained the required flow of *liwu* and would be in a position to request assistance. In this case, the assistance is provided *for* the intermediary, but it is provided *to* the person in need. In many cases, the intermediary arranges a meeting between the seeker of assistance and the superior (as we shall call him). The seeker will discuss his needs, and he will present the superior with *liwu*, thereby beginning a relationship of indefinite duration.

Very commonly, instead of attempting to initiate a *guanxi*, the seeker makes a monetary payment to the superior. While such money transfers would be discomforting to a Westerner, they are quite common as gifts in China for various ritual occasions, including the famous little red envelopes at weddings (Gates 1987). However, unlike the monies that are transferred as *liwu* in various rituals, the payment offered to an official must be of a size appropriate to a specific desired action. It is not determined by relative structural positions within an ego-centered *guanxi* network.

A payment is the purchase of an action, not the initiation of a social relation, and no subsequent flow of *liwu* is implied. Those who offer such payments may subsequently seek to develop a *guanxi* with an official with a flow of *liwu*, but that would be, at least analytically, a separate process. Yet, things are compounded. A payment is accepted because of the superior's trust in the intermediary with whom he possesses good *guanxi*. And the intermediary is ultimately the responsible party and is relied on by the official. Hence, the payment becomes internal to a ritually correct form of *guanxi*.

Some of my informants argue that there is a further complication. There may be ambiguity created by the size of *liwu*. Is it *liwu* or a payment? My response is that this confusion can be only in the minds of third-person observers. If the transfer is actually a payment that is sufficient to induce the desired action, then it must be intended by the client and recognized by the recipient. It is true that a substandard payment may be confused with *liwu*. However, given a culturally recognized code of appropriate *liwu*, it is unlikely (but not impossible) that *liwu* will approximate the required payment. And finally, if the desired action is in fact a violation of procedures, both sides should know it and hence should recognize the form of transaction that is required.

An additional complication is that many observers feel that it is unethical, indeed bribery, if money is offered in relation to an immediately desired action. The argument is that *guanxi*, properly conceived, requires that the potential benefits of a relationship be largely unknown at the initiation of the relation—that *guanxi* is inconsistent with instrumentalism. While it is undeniable that the ethics of *guanxi* are violated by an immediacy of benefit, poor ethics do not convert the transfer into a payment.

Based on the analysis of the last chapter, we now have an analytically complete characterization of payments, for which these ethical issues are irrelevant. In fact, Yang (1994) presents such cases under the rubric of *guanxi-xue*, an instrumental form of *guanxi* that she believes to be increasingly dominant in the urban areas of China. However, if there is an indefinite flow of *liwu* subsequent to the provision of the desired action, then there is *guanxi*, no matter how crudely it is initiated. Bribery should not be alleged simply as a general epithet to be hurled at indiscretion. I would strongly agree, however, that a transfer of money, followed by an official action, with no continuing interaction between the parties could not be *guanxi*.

If the action induced by a payment is conditional on the existence of an intermediary, it is reasonable to presume that the sentimental closeness of the intermediary will affect the willingness of the superior to commit the action and that it will affect the required magnitude of the payment. If a significant rule is to be violated with potential damage to the reputation of the official, the *guanxi* may not be sufficient. We would expect that the magnitude of a payment would be a decreasing function of the importance of the intermediary and an increasing function of the seriousness of rule violation.

Guanxi and Justice Under Law

As I considered the potential legitimacy of payments to superiors in various situations, one domain of action that I thought should be free of payments was civil and criminal justice. Surely, I thought, there can be no cultural rationale for payments in such cases. So I invited to dinner one of my students, Liu Jun, who had mentioned incidentally in class the prevalence of money lending in the small rural village of his birth. His natal village is located in a remote province in northeast China. I had been particularly interested in the resolution of conflicts that would inevitably result from "usurious" loans made to peasants of the village. As he described the issue, the presence of intermediaries was decisive. Not only was an intermediary commonly essential to the securing of a loan, but in the event of a dispute, it was the intermediary who acted as a mediator—his proposal being accepted by both parties. The only dispute Mr. Liu recalled was a situation that was resolved by allowing the peasant to repay the loan without additional interest, given his difficult economic circumstances. We see here the law of relationships operating in a most exemplary manner. While things may be changing in the current period, it had been conventional practice to resolve all such disputes through the intermediary, never taking these issues to formal court proceedings.

Conversations with other informants about dispute resolution in rural China have added considerably to the complexity of the matter. It becomes clear that there are other villages that present a very different institutional context from that in Mr. Liu's village. In more modern villages closer to Beijing, disputes are often resolved by court mediation. In the event of civil cases and even in criminal cases (these categories taken from Western law), it is common for both the plaintive and the defendant to offer "gifts" to the judge-mediator. The judge will often delay his decision in order that the heat of anger may be abated and, perhaps not incidentally, in order to allow time for both sides to offer solicitory gifts, including money.

It is commonly expected that the judge's decision will be affected by the relative size of the offerings from the parties. If one party is strongly in the wrong, he can ensure his position only with a correspondingly large payment. However, if the judge is skillful, the outcome of the proceedings will not be said to be the victory of one side over the other; it will be a settlement that preserves the social order. If the resolution of the case leaves both sides reasonably satisfied, it is unlikely that there will be any complaints about the "use of money" in the proceedings. Rather, there is ritual and customary practice in a generally orderly process.

Philip Huang (1996) has examined the records of conflict resolution in north China villages collected during the 1940s. In these data there were individuals who commonly acted as mediators for all of the conflicts in the village. These people clearly occupied a location within the village relationship structures, defined by *guanxi*. They certainly were not paid for their services. Huang emphasized the fact that community peace through compromise was the central goal. However, there was always, he asserted, the possibility that an unhappy claimant would seek formal court proceedings, in which case, the formal Qing codes would be applied. This fact had the consequence that formal codes remained relevant as boundary conditions on the forms of resolution that would be reached in the informal community mediation. He points out, also, that issues of right and wrong were sometimes relevant, but subordinate to "making peace."

It remains true, today, that an outcome that leaves one party "pleading his misery" is viewed as unfortunate. The dissatisfied party will complain to friends and perhaps to higher-level officials. In these complaints, he may denounce the proceedings as having been affected by the "use of money." Given an outcome that does violence to his expectations, the aggrieved party no longer accepts the money payments as convention and ritual but as an unethical intrusion. The villagers do not employ the term "bribery" in their grievances, they speak disparagingly only of the use of money. But clearly, it is not the use of money, alone, that is the problem. There is a complaint only when decisions are lacking in justice and balance from the perspective of one of the parties.

Similar characteristics may apply to cases that we in the West would call criminal. For example, in a case of homicide in which the family of the assailant offers sufficient compensation to both the police and to the family of the victim, the case may be dropped. There is no sharp demarcation between the criminal and the civil in Chinese practice. And even in these putatively criminal cases, when money payments are an effective means of achieving social peace, there will be no talk of bribery. Indeed, in the T'ang codes and in the codes thereafter, there was a special provision in the special case of accidental homicide that monetary compensation could be paid (in lieu of the same punishment that would be levied if a person were killed in a fight). Hence, the use of payments for homicide found in today's villages has a long history, at least if accident can be suggested as mitigation.

On the surface these Chinese practices are strongly at variance with Western practice. However, within twelve hours I realized the wisdom and legitimacy of it, even within the Western framework. A conception of bribery that has been deservedly influential in the West was offered by Harold Lasswell (1930) in the *Encyclopaedia of the Social Sciences*: "Bribery is the practice of tendering and accepting private advantage as a reward for the violation of duty. To bribe is to control by means of tangible inducements rather than by persuasion or coercion" (p. 690).

By this definition bribery involves a purchase of advantage by means of a transfer of benefit. This aspect of the definition of bribery has been clearly manifested in our discussions of payments to officials and judges in the Chinese village. Many of you may have thought that this criterion was sufficient. However, this is not a sufficient condition to define the process as bribery. There must also be a socially recognized "violation of duty." It is at this point that the social scientist must be careful because "duty" is necessarily socially defined and culturally embedded.

Unfortunately, most observers have imported Western conceptions of judicial and official duty into the Chinese context. In the West judges are expected to make decisions on the basis of codified law and precedent, so an offer of money that affects decision making is unambiguously a violation of duty and hence bribery. This is the consequence of money payments under the "rule of law." However, the tradition in China is a clear ethical alternative: the "rule of relationships." For that reason, the principal goal of the judge's deliberation is to maintain or restore social peace and equilibrium.

It is the common perception that money has contributed to the solutions of disputes that would otherwise disturb the social order. To argue from a comparison case, consider the practice of providing campaign contributions to political candidates in the United States. For over one hundred years, the capitalist class has been able to inure both political parties to the task of furthering the accumulation of capital, and campaign financing has been the major vehicle. Major industries and firms have been able to make conspicuous contributions, often to both of the major political parties, that can be withdrawn and offered to opposition candidates in the event that a politician makes undesirable decisions. Although this system essentially disenfranchises the majority, greatly reducing the range of political alternatives commonly available to the electorate and promoting widespread apathy and nonparticipation in voting processes, it can be said to have stabilized the political order in relation to the management of capital. It has *bought* social peace.

Yet, when contributions become very large and originate from relatively narrow economic interests, the leaders of the system become alarmed and urge "campaign finance reform." So, once again, we have monetary contributions to decision makers that become use of money only when it is feared that the decision-making process is at risk. Notice that the "risk" to which decision making is subjected is not "bribery" but *bias* in decision making. And it is a similar bias that is suggested by use of money by judges in rural China. This is so, because both sides offer money, and neither side is promised a specific action by the judge as a condition for his receiving money. There is no "control" over decisions by use of money, as required by the Lasswell definition.

If we accept the fact that rural courts in China are to be judged by their ability to generate socially equilibrating decisions, then it is reasonable to suggest that the money offered to judges is facilitative in the same way that campaign contributions are facilitative in the United States. Furthermore, even when one claims that there is use of money, one is referring to bias, not to bribery, because the action induced by bias is unpredictable and, in general, is different from the actions most strongly desired by the benefiting parties. Bribery requires a correspondence between payments and outcomes. Hence, the custom in Chinese villages of making monetary transfers to judges is not bribery by Lasswell's definition unless judges allow their actions to be subject to purchase. And that they are not guilty of the use of money unless it can be claimed that decisions are so biased that they fail to produce social peace. The essential point to recognize is that the payments do not necessarily induce either form of failure. Money transfers may, on the contrary, contribute to the solution.

It is additionally instructive to consider the judge's procedure. He conducts a hearing on the issues in court. Then after the formal proceedings, but before making a decision, he will visit the homes of both sides of a dispute, have dinner with the families, and discuss issues of importance to the current circumstances and future plans of each. It is in this way that a judge who did not know the litigants prior to the case gains the ability to play the role of an intravillage mediator—practicing the law of relationships. Judges at all levels are likely to indulge in this process of personal familiarization. The contrast with Western judges is a very strong one. One cannot imagine the Western judge losing his austere dignity, his class position (he was once lord of the manor), and his social distance. As one who must make declarations on the issues of righteousness, he cannot be seen playing silly games with the defendant's children; the Western judge must assume the mantle of God.

It is clear, however, that many urban Chinese observers of this rule of relationships are dismayed by it. Many would argue that the taking of money by officials and by judges is improper and that it is bribery. They presume that something must have been purchased, but they seem uninterested in the nature of the purchased action. Nor have they made the distinction between improper influence through the "use of money" and bribery. It is my impression that many urban and sophisticated Chinese are embarrassed by village culture and that they tend to make rather harsh and broad claims about bribery by imposing a "rule of law" criterion to processes that operate by a different principle.

Chinese informants have indicated considerable puzzlement about the judicial processes in the West. I was asked, "How can judges in your country afford to travel about and investigate cases, who pays for that?" I responded immediately that the state pays for that—an answer that was greeted with incredulity. On a later consideration, I realized that the root of this issue is that judges in China, like waiters in the United States, are often paid very poorly by their employers with the assumption that those who seek their services will add to their income and pay expenses. Therefore, the Chinese State has established a system by which judges *must be* supported by private money as a condition for performing their legitimate functions. In the West the judge works for the state (in a rule of law), and in China he may work more directly for the people (in a rule of relationships).

The fact that the poor are not favored by this system is clear. Hardly any subsystem within social formations favors the poor, in China or elsewhere. Huang (1996) points out that during the Qing village disputes, the mediation had a strong bias toward those who had status in the village. Hence, a wife (having married into the village) had no voice except through her husband or father-in-law, with the consequence that she could not complain effectively against the latter. Similarly, peasants who had lost their land and who suffered as virtual serfs during certain periods would travel from village to village in search of work. These workers would obviously possess no *guanxi* with local mediators or with other village residents and hence would have no effective voice in civil disputes. These observations suggest that the outcome of mediation will generally tend to favor those who are well placed in the village network, systematically favoring the richer villagers.

Thus, it would not be surprising that the poor have some likelihood of "pleading their misery" after a judicial confrontation with the rich. On the other hand, it should be expected that a rich man would offer more substantial financial support for the judge than a poor man, in the same way that a more expensive dinner carries the higher tip. In the United States "small claims courts" have historically had as their principal function the extraction of obligations from the poor by socially advantaged landlords and merchants. In most cases the poor man does not even choose to appear in court, given an inflexible law that does not favor him. For the poor a "law of relationships" is not inevitably less kind than the "rule of law." Certainly, one cannot claim that laws exist to protect the poor.

"From the founding of the Han in 206 B.C. until the fall of the Ch'ing in 1911, Confucianism for most of the time was the orthodox doctrine of the state. . . . [M]ost important was the legal bolstering of the human relationships held to be necessary for the well-being of society" (MacCormack 1996: 7). Top-down rules from the state, backed by threat of punishment, are secondary to education and the cultivation of virtue. "A constant refrain in official declarations on the law is that punishments should supplement, reinforce, or clarify teaching" (p. 11). Magistrates made every effort to discourage litigation and tended to remand issues to the community mediation process for conciliation and compromise. Lawyers were characterized as "litigation tricksters" who would encourage false accusations and bleed the clients of money, with unfortunate consequences for community relations.

On the other hand, beginning with the Sui and continuing into the T'ang, there was a development of law as a necessary supplement of education. In China "law" has meant punishment, and one of the earliest words for law, *hsing*, has a graph that includes the character for "knife." There followed, therefore, a development of specific offenses and specific punishments that were graded in accordance with the perceived severity of the moral infraction, which in turn was a function of the relationship of the parties and the proscribed behavior. Hence, China has not been without law. However, since law has been associated with punishment, rather than with compensation, it has had the aura of criminal sanction from a Western perspective, rather than the form of civil law that developed to facilitate commercial dealings.

According to Norman Cantor (1994), Western law is oriented toward providing a clear statement of right and wrong, as it revealed by "natural law." It is the product of reason, universally conceived (and emanating from God). The Chinese know about right and wrong, but somehow it is not the central issue—a fact that many Westerners find peculiar. If the goal of law is to define a path whose rationale derives from a "natural law" that is independent of and above society, then the appropriate action is to punish and coerce those whose actions deviate from the path.

In this context a peasant who fails to repay the lender should loose his land or suffer fifty lashes. His unpredicted incapacity (to pay interest on the loan) presents no defense. But the more rigid "rule of law" is also oriented toward maintaining the social equilibrium; only this time equilibrium is presumed to require that every citizen be confined to the right path. The equilibrium to be preserved, then, is a moral one in relation to the Christian God, before whom all are equal; it is not an equilibrium among human beings who are arrayed in hierarchically structured social relations.

Cantor (1994: 11) argues that

> Law cannot deal with perceptions and emotion—with love, beauty, joy, or sadness—but it deals well with family property, state power, class privilege, and military force. A familial, paternalistic state is rule conscious, and its inmost meaning is expressed in rules—little wonder that the Romans were the greatest lawyers the world had known. Even today the dominant legal tradition of Europe, from Paris to Moscow, is Roman; every western country (other than England and its former colonies) has a legal system based on Roman law.

China is certainly not in line with Roman tradition. One can say that civil law in China is that which is proclaimed officially as a guide to action. Rather than defining a path of righteousness, based on a universal rationality, it simply places another card on the table for the purpose of influencing decisions and dispositions, carrying the imprimatur of the State. Westerners are often outraged when they see officials deviating from the path defined by law, believing that they must be corrupt. But the Chinese find nothing amiss when proclaiming one thing as law and doing another. It is not that they deny an inconsistency; they simply find consistency unnecessary.

According to my informants, from an early age, Chinese children are taught to distinguish principles from practice. Principles are what you are suppose to say; practice is what people do, and, hence, it is what you are supposed to do.[5] Consequently, when someone else violates principle, they should be condemned, and yes, those officials are indeed corrupt, you should say. In fact, I believe that this explains the popular Chinese conception of bribery that condemns any taking of money as bribery—as a violation of principle. But since the actions of those officials are consistent with common practice, those actions would be appropriate for you and for those within your family and *guanxi* net, in the event that any of you obtained official position.

According to Fei Xiaotung (1992: 78–79):

> The degree to which Chinese ethics and laws expand and contract depend on a particular context and how one fits into that context. I have heard quite a few friends denounce corruption, but when their own fathers stole from the public, they not only did not denounce them but even covered up the theft. Moreover, some went so far as to ask their fathers for some of the money made off the graft, even while denouncing corruption in others. When they themselves become corrupt, they can still find comfort in their "capabilities." In a society characterized by a differential mode of association [a conception by which Fei characterizes Chinese society], this kind of thinking is not contradictory. In such a society, general standards have no utility. The first thing to do is to understand the specific context: Who is the important figure, and what kind of relationship is appropriate with that figure? Only then can one decide the ethical standards to be applied in that context.

Fei is not suggesting that a filial son may regard his father as corrupt and as a thief and be indifferent to that characterization. Rather, the son will rejoice in his father's "capabilities," that is, in the social position by which his father gained the flow of *liwu* and payments. Since anyone who has social position from which to gain advantages is ethically required to use that position for the benefit of himself and family, his father should not be attacked for doing so. However, the fact that officials may have great advantages is irksome to those who must struggle without those advantages. Such advantages would appear to be unfair, and it is customary practice to declare that they are corrupt, even in the absence of concrete evidence. As a sociologist at Peking University explained to me: "Oh, Chinese people always complain." It seems to be a simple problem of envy, as my informants insist; but as I shall argue in the proceeding, it may be more than that.

The ubiquity of *guanxi* and the use of intermediaries mean that such a practice must be found almost everywhere. There is customary practice and there is state law (principle). State officials may claim that people should be guided by the rule of law, so that decisions that are influenced by money are unethical. Technically, gifts of money are illegal. Yet those same officials understand that the rule of law is not the norm in China; they know that the rule of law is not customary practice. Consequently, everyone can be presumed to have violated *principle* and to be guilty of bribery and corruption, as defined by law. Indeed, as I have pointed out, the decentralization strategies of the state have actively created the potential for these customary practices.

In a struggle of cliques, one group may successfully accuse another of bribery, making strategic use of state law. However, even here, the accusation will be joined with an assertion that the other clique is of low moral character. This being so, it is deemed to be unfortunate that they follow customary practice. Given their low moral character, their receipt of money can only induce bad decisions. So the critical issue is not simply the amount of money but also the integrity of the official. The receipt of money by the victorious clique creates no ethical problem since its integrity has not been destroyed.

Relative to the differences between principle and practice, it would appear that accusing other cliques of being corrupt (in violation of principle) is common practice. That is, it is *common practice* that "people complain" about the violation of principle.[6] However, in most cases this is a matter of mutual recriminations that goes nowhere. If, however, the equilibrium is disturbed, decision makers at a higher level may step in to declare the victory of one side. It is by this mechanism that the losing side becomes officially recognized as corrupt. We may conclude, then, that in the countryside and in Beijing receipt of money by an "ethical and effective" official is not bribery. Bribery implies the recognition of ethical violations by a sufficiently powerful authority. In this way violation of duty is required not only by Lasswell's (Western) definition, but also by the definition that is implicit in Chinese practice.

I have spent many hours pondering this issue, with little hope of a complete resolution, but the key to this puzzle may lie in an assertion made by Fei (1992) from which I had previously taken a narrower interpretation. Fei indicated that the Chinese do not recognize a public domain as a locus of personal responsibility. This issue can be considered, however, only in comparison with Western conceptions. In the West there is a public that contains everyone *as unrelated* individuals—it is the megabundle referred to earlier in this chapter. It is true that Western institutions of family, work, education, and the state are structured as complementary associations within which individuals are related to others. And some individuals may be so burdened by institutional expectations that there is little time or few resources for indulgence into relations that are outside of the socially prescribed set.

Nevertheless, there is still a Western conception of self that places each person into the public as an individual who is related only to the state or God or both and *not to any other individuals*. Hence, when Aristotle discusses friendships between Good Men, he presumes that these men are affluent, socially unburdened, and functionally independent. In a word, they are *atomistic* individuals, at least in relation to their desire for friends. Women and lesser men are able to have friendships of only a less noble kind, resting on some form of deficiency. Indeed, Aristotle recognizes Good Men to be rare, so that friendships among them are eagerly and in many cases vainly sought.

Western ideology focuses on this Good Man as the model and on his friendships as the closest approximation of perfect virtue. The effusiveness with which friendship was described prior to the current period was without sensible bounds. The critical factor was that it was a love for the other for the sake of the other, most unlike the self-interested love that a man might have for a woman or the asymmetrical love that he has for his children. Only when a man is unrelated to others by institutional construction can he fully realize himself and be in a true reciprocal relation of friendship. In this context a man can be equivalent to similar others. We can say, then, that the Western, or Aristotelian, man seeks to relate to other men from within a domain of complete unrelatedness. It is this domain that defines the *public* in Western thought. As an atomistic individual, he is dependent only on God (and the state). It is this "atomistic" individual who is recognized by *methodological individualism*.

The contrast with the Chinese conception of self could not be more dramatic, for here one's social position is defined by relatively proximate relationships, not from an abstract and distant source, and the individual is never allowed to stand alone in a public. This relational self is always a self in multiple enactment of complementarity, as defined by the *wu-lun*. There can be no public location for this self. A purely public self would be a nonperson, lacking the essential qualities of humanity. There may be a public park, but no public, atomized self.

Social relations of reciprocity are feasible only for a nonrelational self ("nonrelational" in the sense of Fei). Thus, for a Chinese person reciprocity in its Western sense cannot be experienced. Yet many Chinese persons feel compelled to deny this impossibility, being unable, I believe, to imagine the actual characteristics of Western reciprocity. There is a presumption that if the powerful West possesses a cultural characteristic, then this characteristic is also present in Chinese culture. Chinese "exceptionalism" would imply inferiority. Therefore, reciprocity becomes a conceptual "black hole" that must be covered immediately in order to avoid an ideational crisis. The necessary cover is provided by *guanxi*, a word that is allowed to mean *relationships in general* rather than the specific form of relation discussed in the beginning of this chapter.

Furthermore, the Chinese translation of "reciprocity" is *hu hui*, meaning mutual benefit. It does not connote a social relation modeled on exchange (as presented in the last chapter) since such a relationship is largely inconceivable and would imply a nonrelational being whose personhood resides in a public. However, since mutual benefit is characteristic of all voluntary forms of relation, those governed by complementary and by balanced reciprocity, reciprocity in its *hu hui* form is foundational to all forms of relation in both China and the West. For this reason, the Chinese can easily accept the "norm of reciprocity" without knowing that its meaning is completely different in the West. There is, indeed, no word in Chinese for reciprocity, as defined in the last chapter.

On the other hand, Westerners are ideologically committed to the universality of reciprocity in a public (nonrelational) domain. As a result, Westerners and Chinese with Western training are likely to impose the reciprocity (gift exchange) model on *guanxi*. And prior to going to China, I feared that the imposition of this model on Chinese decision makers would have unfortunate consequences for their management of an ongoing process of capital accumulation in this period of globalization. However, it now seems more likely that a conventional difference between principle and practice will allow them to speak the language and ideology of the West while continuing to develop with Chinese characteristics.

Development with "Chinese Characteristics"

As an economic anthropologist, I am particularly concerned with the role of national cultures as factors that differentiate the evolution of social formations, and it appears that Chinese culture is a powerful influence in the modernization process. In this respect I join forces with scholars who stress the impact of culture on national development. For example, Jones (1994: 199) challenges the notion that a successful market economy requires the rule of law, suggesting that

> developments in China and East Asia indicate an alternative trajectory. Contrary to the predictions of modernization theory, emergent property forms in China suggest that the structural cleavage is created not between citizens and officials, but between local officials and the national political hierarchy; the mechanism of change is not resistance by citizens but . . . the interest and behaviour of local officials (Walder 1993: 22). Second the impact of globalization on China and East Asia is mediated by cultural values and practices such as *guanxi* and familism, which limit the penetration of globalization into Chinese society.

The argument, essentially, is that there may be radically different, yet efficient, paths toward economic development. The Western path, featuring civil society and a putatively rule-following administrative system, are the product of Western culture and need not be compelling paths to follow within other cultural contexts.

While China has proven to be reliably unpredictable, it is our hypothesis that the evolution of law in China will eventuate in a special

Chinese form of modernity—a path whose terminus will continue to contain "Chinese characteristics." Moreover, the trajectory of that path, we hypothesize, will be determined by the energies and modalities presented by the unique social form called *guanxi*. Indeed, the political structure of the current reform process is precisely an illustration of this tendency. Chinese society presents especially valuable opportunities for the consideration of an effective alternative to Western social forms. However, the models and definitions that I am presenting for this discussion were developed without particular reference to China. I have focused on developing a language and tools of analysis that can be used in understanding any system of social relations, given the characteristics of its system of "wealth-accumulation."

Since every society reaches the present with a cultural heritage that was developed in the past, differences in historical paths provide unique bases for the construction of the social structures of the future, allowing each cultural group to articulate the processes of wealth-accumulation with a social formation that differs from those of other groups. Hence, there is no one-to-one relation between the "economic base" and the system of social relations, as suggested by some vulgar Marxists, nor is the mode of Western capital a logical imperative for development, as suggested by those who would advance Western hegemony.

NOTES

Chapter 2

1. See my discussion of this matter in chapter 8.

2. Yang Yudong pointed out in class that mine was not a definition.

3. The drain on the consumption group, as indicated here, is in some way comparable to the drain in the wealth domain that arises with bridewealth among the owners of animal stock.

4. The reader may note that Marx did not give primacy to the wealth-assets as an independent force, having characterized capital as "congealed labor." However, the same obviously could not be said about other forms of wealth (and I do not believe that it should be said here).

Chapter 3

1. This chapter was initially published as "Polanyi and the Definition of Capitalism" in *Theory in Economic Anthropology*, edited by Jean Ensminger, AltaMira Press 2002 (see Bell).

Chapter 5

1. According to my friend, Dr. Khalid M. Al-Aiban, the official host of such a feast is the man of highest rank, regardless of the source of meat. If the provider of the meat is low ranking, he does not sit during the meal, in deference to the host!

2. In general this discussion will treat the domestic consumption group as a largely undefined entity. For an extended discussion of various concepts of the "household," see Netting, Wilk, and Arnould (1984).

3. For simplicity of diagrammatic exposition, we shall assume in the present discussion that the "social pressures for increased shares" are interpersonally independent. That means that pressure to increase one person's shares is not affected by the size of share received by others in the household. This is a fairly

absurd assumption, and it is useful only in simplifying figure 5.2. In a purely mathematical presentation, this assumption would not be necessary. Also, for diagrammatic simplicity, we assume that allocation schemes are very well defined. Figure 5.2 posits functional relations between social pressure and the level of consumption for each individual. In fact, such functions do not exist. Customary practices generate indications of the general shape of things, but they do not generate functional relations of an analytic kind. Hence, if Figure 5.2 were more emphatically descriptive, it would present much "fuzzier" relationships among variables. In my view such increased accuracy would provide no improvement in our understandings at this point.

4. For those who know the calculus, we are assuming that the first partial derivatives of $S(\cdot)$ are positive and that the second partial derivatives are negative.

Chapter 6

1. I would like to recognize Liang Yongjia as the source of the term "imposed," replacing a distinctly inferior term that I had previously employed.

Chapter 7

1. E. E. Evans-Pritchard (1990 [1951]) should have used the term "ghost fatherhood," since the husband is not a ghost.

2. I include in "reproductivity" the subsistence production that may be required of a woman in raising a child to maturity. This argument does not contradict the fact that there may be some nonbeggars who are worse off than some beggars, at least when "worse off" is defined by the consumption of "basic essentials." Indeed, some nonbeggars may be the victims of foolish pride in refusing their (material) best option.

3. It is typical of marriage rules that they are structured by the ambitions of dominant classes. Among the Nayar, it was those of higher rank who induced the abandonment of their traditional matrilocal marriage in order to have Nambiduri Brahman as the ritual husbands of their daughters.

Chapter 8

1. An earlier version of this chapter was published as Bell (1995).

Chapter 9

1. Since latrine cleaners are a subcaste within the village, their "supply" depends on the fertility of the women in that group. It is not unreasonable to spec-

ulate on the effect of the living standards of caste members on the fertility of women and, hence, the effect of the number of chapatis per latrine on the availability of latrine cleaners. This mechanism does not correspond to our usual supply-demand process. It is assumed, here, that the number or thickness of the chapatis will vary with the availability of grain to the community.

2. It is a characteristic of domestic groups that membership can be transient and episodic. The admission of an adult into a domestic group is always conditional on the performance of some kind of responsibility that validates membership.

3. We may see this point more readily by noting that the appropriate wage might be insufficient to purchase a meal, whereas one cannot imagine feeding this man without concern for his hunger.

Chapter 10

1. Gong Haoqun has suggested (in class) that this discussion appears to be consistent with an individualistic perspective on social process. And she is quite correct. The domain of exchange is precisely the domain in which the individualistic perspective has validity. It loses that validity as we begin to consider complementarity. In other words, the individualist perspective denies the existence of complementarity and culturally derived rules of allocation within groups.

Chapter 11

1. Ambrose King (1985) attributes to James Legge the translation of *jen* as virtue or perfect virtue. However, *jen* appears often to have a narrower meaning, referring primarily to kindness or humaneness (especially in relation to subordinates). The term *de* has broader reference to virtue in general. I thank an anonymous reviewer for raising this issue.

2. According to Ambrose King (1985: 63), there is a more basic term *"lun."* "Confucian thinking," he [Liang Sou-ming] writes, "is deeply concerned with one basic principle, which consists of two primary problems: the kind of differentiation to be made between individuals and the kind of relations to be established between individuals. He said the totality of these two issues is the principle of *lun.*"

3. The amount contributed by each family is recorded by the host. The significance of this is not, as some have suggested, to record a debt owed to the donor, but to maintain an indication of the form of relation that the contribution implies. On some subsequent occasion, the host may need to know that a given family presented itself as simply a "fellow villager," rather than as a "close neighbor," etc., and, of course, to record the fact that a contribution was made.

NOTES

4. I must thank Mikkel Bunkenborg and Lui Ping for reminding me of this feature during class discussion.

5. An application of this approach is the common failure to offer a new employee formal guidelines for performance of duties. A person is expected to learn by watching the actions of others.

6. The professor's assertion that "Chinese people always complain" was in response to my declared interest in popular conceptions of administrative behavior. I now understand his meaning: My inquiries would elicit only customary complaints of questionable sociological value.

REFERENCES

Arrow, Kenneth J.
1994 Methodological Individualism and Social Knowledge. *American Economic Review* 84 (2): 1–9.

Becker, Gary
1991 *A Treatise on the Family.* Cambridge, Mass.: Harvard University Press.

Beckoff, M.
1974 Social Play and Play-Soliciting by Infant Canids. *American Zoologist* 14: 323–40.

Bell, Duran
1987–1988 Production and Distribution within Hierarchically Structured Cooperative Groups. *Journal of the Steward Anthropological Society* 16: 1–20.

1995 The Structure of Rights in the Context of Private Property. *Journal of Socio-Economics* 24 (4): 607–21.

1997 Defining Marriage and Legitimacy (plus commentaries). *Current Anthropology* 38 (2): 237 53.

1998 Wealth Transfers Associated with Marriage. In *Kinship, Networks and Exchange.* Edited by T. Schweizer and D. R. White. Cambridge: Cambridge University Press.

2002 Polanyi and the Definition of Capitalism. In *Theory in Economic Anthropology: Theory at the Turn of the Century.* Edited by Jean Ensminger. Lanham, Md.: Altamira Press.

Bell, Duran, and Shunfeng Song
1990 Growth and Process in a Lineage-Based Social Technology. *Journal of Quantitative Anthropology* 2: 17–45.

1992–1993 Sacrificing Reproductive Success for the Primitive Accumulation of Cattle. *Journal of Quantitative Anthropology* 4 (1): 175–84.

REFERENCES

1994 Explaining the Level of Bridewealth. *Current Anthropology* 35 (3): 311–16.

Blau, Peter M.
1964 *Exchange and Power in Social Life*. New York: Wiley.

Block, Fred
1997 Polanyi and the Concept of Capitalism. Paper read at the 1997 meetings of the Social Science History Association.

Boserup, Ester
1965 *The Conditions of Agricultural Growth: The Economics of Agrarian Change under Population Pressure*. New York: Aldine.

Bromley, Daniel W.
1989 *Economic Interests and Institutions: The Conceptual Foundations of Public Policy*. New York: Basil Blackwell.

Burton, Captain Sir Richard F.
1864 *A Mission to Gelele: King of Dahomey*. 2 vols. London: Tinsley Brothers.

Burton, M. L., and D. R. White
1984 Sexual Division of Labor in Agriculture. *American Anthropologist* 86: 568–83.

Cai Hua
2001 *A Society without Fathers or Husbands: The Na of China*. New York: Zone Books.

Cantor, Norman F.
1994 *The Civilization of the Middle Ages*. New York: HarperPerennial.

Carloni, Alice S.
1981 Sex Disparities in the Distribution of Food within Rural Households. *Food and Nutrition* 7 (I): 3–12.

Chen, L. C., E. Huq, and S. D'Souza
1981 Sex Bias in the Family Allocation of Food and Health Care in Bangladesh. *Population and Development Review* 7.

Coase, Ronald H.
1960 The Problem of Social Cost. *The Journal of Law & Economics* 3 (l): 1–69.

Collier, Jane F.
1988 *Marriage and Inequality in Classless Societies*. Stanford, Calif.: University Stanford Press.

Dahl, G. and A. Hjort
1976 *Having Herds: Pastoral Herd Growth and Household Economy*. Stockholm: Department of Social Anthropology, University of Stockholm.

Dasgupta, Partha
1993 *An Inquiry into Well-Being and Destitution*. Oxford: Oxford University Press.

De Allessi, L.
1980 The Economics of Property Rights: A Review of the Evidence. *Research in Law and Economics* 2 (1): 17.

Demsetz, Harold
1967 Toward a Theory of Property Rights. *American Economic Review* 57 (2): 347–59.

Dickinson, Henry D.
1939 *Economics of Socialism*. London: Oxford University Press.

Douglas, Mary
1990 Foreword to *The Gift* by M. Mauss. New York: Norton.

Dumont, Louis
1983 *Affinity as a Value: Marriage Alliance in South India, with Comparative Essays on Australia*. Chicago: University of Chicago Press.

Dunbar, Robin I. M.
1983 Relationships and Social Structures in Gelada Baboons. In *Primate Social Relationships*. Edited by Robert A. Hinde. Oxford: Blackwell Scientific Publications.

1984 *Reproductive Decisions: An Economic Analysis of Gelada Baboon Social Structures*. Princeton, N.J.: Princeton University Press.

1988 *Primate Social Systems*. London: Croom Helm.

Ebrey, Patricia
1991 *Marriage and Inequality in Chinese Society*. Berkeley: University of California Press.

Edgerton, Robert B.
2000 *Warrior Women: The Amazons of Dahomey and the Nature of War*. Boulder, Colo.: Westview.

Engels, Friedrich
1972 [1884] *The Origin of the Family, Private Property, and the State*. New York: Pathfinder Press.

REFERENCES

Evans-Pritchard, E. E.

1990 [1951] *Kinship and Marriage among the Nuer*. Oxford: Clarendon Press.

Epstein, S.

1973 *South India Yesterday, Today and Tomorrow: Mysore Village Revisited*. London: Macmillan Press.

Etzioni, Amitai

1988 *The Moral Dimension: Toward a New Economics*. New York: The Free Press.

Fei Xiaotung

1976 [1939] *Peasant Life in China*. London: Routledge & Kegan Paul.

1992 [1947] *From the Soil*. Berkeley: University of California Press.

Fentress, John C., and Jenny Ryon

1979 A Long-Term Study of Distributed Pup Feeding in Captive Wolves. In *Wolves of the World: Perspectives on Behavior, Ecology, and Conservation*. Edited by Fred H. Harrington and Paul C. Pacquet. Park Ridge, N.J.: Noyes, 1982.

Friedl, Ernestine

1963 Some Aspects of Dowry and Inheritance in Boeotia. In *Mediterranean Countrymen: Essays in the Social Anthropology of the Mediterranean*. Edited by Julian Pitt-Rivers. Chicago: University of Chicago Press.

Fruzzetti, Una M.

1982 *The Gift of the Virgin: Women, Marriage and Ritual in a Bengali Society*. New Brunswick, N.J.: Rutgers University Press.

Gates, Hill

1987 Money for the Gods. *Modern China* 13 (3): 259–77.

Giesen, Deirdre

1994 Legal Arrangements of Intimate Relationships. Paper presented at the 13th World Congress of Sociology, Bielefeld, Germany.

Gilby, Thomas, ed.

1960 *St. Thomas Aquinas, Philosophical Texts*. New York: Oxford University Press.

Godelier, Maurice

1986 The Making of Great Men: Male Domination and Power among the New Guinea Baruya. Cambridge: Cambridge University Press.

Gold, Thomas B.
1985 After Comradeship: Personal Relations in China since the Cultural Revolution. *An International Journal for the Study of China* 104: 657–75.

Goodenough, Ward Hunt
1970 *Description and Comparison in Cultural Anthropology*. Chicago: Aldine.

Goody, Jack
1973 Bridewealth and Dowry in Africa and Eurasia. In *Bridewealth and Dowry*. Edited by J. Goody and S. Tambiah, 1–58. Cambridge: Cambridge University Press.

Gotter, Michael G.
1968 Toward a Social History of the Vietnamese Southern Movement. *Journal of South East Asian History* 9 (1): 12–24.

Gough, E. Kathleen
1959 The Nayars and the Definition of Marriage. *Journal of the Royal Anthropological Society* 89: 49–71.

Gouldner, Alvin W.
1960 The Norm of Reciprocity: A Preliminary Statement. *American Sociological Review* 25 (2): 161–78.

Gregory, C. A.
1982 *Gifts and Commodities*. New York: Academic Press.

Guemple, Lee
1988 Teaching Social Relations to Inuit Children. In *Hunters and Gatherers 2: Property, Power and Ideology*. Edited by Tim Ingold, David Riches, and James Woodburn. Oxford: Berg.

Hakansson, N. Thomas
1994 Grain, Cattle, and Power: Social Processes of Intensive Cultivation and Exchange in Precolonial Western Kenya. *Journal of Anthropological Research* 50: 249–76.

Halperin, Rhoda
1998 Reading Karl Polanyi: The Institutional Paradigm in the Context of Contemporary Culture Theory and Practice. Unpublished manuscript.

Harris, Marvin
1993 The Evolution of Human Gender Hierarchies: A Trial Formulation. In *Sex and Gender Hierarchies*. Edited by Barbara D. Miller. New York: Cambridge University Press.

REFERENCES

Herskovits, Melville J.
1967 *Dahomey, an Ancient West African Kingdom*. Evanston, Ill.: Northwestern University Press.

Hoebel, E. Adamson
1967 *The Law of Primitive Man: A Study of Comparative Legal Dynamics*. Cambridge, Mass.: Harvard University Press.

Huang, Philip C. C.
1996 *Civil Justice in China*. Stanford, Calif.: Stanford University Press.

Ingold, Tim
1980 *Hunters, Pastoralists and Ranchers*. Cambridge: Cambridge University Press.

Jeudwine, J. W.
1975 [1918] *The Foundations of Society and the Land*. New York: Amo Press.

Jones, Carol A. G.
1994 Capitalism, Globalism and Rule of Law: An Alternative Trajectory of Legal Change in China. *Social & Legal Studies* 195–221.

Keegan, John
1993 *A History of Warfare*. New York: Alfred A. Knopf.

Kehoe, Alice B., and Dody H. Giletti
1981 Women's Preponderance in Possession Cults: Tl.e Calcium Deficiency Hypothesis Extended. *American Anthropologist* 83: 549–60.

Kemper, Theodore D.
1990 *Social Structure and Testosterone: Explorations of the Socio-Bio-Social Chain*. New Brunswick, N.J.: Rutgers University Press.

King, Ambrose Y. C.
1985 The Individual and Group in Confucianism: A Relational Perspective. In *Individualism and Holism: Studies in Confucian and Taoist Values*. Edited by D. J. Munro, 57–69. Ann Arbor: University of Michigan Press.

Kipnis, Andrew B.
1997 *Producing Guanxi*. Durham, N.C.: Duke University Press.

Kruuk, Hans
1972 *The Spotted Hyena: A Study of Predation and Social Behavior*. Chicago: University of Chicago Press.

Kummer, Hans

1968 *Sociological Organization of Hamadryas Baboons*. Chicago: University of Chicago Press.

1970 Cross-Species Modification of Social Behavior in Baboons. In *Old World Monkeys*. Edited by J. H. Napier and P. Napier. London: Academic Press.

Lacey, W. K.

1968 *The Family in Classical Greece*. Ithaca, N.Y.: Cornell University Press.

Lange, Oscar, and Fred Taylor

1938 *On the Economic Theory of Socialism*. Minneapolis: University of Minnesota Press.

Lasswell, Harold D.

1930 Bribery. In *Encyclopaedia of the Social Sciences*. Edited by E. R. A. Seligman and A. Johnson, 690–92. New York: Macmillan.

Leach, E. R.

1955 Polyandry, Inheritance and the Definition of Marriage. *Man* 54: 182–86.

Leacock, E.

1954 The Montagnais "Hunting Territory" and the Fur Trade. *American Anthropologist* 56 (5), pt. 2, Memoir no. 78.

Lerner, Abba P.

1944 *The Economics of Control*. New York: Macmillan.

Levi-Strauss, Claude

1969 [1949] *The Elementary Structures of Kinship*. Boston, Mass.: Beacon.

MacCormack, Geoffrey

1996 *The Spirit of Traditional Chinese Law*. Athens: University of Georgia Press.

Malinowski, Bronislaw

1922 *Argonauts of the Western Pacific*. New York: Dutton.

Manser, M., and M. Brown

1980 Marriage and Household Decision-Making: A Bargaining Analysis. *International Economic Review* 21 (3): 31–44.

Marglin, F. A.

1985 *Wives of the God-King*. Dehli, India: Oxford University Press.

REFERENCES

Marris, Peter
1962 *Family and Social Change in an African City*. Evanston, Ill.: Northwestern University Press.

Marx, Karl
1906 *Capital: A Critique of Political Economy*. New York: The Modern Library.

Mauss, Marcel
1990 [1950] *The Gift*. New York: Norton.

McCay, Bonnie J., and James M. Acheson, eds.
1987 Human Ecology of the Commons. In *The Question of the Commons: The Culture and Ecology of Communal Resources*. Edited by B. J. McCay and J. M. Acheson, 195–216. Tuscon: University of Arizona Press.

McComb, Karen, Craig Packer, and Anne Pusey
1994 Roaring and Numerical Assessment in Contests between Groups of Female Lions. *Animal Behaviour* 47 (2) (February): 379–87.

McCreery, John L.
1976 Women's Property Rights and Dowry in China and South Asia. *Ethnology* 15: 163–74.

McElroy, Marjorie, and Mary J. Horney
1981 Nash-Bargained Household Decisions: Toward a Generalization of the Theory of Demand. *International Economic Review* 22 (2) (June 1981): 333–49.

McKeon, Richard, ed.
1980 *The Basic Works of Aristotle*. New York: Macmillan.

McPherson, C. B.
1985 *The Rise and Fall of Economic Justice and Other Papers*. Oxford: Oxford University Press.

Munro, Donald J.
1985 Introduction to *Individualism and Holism: Studies in Confucian and Taoist Values*. Edited by Donald J. Munro, 1–30. Ann Arbor: Center for Chinese Studies, University of Michigan.

Musil, Alois
1978 [1928] *The Manners and Customs of the Rwala Bedouins*. New York: AMS Press.

Netting, Robert, Richard R. Wilk, and Eric J. Amould
1984 *Households: Comparative and Historical Studies of the Domestic Group*. Berkeley: University of California Press.

Nicolaisen, Johannes

1963 *Ecology and Culture of the Pastoral Tuareg*. Copenhagen: National Museum.

Oxby, Clare

1986 Women and the Allocation of Herding Labour in a Pastoral Society (Southern Kel Ferwan Twareg, Niger). In *Le Fils et Le Leveu: Jeux et enjeux de la pente touareque*. Edited by S. Bernus, P. Bonte, L. Brock, and H. Claudot. Cambridge: Cambridge University Press.

Pacquet, P. C., S. Bragdon, and S. McCusk

1979 Cooperative Rearing of Simultaneous Litters in Captive Wolves. In *Wolves of the World: Perspectives on Behavior, Ecology, and Conservation*. Edited by Fred H. Harrington and Paul C. Pacquet. Park Ridge, N.J.: Noyes Publications.

Pahl, Jan

1980 Patterns of Money Management within Marriage. *Journal of Social Policy* 9 (3): 313–35.

Parr, C. W. C., and W. H. Mackray

1910 Rembau, One of the Nine States. *Journal of the Straits Branch of the Royal Asiatic Society* 56.

Parsons, Talcott

1951 *The Social System*. Glencoe, Ill.: Free Press.

Peters, P. E.

1994 Common Property, Property and Social Analysis. Paper presented at the meeting of the Society for Economic Anthropology, March.

Polanyi, Karl

1944 *The Great Transformation*. Boston, Mass.: Beacon

1966 *Dahomey and the Slave Trade*. Seattle: University of Washington Press.

Polanyi, Karl, and Conrad M. Arensberg

1957 Introduction to *Trade and Market in the Early Empires*. Edited by Karl Polanyi, Conrad M. Arensberg, and Harry W. Pearson. Glencoe, Ill.: Free Press.

Proudhon, P. J.

1840 *Qu'est-ce que la propriété*. Paris.

Pye, Lucian W.

1995 Factions and the Politics of *Guanxi*: Paradoxes in Chinese Administrative and Political Behavior. *The China Journal* 34: 35–53.

REFERENCES

Pyke, Karen D.
1996 Class-Based Masculinities: The Interdependence of Gender, Class, and Interpersonal Power. *Gender & Society* 10 (5): 527–49.

Richards, Audrey I.
1948 *Hunger and Work in a Savage Tribe: A Functional Study of Nutrition among the Southern Bantu.* Glencoe, Ill.: Free Press.

1950 Some Types of Family Structure amongst the Central Bantu. In *African Systems of Kinship and Marriage.* Edited by A. R. Radcliffe-Brown and Daryll Forde, 207–51. London: Oxford University Press.

Rivers, William H. R.
1967 [1906] *The Todas.* Oosterhout, the Netherlands: Anthropological Publications.

Rivière, P. G.
1971 Marriage: A Reassessment. In *Rethinking Kinship and Marriage.* Edited by R. Needham. London: Tavistock.

Rosner, Peter
1990 Karl Polanyi and Socialist Accounting. In *The Life and Work of Karl Polanyi.* Edited by Karai Polanyi-Levitt, 55–65. New York: Black Rose Books.

Rudnai, Judith A.
1973 *The Social Life of the Lion: A Study of the Behaviour of Wild Lions.* Lancaster: Medical and Technical Publication Company.

Sahlins, Marshall
1972 *Stone Age Economics.* New York: Aldine de Gruyter.

Sanday, Peggy R.
1981 *Female Power and Male Dominance: On the Origins of Sexual Inequality.* Cambridge: Cambridge University Press.

Scheper-Hughes, Nancy
1985 Culture, Scarcity and Maternal Thinking: Maternal Detachment and Infant Survival in a Brazilian Shantytown. *Ethos* 13 (4): 291–317.

Sen, A.
1966 Peasants and Dualism with or without Surplus Labour. *Journal of Political Economy* 74 (5).

Shirk, Susan L.
1993 *The Political Logic of Economic Reform in China.* Berkeley: University of California Press.

Sigg, H., A. Stolba, J.-J. Abegglen, and V. Dasser
1982 Life History of Hamadryas Baboons: Physical Development, Infant Mortality, Reproductive Parameters and Family Relationships. *Primates* 23: 473–87.

Siskind, J.
1973 *To Hunt in the Morning*. New York: Oxford University Press.

Smart, Alan
1993 Gifts, Bribes and *Guanxi*: A Reconsideration of Bourdieu's Social Capital. *Cultural Anthropology* 8 (3): 388–408.

Smuts, Barbara B.
1985 *Sex and Friendship in Baboons*. New York: Aldine.

Smuts, Barbara B., et al.
1987 *Primate Societies*. Chicago: University of Chicago Press.

Sorokin, Pitirim A.
1975 [1922] *Hunger as a Factor in Human Affairs*. Gainesville: University Press of Florida.

Stepniak, S.
1888 *The Russian Peasantry*. New York: Harper & Brothers.

Strathern, Marilyn
1988 *The Gender of the Gift*. Berkeley: University of California Press.

Taylor, Sandra C.
1999 *Vietnamese Women at War: Fighting for Ho Chi Minh and the Revolution*. Lawrence: University of Kansas Press.

Tucker, Robert C., ed.
1972 *The Marx-Engels Reader*. 5th ed. New York: Norton.

Turner, Terence S.
1979 The Gê and Bororo Societies as Dialectical Systems: A General Model. In *Dialectical Societies*. Edited by David Maybury-Lewis, 147–78. Cambridge, Mass.: Harvard University Press.

Vaughan, Megan
1987 *The Story of an African Famine*. Cambridge: Cambridge University Press.

Von Mises, Ludwig
1920 Die Wirtshaftsrechnung und sozialistischen Gemeinwesen, Archiv für Sozialwissenschaften und Sozialpolitik Bd. 47: 86–121.

REFERENCES

Walder, A.
    1993 China's Trajectory of Economic and Political Change: Some Contrary Facts and Their Theoretical Implications. Paper presented at miniconference on "Chinese and East European Transitions: On Divergent Roads?" at the Center for Chinese Studies, University of California at Los Angeles, June 7.

Wank, David L.
    1996 The Institutional Process of Market Clientelism: *Guanxi* and Private Business in a South China City. *The China Quarterly* 147: 820–38.

Ward, Benjamin
    1967 *The Socialist Economy*. New York: Random House.

Watson, Rubie S.
    1991 Wives, Concubines, and Maids: Servitude and Kinship in the Hong Kong Region, 1900-1940. In *Marriage and Inequality in Chinese Society*. Edited by R. S. Watson and P. B. Ebrey. Berkeley: University of California Press.

Weiner, Annette B.
    1976 *Women of Value, Men of Renown*. Austin: University of Texas Press.

Weyer, E. M.
    1962 [1932] *The Eskimos*. Hamden, Conn.: Archon Books.

Whitehead, Harriet
    1981 The Bow and the Burden Strap: A New Look at Institutionalized Homosexuality in Native North America. In *Sexual Meanings, the Cultural Construction of Gender and Sexuality*. Edited by Sherry B. Ortner and Harriet Whitehead. New York: Cambridge University Press.

Wiegersma, Nancy
    1988 *Vietnam—Peasant Land, Peasant Revolution: Patriarchy and Collectivity in the Rural Economy*. New York: St. Martin's Press.

World Health Organization
    www.who.int/, data for September 1, 2001 [accessed June 2, 2003].

Yan Yunxiang
    1996 *The Flow of Gifts: Reciprocity and Social Networks in a Chinese Village*. Stanford, Calif.: Stanford University Press.

Yang, Mei-hui
    1994 *Gifts, Favors and Banquets*. Ithaca, N.Y.: Cornell University Press.

INDEX

219

INDEX

BIOGRAPHY OF GYULA DERKOVITS

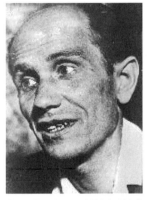

Gyula Derkovits (1894–1934)

Painter, graphic artist. He was an apprentice in his father's joiner shop. He began drawing very early and was taught to paint by a sign painter. His left arm became paralyzed in World War I. From 1916 onwards, he lived in Budapest. He learned to paint and do copper engravings in Károly Kernstock's school. He produced mostly pencil and tint drawings during 1916–1918. He met left-wing emigrants in Vienna and joined the Austrian Communist Party. His works reflected the influence of German expressionists and his political experiences in Vienna in 1928–1929, when his most significant graphic work, *1514*, wood engravings inspired by the Dózsa peasant revolt, was finished. His final period is best represented by *Orders* (1930), *Sleeping* (1932), *Execution* (1932), *By*

This selection is reprinted from the website: Fine Arts in Hungary, http://hungart .euroweb.hu/index2.html *the Rails* (1932), and *Mother* (1934). His Dózsa-series were transformed in copper engravings around 1931. Poverty and diseases put an end to his life. His art was influenced by expressionism, but he created an entirely individual style of his own in the last years of his life uniting strict composition and lyrical colors with portrayal.

ABOUT THE AUTHOR

Duran Bell began his work as an economic anthropologist after nearly twenty years as an economist, holding a Ph.D. in agriculture economics from University of California, Berkeley. He was lured into anthropology by an interest in intrahousehold resource allocation, a subject on which anthropology presents an abundance of culture variation. Dr. Bell then became interested in bridewealth and dowry and, consequently, with the nature of lineage organization as wealth-holding social entities, which led finally to a more general interest in wealth-assets and their concomitant social implications. Having developed the set of necessary and sufficient conditions that must characterize any forms of wealth, he presents his current understanding of the fundamental dynamic that orients the development and management of lineages, tribes, and states. There is now a basis for investigating the dynamics and the evolution of social formations, using wealth as the central instrumental variable and positing the survival of wealth-holding groups as the central criterion.